RURAL WOMEN AT WORK

RURAL WOMEN AT WORK

Strategies for Development in South Asia

Ruth B. Dixon

Published for RESOURCES FOR THE FUTURE
by the JOHNS HOPKINS UNIVERSITY PRESS

Baltimore and London

Copyright © 1978 by The Johns Hopkins University Press
All rights reserved. Manufactured in the United States of America.

Library of Congress Catalog Card Number 78–5825
ISBN 0–8018–2124–X

CONTENTS

TABLES AND FIGURE

FOREWORD

This study is one of several research projects on population policy that have been sponsored by Resources for the Future (RFF) and funded by a grant from the Rockefeller Foundation. RFF's first effort in this direction was a volume of essays related to various hypothesized socioeconomic determinants of fertility.[1] Each author was asked to review the theoretical and empirical evidence about the relationships between fertility and those determinants of fertility that might be amenable to policy manipulation, to consider what policies might be appropriate to move these determinants in a favorable direction, and to discuss research needs and how best to fulfill them.

One of the most promising areas identified in our initial study was female labor-force participation. If good jobs at decent wages were offered to women, particularly those living in rural areas, would such employment have an effect on family size? Would their jobs compete for the women's time as mothers and housewives, offer them an alternative route to acquiring status and a sense of purpose, and perhaps also provide the women with an independent source of income which would enable them to achieve more control over their lives?

But, as our original volume makes clear, the situation is more complicated than it first appears to be. The available empirical evidence is ambiguous, suggesting that not all jobs in all cultural settings affect family size. Moreover, even if future studies develop evidence that is more encouraging, how can the policy questions be answered? How can the appropriate jobs be identified? How can cultural and economic resistance, particularly strong in areas with high male unemployment, be overcome? Where are the capital, markets, raw materials, and technical and managerial skills to come from? What has been the experience of past efforts to set up jobs for women; and what factors distinguish successful from unsuccessful efforts? To all such questions we must admit ignorance. Yet without answers, this possibility for reducing fertility—even with adequate evidence to support the basic proposition—is likely to remain in the "promising" category for many years to come.

---

[1] Ronald G. Ridker, ed., *Population and Development: The Search for Selective Interventions* (Baltimore, Johns Hopkins University Press for Resources for the Future, 1976).

Fortunately, Ruth B. Dixon, who had participated in our original study, was eager to look for answers to these questions. Initially, her task was to search through the relevant literature and to learn what she could from her firsthand observation and discussions with persons engaged in current efforts. This background information has enabled Dixon to suggest solutions to these problems and to propose research by which her recommendations can be tested.

Her findings suggest that jobs for women, while useful for many other reasons, may have little impact on fertility unless they are combined with other changes. For maximum effectiveness, Dixon recommends that efforts be concentrated on young, preferably unmarried women and that, for best results, the new employment opportunities should move the women out of their traditional home and agricultural settings and into central work places located in villages or small towns. She also recommends that women be provided with a financial stake and a voice in the operation of the business venture. Supporting services such as job training and functional literacy classes, along with family-planning, health, and child-care facilities, should be made available. In some circumstances it may be important to provide living quarters for female workers and incentives to encourage delayed marriage and birth control.

These considerations quite naturally lead to Dixon's central proposal— the development of producer cooperatives owned and operated by women. At first glance, this proposal is likely to appear too radical to have much chance of implementation, even on a small scale, in the Muslim and Hindu cultures on which Dixon concentrates. But it begins to sound more plausible as we follow the author's review of case studies which incorporate some of her recommended changes and her discussion of the pros and cons of specific approaches to such problems as choosing products, acquiring credit, and overcoming the cultural barriers to female employment.

There have been some remarkable successes: on a large scale in the case of the Indira Mahila Cooperative Bank of Bombay, owned and operated solely by women; on an individual level in the case of Medina, an unmarried Muslim of eighteen who has resisted parental and social pressures for early marriage and the observation of purdah in order to obtain a secondary education and a good job; a financial one in the case of 2,700 Indian peasant women who cooperatively make and sell papads, a local appetizer, in foreign and domestic markets; and a dramatic one in the case of Mrs. Begum, a member of a handicraft cooperative in Bangladesh, who, with the help of her daughter and husband, frequently earns over $200 per month making jute handbags.

One also learns of failures, misplaced efforts, and the draining effects of ingrained suspicions. In the end, the reader is likely to conclude that Dixon is on the right track, and that while the package she recommends will be far from easy to assemble, there are enough precedents around to make it worth trying. But if her recommendations are tried out, an evaluation effort should be implemented along with them in order to ensure that everything possible is learned from future successes and failures.

This is a carefully researched, thoughtful, and sympathetic book about efforts to effect social change at the grass roots in an important part of the world. It should prove enlightening for those who want to understand the process and practical for those who want to influence it.

Washington, D.C.   Ronald G. Ridker
                                      Senior Fellow
                                      Renewable Resources Division

PREFACE

This report evolved from an essay commissioned by Resources for the Future for a conference on the Socioeconomic Determinants of Fertility held in Washington, D.C., in February 1975. The conference papers appear in *Population and Development: The Search for Selective Interventions,* edited by Ronald G. Ridker. The experience of writing that essay and an earlier report for the United Nations on the *Status of Women and Family Planning* impressed me with the inadequacies of our knowledge of how rural women live in most parts of the world. In particular, the experience increased my own bewilderment about the conditions under which the various proposals (including my own) for improving the status of rural women and reducing birthrates might really work.

To satisfy their curiosity as well as mine, Resources for the Future kindly provided funds for me to travel to Bangladesh, Pakistan, India, and Nepal from January through April of 1976. There, I talked with dozens of women and men in international agencies, governments, foundation offices, population institutes, family-planning clinics, and rural community development programs. I also spent weeks tracking down promising projects in which village women were organized into producers' cooperatives that provided them with an independent source of income. This report is based on those observations as well as on a variety of published and unpublished materials relating to development, the status of women, and population processes.

Although *Rural Women at Work* has been written primarily for development planners and community organizers searching for ideas on how to upgrade rural women's economic activities, the research proposals should attract wider interest. During my information-gathering forays to foundations and agencies (indigenous and foreign) involved in development projects, those being interviewed often turned the tables to question me avidly about projects I had seen. I was uncomfortably cast into the role of instant expert and asked for suggestions that I was totally unprepared to make.

Now, more than a year later, most of the smaller pieces have settled into place, although the larger questions still loom unanswered. I hope that this report will offer some new information about what programs might be possible, and that it will stimulate others to explore more fully some of the theoretical and practical issues it raises.

It is impossible to list all those—from dispensers of millions of dollars of international funding, to harried occupants of district government posts, to illiterate village women weaving jute mats while their children beg for attention—who have given me so much assistance throughout this study. Those who read English and have access to reports of this nature will undoubtedly recognize their own contribution in its pages; the rest cannot know how invaluable their help has been. A note of special thanks goes to Ronald G. Ridker, of Resources for the Future, for his continued interest in and very direct support of this work.

Davis, California   Ruth B. Dixon

RURAL WOMEN AT WORK

1

INTRODUCTION

Problems of persistent poverty and high birthrates appear to be inextricably bound together in developing countries that have not yet reached that magic breakthrough or takeoff point once so fondly countenanced by economic and demographic forecasters. Extreme poverty induces couples to give life to many children for their later economic and social support and for the few personal pleasures that life may hold; dependence on large families requires the early and universal marriage of females and a life of constant childbearing to ensure that enough children, especially sons, will survive to their parents' old age; heavy domestic responsibilities, along with economic and cultural factors, frequently restrict women to the home; and the resulting high dependency ratios weigh heavily upon male providers who, themselves largely illiterate and unskilled, have access to only the poorest of paid employment or subsistence agriculture.

The circle seems unbreakable. Certainly, family planners have long confronted the reality of resistance to birth control in countries where cultural and structural pressures for large families remain strong,[1] and development planners have long confronted the reality of runaway rates of population growth that seem to entangle their every effort at change.[2] The 1974 World Population Conference was nevertheless marked by conflict between "population" proponents who defined high fertility as the key problem and more effective population programs as the solution, and "development-first" proponents who defined poverty as the key problem and an end to economic exploitation of poor countries by the rich as the solution.[3] Although some observers strove valiantly to find consensus in the debates (Teitelbaum, 1974), few participants came away with a clear vision of just what was to be done in programmatic terms. It seemed that the heat of the debate itself had already consumed much of the energy

---

[1] See, for example, Davis's (1967) critique of the assumptions of family-planning program in *Science*.

[2] One of the earliest investigations into the economic consequences of population growth in developing countries is found in Coale and Hoover (1958).

[3] For identification of the various positions taken at Bucharest, see Mauldin and coauthors (1974), and Finkle and Crane (1975).

needed to attack the dilemma of interlocking poverty and high fertility in all its complexity.

This report offers one small piece to fit in the complex of proffered solutions. It proposes that a promising point of intervention in the circle of rural poverty and high fertility in economically stagnant rural economies is through women—specifically, through upgrading women's productive activities from the household and subsistence sectors to income-generating employment outside the home. The argument, which is elaborated in some detail in the following chapters, contends that non-agricultural employment that expands the range of economic and social rewards available to women outside the home can promote rural development, raise the status of women, and alter reproductive behavior. Furthermore, programs specifically incorporating women as decision makers and beneficiaries should stimulate more immediate and direct social and economic changes than would similar programs aimed primarily at men. Substantiated by statistical studies and case examples from four South Asian countries—India, Pakistan, Bangladesh, and Nepal—the argument has wider practical and theoretical applicability as well.

NONAGRICULTURAL EMPLOYMENT FOR RURAL WOMEN IN SOUTH ASIA

The countries of South Asia under discussion here—India, Pakistan, Bangladesh, and Nepal—include some of the highest population densities per unit of arable land in the world.[4] Pressure on rural land is exacerbated by the rapid population growth produced by continued high birthrates and dramatically declining death rates. The low status of most Hindu and Muslim women is reflected in their early and universal marriage and in strong cultural forces toward high marital fertility. Even if by the end of the century couples bear one or two fewer children on the average (the total fertility rate shown in table 1-1), rates of natural increase in the populations of India, Bangladesh, and Pakistan will rise before they begin to drop. In Nepal the rate of natural increase will continue to grow to the year 2000, even if couples reduce their family size from six to just over four children. With moderate fertility declines, the four countries together

---

[4] Sri Lanka is excluded from the discussion because its cultural and structural conditions differ considerably from those of its northern neighbors, and because the average age at which women marry is remarkably high—23.5 years in 1971 (Baldwin, 1977, p. 1). For an extended discussion of the uniqueness of Sri Lanka, with respect to the determinants of marriage patterns, see Duza and Baldwin (1977), and Dixon (1970).

can be expected to add about 560 million to their numbers in the last twenty years of the century.[5]

Agriculture cannot absorb the rural population increase because in most areas too many people already depend on farm occupations for their sustenance. Nepal, in 1971, employed 420 males in agriculture per square mile of arable land (Davis, 1975, page 16), compared with 335 in Taiwan, 173 in Sri Lanka, and 30 in Costa Rica in 1960. Cities are barely

Table 1-1. Population Projections for India, Bangladesh, Pakistan, and Nepal to the Year 2000, Based on an Assumption of Moderate Fertility Decline

Country and year	Total population (in thousands)	Crude birthrate	Crude death rate	Rate of natural increase	Total fertility rate
India					
1970	537,845	38.8	15.4	2.34	5.4
1980	680,617	34.6	11.4	2.32	4.7
1990	860,727	32.7	9.1	2.36	4.3
2000	1,084,571	30.4	7.8	2.26	4.0
Bangladesh					
1970	71,552	43.5	21.2	2.22	6.3
1980	92,852	45.8	15.4	3.04	5.9
1990	124,827	39.0	10.9	2.81	5.1
2000	164,616	36.1	8.6	2.75	4.6
Pakistan					
1970	60,269	43.3	15.7	2.76	6.8
1980	81,992	45.3	11.6	3.37	6.5
1990	115,139	41.4	8.4	3.30	5.9
2000	158,001	37.2	6.5	3.07	5.1
Nepal					
1970	11,240	43.2	22.0	2.13	6.1
1980	13,996	40.7	18.3	2.24	5.4
1990	17,501	37.2	14.6	2.26	4.8
2000	21,958	34.1	11.2	2.29	4.3

Source: Zachariah and Cuca (n.d.).

Note: Moderate fertility declines are set halfway between a constant gross reproduction rate (GRR) and a fast-declining GRR based on the following schedule:

1970 GRR	Projected percentage of decline per year
1.5 or less	1
1.5–2.0	2
2.0–2.5	3
2.5–3.0	2
3.0 or more	1

Mortality declines also depend on the initial levels of mortality, with slower rates of decline projected for countries with the highest and lowest life expectancies in 1970.

[5] Lower projections are based on an assumption of a fast fertility decline (Zachariah and Cuca, n.d.). To my mind, the moderate estimates are more reasonable, considering the slow pace at which deliberate birth control is being adopted in these countries.

able to provide jobs and services for their own expanding populations. Clearly, rural birthrates need to be drastically reduced and nonagricultural employment simultaneously expanded.

Although the diagnosis is hardly new, I am proposing a particular cure. A key strategy for intervening in the mutually compounding forces of rural poverty and high fertility is to generate nonagricultural employment for rural women. Such a strategy should promote development by adding new sources of income to village households. It should also create conditions favorable to delayed marriage and lower marital fertility by radically altering the social and economic status of rural women.

If the new employment is to have maximum impact on social, economic, and demographic behavior, it should include all the following elements:

1. Produce income over which women have some control
2. Provide employment in small towns and villages
3. Create jobs outside the agricultural sector
4. Introduce small-scale, labor-intensive light industries
5. Locate production in a central workplace outside the home
6. Recruit new workers, especially those women in their early reproductive years
7. Organize production on principles of economic and social cooperation
8. Offer additional services and incentives.

Outlined in the next chapter is the precise nature of each of these elements, and the reasons they can be expected to promote rural development, raise the status of women, and reduce birthrates. Because social scientists have only recently turned their attention to the complex relationships among population processes, development, and the status of women, solid evidence remains scarce.[6] Consequently, most of the arguments presented here are rather speculative: they take the form of propositions which remain to be tested in a variety of settings rather than being facts upon which we can placidly rely. Nevertheless, I have chosen to argue strongly for a particular configuration of elements in the hope that planners and researchers will be moved to action—or reaction—rather than waiting for that elusive millennium when all the data are in. If some statements seem cloaked in a higher degree of certainty than is warranted by the state of the art, it is with this provocative intent in mind.

[6] The pioneering work on women in development is that of Boserup (1970); for more recent works, see Buvinic (1976). Much of the literature and debate on women and population has been summarized by the UN Department of Economic and Social Affairs (1975), and by Birdsall (1976).

A MATTER OF DEFINITIONS

The particular model of female employment described above is designed to achieve advances in rural development, improvements in the status of women, and modifications in reproductive behavior. Here, *development* refers not to the traditional indicator—the growth of per capita gross national product (GNP)—but to a broader conception that includes, in Mahbub ul Haq's words, "Progressive reduction and eventual elimination of malnutrition, disease, illiteracy, squalor, unemployment, and inequalities" (Rich, 1973, page 23). Kocher (1973, page 5) defines development as "(1) a general improvement in levels of living, together with (2) decreasing inequality of income distribution, and (3) the capacity to sustain continuous improvements over time. *The components of socioeconomic well-being are the substance of development"* (italics added).

But how are these components of development to be measured? Tailored to local conditions, general improvements in levels of living would include not only the reduction of malnutrition, disease, illiteracy, squalor, and unemployment, but also increases in the regularity, amount, and purchasing power of incomes in kind or in cash, and in land ownership or access; reduction in the number of hours of labor expended for subsistence needs and in the arduousness of the heaviest tasks; improvements in labor productivity, including domestic labor; improved housing; access to medical care, and so on. Authentic development would spread improvements across all of these areas rather than concentrating them in one. Increased incomes clearly bring little benefit if they only stimulate a more rapid rise in the price of food, for example. Nor does a woman's life improve if she simply adds the hours of her new employment to an already burdensome round of domestic work and has no control over how her earnings are spent.

The reduction of inequalities refers generally to the distribution of economic and social resources (of which income is only one ingredient) across geographic regions (nations, subnational regions, districts, communities, rural and urban areas) and across major class and ethnic–racial–caste groupings within each region or community. Of particular concern here, is the potential impact of female employment on the distribution of resources *within the family,* especially as it affects the inequalities between men and women, boys and girls. The extent to which the income-earning capacity of adult women brings about a more egalitarian investment between sons and daughters in schooling, food, and medical care, for example, is a crucial aspect of this distributional component of development.

The concept of the capacity to sustain continuous improvements over time is more difficult to measure directly. Such so-called improvements could be economic, social, and political, inhering in the individual, the family or household, the larger social group, or the community as a whole. We would want to tap a wide range of behavior, from an individual's new discovery of her own capacity for making independent decisions or earning enough money to keep her children in school, to the political mobilization of a group of workers who demand reforms in community government, to the creation of an economic infrastructure of buildings, equipment, and credit that will require or stimulate additional productive activity. (A number of these specifically economic spin-offs are discussed in chapter 4.)

The *status of women* is a similarly elusive concept. It is defined here as the degree of women's access to (and control over) material resources (including food, income, land, and other forms of wealth) and to social resources (including knowledge, power, and prestige) within the family, in the community, and in the society at large. It is measured *de facto* rather than *de jure,* both in absolute terms and relative to men. Clearly, there are societies in which women's legal rights are extensive, but their exercise is considerably constrained by economic and cultural considerations. And while there are societies and groups in which neither women nor men have much control over economic and social resources, in others, women as a group have experienced considerable improvements in socioeconomic well-being, only to find that they are relatively worse off in view of the even faster improvements for men. These qualifications must be kept in mind in any discussion of women's status.

The concept becomes even more elusive when we try to develop measures sensitive to differences in structural and cultural conditions across societies and groups. In addition, one must deal with the differences between the interpretations of the outside observer and the perceptions of the actor herself in her own cultural milieu. These objective-subjective distinctions become extremely complex in the South Asian context. Whereas the Western-trained social scientist is likely to interpret practices such as the arranged marriage of young girls, extravagant dowries, and female seclusion as reflections of women's *low* status (that is, the lack of control over one's own life decisions), a young Hindu or Muslim woman may take great personal pride in the size of her dowry and in her ability to observe purdah. In societies valuing female seclusion as the ideal, the employment of women outside the home may represent a decline in status that brings dishonor to the entire family. And among people valuing early marriage and high fertility, shifts toward delayed marriage and less-frequent childbearing may be, at least initially, similarly scorned.

It would appear that there is no way to arrive at a culture-free definition of *status,* particularly one which reflects its many dimensions. For simplicity, then, this report seeks to examine the extent to which women can transform material and social resources (from any source) into a particular kind of behavior—the ability to shape major decisions about their own lives in a relatively autonomous manner. Note, however, that I am not referring here to control over others, but rather, control over oneself.

Under *reproductive behavior* I include the timing of marriage, knowledge and practice of family-planning methods, the timing of the first birth, the spacing of subsequent births, and the total number of births. I argue that the introduction of income-generating employment outside the home for rural women provides a source of material and social resources that, under certain conditions, can be translated into greater decision-making power within the family. This increased autonomy, exercised in the context of perceived social and economic alternatives to early marriage and frequent childbearing, should enable young women to delay their marriages and to seek information permitting them to space and limit births. The argument linking female employment with fertility through a shift in decision-making patterns admittedly rests on sketchy research findings, some of them contradictory. This volume should thus be viewed not as a final synthesis, but as a step in building upon our knowledge of relationships among rural development, the status of women, and reproductive behavior. (The appendix includes a number of specific proposals for further research.)

The proposition that a specific type of economic activity (that is, rural women's income-earning employment outside the home) will create conditions favorable to delayed marriage and fertility control in currently early-marrying and high-fertility societies needs to be clearly specified so that the implied causal mechanisms can be tested under a variety of cultural and structural conditions. Recent research has leaned heavily toward the interpretation that, in almost all settings, fertility influences female labor-force participation more than vice versa.[7] That is, the lower fertility of employed women compared with that of currently nonemployed women is attributed to a selectivity factor, by which women who (for whatever reason) have no children, or only one or two, are more free than those with more children to seek employment outside the home

---

[7] For a summary of causal paths operating in the relationship, see Terry (1974 and 1975), and Fong (1976). The literature on female employment and fertility is reviewed by Birdsall (1974); Dubey, Bardhan, and Garg (1975); Piepmeier and Adkins (1973); and the UN Department of Economic and Social Affairs (1975), among others.

and to remain there.[8] Even in industrial societies offering career options for females in the manufacturing and service sectors of the economy, studies find that very few women claim to be limiting their fertility for the purpose of remaining in the labor force.[9] More typically, aspirations for their own and their children's material and social well-being induce couples both to limit their fertility and seek additional income through the wife's employment.

In rural and urban areas of developing countries another body of research reveals no association at all between female labor-force participation and fertility when women's occupations do not directly compete with their traditional roles as wives and mothers, as in agricultural work, handicrafts, some service work, and market activities.[10] Still others find a positive relationship between fertility and female employment in agriculture.[11]

Contradictory findings can no doubt be partially explained by the use of very different methodological approaches. Some studies use aggregate national or subnational data in ecological correlations; others use census data for comparisons across major population subgroups or for analyses of aggregate changes over time; still others are based on lengthy personal interviews, including work and pregnancy histories. Too, the dependent variables differ. Some use actual measures of fertility such as the number of children ever born (controlling for woman's age and duration of marriage); others use the number of additional births expected or wanted, ideal family size, or family-planning knowledge, attitudes, or practices.

Still, conclusions of reverse or indirect causality, or of no causality at all, cannot be denied. But do they throw into doubt the entire proposition that female employment can affect fertility in very important ways, a proposition that only recently has begun to win recognition in planning circles. Indeed, if these reverse or indirect causal paths were to represent

[8] The relationship in some cases is curvilinear, however; women with large families can be forced into the labor force by economic necessity because of their high fertility, or, more accurately, their poverty can "cause" both high fertility and labor-force participation.

[9] For example, although cross-sectional analysis of census data from Melbourne, Australia, shows a strong negative relationship between a wife's current employment and fertility, interviews with 2,652 women found no relationship between employment status and wanting more children or practicing family planning. Fewer than 10 percent of the sample could be said to have careers, even under the most liberal definition (Ware, 1965).

[10] For India, see Dandekar (1959), and Mukherjee (1975b); for urban Latin America, see Hass (1972); for Japan and Puerto Rico, see Jaffe and Azumi (1960); for Pakistan, see Shah (1975a); for Lima, Peru, see Stycos (1965); and for Turkey, see Stycos and Weller (1967).

[11] For Egypt, see Bindary, Baxter, and Hollingsworth (1973); and for Thailand, see Goldstein (1972).

the entire range of possibilities, there would be little point in proposing female employment as a purely demographic policy, even though there are compelling arguments on other grounds. This is not a simple proposal for increasing female employment, however. Rather, I am suggesting that the employment created should be of a particular type which will maximize the potential for positive change in reproductive behavior as well as encouraging self-reliance among women and promoting rural development. Since so few tasks in which women are currently engaged in most developing countries come even close to this model, the proposition has hardly been tested.

AN OUTLINE OF WHAT FOLLOWS

Rural women's producer cooperatives are only one small piece in the puzzle. They are certainly no panacea and cannot be considered apart from other development plans with which they should be integrated. These include the extension to rural areas of appropriate health and educational facilities; the upgrading and diversification of agricultural production; the narrowing of income inequalities between urban and rural areas and within rural communities; genuine land reform; and the expansion of jobs for both men and women in the rural industrial and service sectors.[12] The governments of India, Pakistan, Bangladesh, and Nepal, for example, have all outlined plans for promoting rural development through such means as the extension to farmers of low-interest loans, the organization of multipurpose cooperatives, land reform, rural industries, and the promotion of the back-to-the-village panchayat government or Swanirvar self-reliance. They have expressed at least formal interest in integrating women into the development process; and they have all adopted policies for reducing birthrates through the spread of family-planning information and services, as well as through other incentives.[13] Yet strong cultural and structural, as well as political, factors continue to impede the achievement of these goals.

Increasingly, international agencies are turning their attention to the integration of women in development as a strategy for improving economic conditions and promoting the adoption of family planning. Attesting to this concern are numerous resolutions from the 1974 World Population Conference in Bucharest, from the 1975 International Wom-

[12] A number of strategies for intervention through employment, education, health-care systems, and other institutions are analyzed in Ridker (1976).

[13] The governments' positions on population growth and family planning are summarized by Nortman and Hofstatter (1975, pp. 23–25).

en's Year Conference in Mexico City, and from the voluminous background papers and UN agency reports preceding and following these conferences. Individual donor governments, too, are expressing interest in policies linking development with the status of women and population questions. The Percy Amendment to the U.S. Foreign Assistance Act, for example, requires that the provisions of the act "shall be administered so as to give attention to those programs, projects, and activities which tend to integrate women into the national economies of foreign countries, thus improving their status and assisting the total development effort."[14] The leverage of good intentions already exists at the international level and, indeed, in many cases at the national level; what is needed are concrete proposals for action and research.

In chapter 2 a model of female employment is outlined which incorporates elements designed to achieve the goals of promoting rural development, improving the status of women, and encouraging delayed marriage and birth planning. The key points have been set forth in this introduction, that is, the employment should generate income over which women have some control, provide jobs for young rural women in small-scale, labor-intensive light industries, organize the work along cooperative principles in a centralized workplace outside the home, and offer additional social services and incentives such as literacy training, child care, and family planning. The reasons for including each of these are set forth in some detail, although it is difficult to sort out their independent effects in promoting change. Each is somewhat controversial. For example, the idea of restricting employment to women, and especially to unmarried women or to those with only one or two children, is bound to elicit some disagreement. Locating work outside the home, emphasizing industry over agriculture, encouraging cooperatives, and providing child care on the job, are debatable proposals, even in the South Asian context. The model is not rigid, however, and alternative forms have been suggested where appropriate.

Chapter 3 consists of five case studies of employment schemes in South Asia in which rural women are currently earning money. These are described in some detail to convey the flavor of the local culture and the vivid personalities of some of the women whose lives have changed as a result of their employment. The programs include small agricultural cooperatives for raising vegetables and poultry, sponsored by the government of Bangladesh; the Anand Milk Union Ltd. (AMUL) Dairy cooperative in India, with tens of thousands of members, in which women sell milk to the cooperative for a daily cash return; the rapidly growing jute

---

[14] Quoted in Papanek (1975, p. 196, n. 1).

handicraft industry in Bangladesh, which is organized around village cooperatives; several food-processing cooperatives in India, one of which
brings young tribal women out of their homes to a central workplace
every day; and the Nepalese carpet-weaving factories. None of these projects perfectly fits the model proposed here—some are agricultural, some
are home-based, some employ men as well as women, and some offer only
irregular incomes. Although systematic data are not available, each of the
projects is informally evaluated for its current and potential social, economic, and demographic impacts.

Chapter 4 outlines a number of issues relevant to some very basic questions. What type of small industry is viable in a particular village? Where
are the raw materials to come from, and how are products to be marketed? Where can one turn for long-term development loans and for
operating expenses? Some rural regions appear to be so devoid of resources and so plagued with calamities that the creation of self-sustaining
industries is out of the question. Others show more promise. Chapter 4
offers suggestions for products and credit that could be adapted to the
unique conditions of different locales.

Chapter 5 proposes strategies for overcoming structural and cultural
obstacles to women's employment outside the home, such as the already
heavy domestic (and sometimes agricultural) burdens of rural women
and the pervasive cultural restrictions of Hindu and Muslim origin on
women's physical mobility. Chapter 6 addresses the problems of creating
a cooperative work group, building a viable organizational structure, and
training workers in production and administration, based on principles of
self-management. The final chapter presents an overview of the broader
questions of socioeconomic development in an attempt to place this set
of proposals in a larger context. Obviously, any specific suggestion for
investment of money and energies must deal with the issue of finite
amounts of both, of priorities, and of the returns from alternative forms of
investment.

Every chapter raises more questions than it answers. Some of these are
included in the appendix, which sets forth a variety of research proposals
for investigations prior to deciding on a project site, for evaluations of
ongoing programs of female employment, and for assessing, on a comparative basis, the causal relationships implied in the model of female
labor-force participation and fertility. What emerges most clearly is that
the state of our knowledge remains highly tenuous. We need to arrange
a closer marriage between theory and practice.

2

CREATING NONAGRICULTURAL EMPLOYMENT FOR RURAL WOMEN

If they are to serve as authentic channels for social change, strategies for integrating women into the development process must be sensitive to differences in social and economic structures as well as in cultural values and beliefs. The strategy outlined in this chapter has a particular thrust in contending that one must begin with the creation of employment for rural women, and that this employment should produce income over which women have some control. In addition, it should be located in small towns and villages; create jobs outside agriculture in small-scale, labor-intensive light industries; draw women out of their homes into a central workplace; organize production cooperatively; and offer additional services and incentives.

This particular combination of elements derives from observations of four countries (India, Pakistan, Bangladesh, and Nepal) that share certain characteristics such as their extreme poverty, relatively high rates of population growth, early and universal marriage patterns among women, and cultural systems valuing female seclusion. But structural and cultural conditions differ widely within these countries both by geographical region and by religion, caste, and class. Thus, the several parts of the model will have to be adapted to local situations, even in the South Asian context. The model is certainly not designed to be transplanted intact to other settings, although in some parts of Africa, Latin America, or elsewhere in Asia or the Middle East, conditions may resemble those described here more than one would initially suspect.

Before determining which projects are feasible, it is necessary to obtain information on the current productive activities of rural women. It is amazing how little we know, in general, about how rural women in most parts of the world spend their time. A few valiant attempts have been made to compile comparative international data on women's access to schooling, employment in the formal and informal sectors, income, political power, and other resources, or to explore in diverse settings their decision-making roles in agriculture, small rural industries, marketing, community projects, and family care.[1] Information from seven African and Latin American countries suggests certain similarities. For example, even where women play an active role in agriculture as workers and decision makers, joining agricultural cooperatives or obtaining credit appears to be the prerogative of men (Mickelwait, Riegelman, and Sweet, 1976, pages 40–45). Thus, even in cultures setting few restrictions on women's mobility outside the home, programs may have to be aimed specifically at women in order for them to benefit directly as active participants.

In the sections that follow, I will explore the conditions under which it would be more appropriate to integrate women more fully into the agricultural sector rather than creating jobs for them in small industries, or to mingle the sexes in the workplace rather than restricting employment to women only, or to organize production more loosely or more rigidly rather than insisting on cooperatives. Also, it may be more appropriate under some conditions to pay women workers partly or solely in kind rather than cash in order to avoid their having to turn over their earnings to the male household head, and to bypass inflationary increases in the cost of food staples.[2] For most rural settings in Asia, Africa, Latin America, and the Middle East, it can be argued that upgrading women's domestic and subsistence activities to income-generating production is central to improving their status, promoting rural development, and altering reproductive aspirations and behavior.

THE IMPORTANCE OF EARNING MONEY

After months of discussions with women in her natal village in the Punjab, Syeda Abida Hussain decided ten years ago that the key to women's problems was their lack of control over money.[3] She began, on a very small

---

[1] Among the major contributions are Boserup (1970); Boulding (1977); Boulding and coauthors (1976); Giele and Smock (1977); and Mickelwait, Riegelman, and Sweet (1976).

[2] As Epstein has suggested (1973, pp. 261–263), paying workers in quantities of grain rather than cash is not a regressive step. Cancian (1977, p. 7) calls it "the rural society's equivalent to wage rates tied to the consumer price index." An additional advantage is that cooperatives could buy wheat or rice in bulk for lower prices and thus save two ways. Inasmuch as most poor women working essentially out of economic need are likely to spend most or all of their income on daily subsistence requirements, payment in kind on the basis of the family's needs and in cash beyond that point could eliminate one profit-taking step in the transformation of cash to food (Mickelwait, Riegelman, and Sweet, 1976, p. 64; and Singh, 1977, p. 255). It also provides a highly visible symbol of a woman's earning power if she brings home food every day, and helps her to maintain control over her earnings.

[3] An April 1976 interview with Syeda Abida Hussain, member of the Provincial Assembly, Punjab, Pakistan.

scale, to encourage an embroidery industry which now provides income for some two hundred Muslim girls and women in the village. Several of the original workers have saved enough money to buy their own homes. Many save for their own or their daughters' dowries. One girl loaned money to her father to start a vegetable shop. Parents are said to look on the birth of girls far more favorably now than was customary in the days when an unmarried daughter contributed nothing. The women themselves are proud of their skills and their ability to earn money.

It is remarkable how rarely people have come to this particular conclusion regarding the needs of rural women. Community development experts, in spite of the obvious and desperate financial need of many wives and widows, rarely suggest programs that would enable women to earn money. A 1975 seminar on Rural Women and Social Development, sponsored by the Family Planning Association of India, for example, drew up a plan for the Mahila Mandals (village women's associations). This plan, though promoting self-reliance, recommended merely (1) more awareness of community social problems, (2) more female participation in voluntary labor programs, and (3) more contraceptive centers with family-counseling services. Yet it could be argued that the lack of money in poor households is the single most important factor retarding rural development, and that the lack of control over what money exists contributes to the low status of women and increases their motivation for frequent childbearing.

The redistribution of income, land, wealth, and services may be essential to creating conditions favorable to socioeconomic development and fertility decline in developing countries.[4] Income distribution within nations appears to explain the different fertility levels across countries more adequately than does per capita GNP.[5] At given levels of per capita GNP, those nations in which the poorest sector of the population receives a relatively higher percentage of the total income tend to have lower birthrates than those in which the poorest sector receives a smaller share. One direct method of raising the level of living for the poor is to reduce the ratio of dependents to workers by generating income-earning employment for women. This strategy is especially important where cultural restrictions limit women's mobility outside the home, or where women working outside the home receive little more than their midday meal in payment. Such

----

[4] This argument is expanded by King (1974, pp. 147–148); Kocher (1973); and Rich (1973), among others.

[5] Repetto's (1974, p. 147) study of sixty-four countries found that each additional percentage point of GNP going to the poorest 40 percent of the population reduced the number of births per thousand women of reproductive age by 2.9 points.

conditions force male workers to support numerous dependents, including adult women, on impossibly small incomes.

Some economists have argued that, other things being equal, increasing household income is pronatalist because of its "pure income effect." In rural Pakistan at very low income levels, fertility tends to rise as income rises, although the net statistical effect of income on fertility overall is near zero (Khan and Sirageldin, 1975). The pure income argument assumes that the fertility constraints induced by low incomes weaken as incomes rise and couples are able to afford more children. The question is whether the poor voluntarily limit childbearing or whether extreme destitution causes maternal malnutrition which, in turn, reduces fecundity and thus, involuntarily, fertility. In any case, conditions are rarely as equal as the economists would wish. Incomes generally rise in the context of changing living conditions and altered tastes and aspirations, which simultaneously affect reproductive motivation and behavior.

The effect of income on fertility also depends on which household member is earning and controlling the money. Income distribution between husband and wife or parent and child may be crucial to determining the power structure of the decision-making unit. A woman earning half the household income will likely have more bargaining power than the woman who earns none, even when total household earnings are the same. Whether the woman directs her power toward delaying marriage for herself or her daughter, or practicing birth control, would depend on the extent to which she is exposed to social rewards other than marriage and childbearing.

Earning money may help to delay the marriage of young girls by persuading their parents not to marry them off so early as long as they are contributing to household earnings, and by improving the young women's bargaining position over the timing of marriage and the choice of a mate (Dixon, 1976b). The strong preference for sons that is characteristic in so many parts of South Asia should also weaken if unmarried girls earn money, which would reduce fertility indirectly. Married women earning their money may exercise more choice about childbearing and feel less dependent on family members, particularly sons, for economic survival. The emphasis of the Integrated Rural Development Program in Bangladesh on raising women's routine subsistence activities to the commercial level is premised on precisely this assumption: "The hypothesis is that a woman's income-earning capacity will of necessity give her an equal right to decide the largeness of her family, and provide her recognition for activities other than childbearing" (Ahmad, 1976, page 23). In some situations, strong cultural values favoring male dominance may override the effects of women's economic independence on the decision-making power within the family (Safilios-Rothschild, 1970). But patriarchal power relations within the rural family are not likely to be substantially altered if women do not earn and control some money.

Raising women's subsistence activities to the level of providing income is probably a highly unrealistic goal for some areas, especially for isolated communities far removed from sources of raw materials and from markets. The Bangladesh Rural Advancement Committee project, covering two hundred villages in the Sulla area near Sylhet, encourages self-sufficiency in agriculture and in basic household goods rather than promoting production aimed at a larger market. If women can grow vegetables for their own consumption or make baskets or fishnets for local use, then the cause of rural development will be served; households will be better off, even in the absence of women's earned incomes. Under other conditions, however, the generation of income for rural women is a viable possibility that can simultaneously create an effective demand for new goods and services within the village.

THE RURAL SITE

The rationale for locating income-generating employment in rural areas is simple. The vast majority of the South Asian population is rural: 81 percent in India in 1971, 74 percent in Pakistan, 93 percent in Bangladesh, and 96 percent in Nepal.[6] Rural inhabitants experience more extreme poverty than do urban residents, in part because of the frequently high levels of both seasonal and permanent under- and unemployment in the agricultural sector. In addition, rural women marry earlier and bear slightly more children on the average than do women in towns and cities. If national birth rates are to be substantially reduced, opportunities for rural women must be expanded beyond their current subsistence limits.

The decentralization of industrial development creates a diffusion effect by dispersing the sources of economic and social change throughout the country rather than concentrating them in urban centers. As a result of such dispersal, migration from the countryside to overcrowded cities will be slowed. But where should the new employment be located? Staley and Morse (1965, pages 310–316) argue that villages are too small and too

---

[6] Chesnais and Vallin (1975, p. 1066) note that the Indian census defines as urban all cities with municipal statutes, and localities of more than 5,000 inhabitants, having a density greater than 386 persons per square kilometer, and with less than one-fourth of the active male population in agriculture. In Pakistan and Bangladesh, towns with municipal statutes and localities of more than 5,000 inhabitants with an "urban character" are defined as urban. The definition for Nepal is not specified.

culturally conservative to serve as appropriate locations for most new rural industry, whereas intermediate-sized towns are more receptive to innovation and more easily linked with urban markets. It may be, however, that certain small-scale industries or agro-industries, such as fruit preservation or dairy processing, can be more efficiently sited close to the source of raw materials, that is, in villages rather than towns. One could also question the assumption that villages are necessarily more culturally conservative than towns, especially in their attitudes about women's roles. One study (Gore, 1968, page 160) of several Hindu Agarwal communities found that 50 percent of rural women accepted without qualification the statement, "Women may work for money if they so choose," while only 37 percent of women living in urban fringe areas and only 30 percent living in Delhi agreed with the statement. (It should be noted that no men were in agreement with this idea.) Muslim families of the urban lower-middle class frequently adhere more strictly than do villagers to the observance of purdah in order to protect their tenuous social standing (Papanek, 1971, pages 294 and 322). Village women may consequently be more amenable to recruitment for income-generating employment outside the home than are women in towns.

NONAGRICULTURAL EMPLOYMENT

In regions or among socioeconomic or ethnic groups in which women currently play an important role in agriculture—in the Himalayan regions, for example, or among the tribes and lower castes of India—the best strategy may well be to integrate women more fully into the agricultural process. Programs would aim at ensuring that women receive appropriate training in new methods of planting, cultivation, harvesting, storage, and processing, and in animal and poultry husbandry; that they have equal access with men to new technology, especially labor-saving methods and equipment; that they have equal access to membership in agricultural cooperatives, to land ownership and tenant status, to credit and marketing facilities; and that they receive equal wages for agricultural labor. In many cases this would require that female agricultural extension workers be trained specifically to reach out to women clients.

As a development strategy for India, Mazumdar (1975) proposes integrating—or, more accurately, *rehabilitating*—women in agriculture, on the grounds that agriculture is the most important productive sector of the economy, that women have acquired skills and an attachment to agricultural production by long tradition, and that the alternatives (rural industry, handicrafts, or the service sector) can employ a small minority only.

Recognizing that agricultural employment is frequently seasonal, unpredictable, and exploitative, Mazumdar argues that the answer is to ensure adequate wages, security of employment, and maternity benefits and child care for women workers, concluding that "agro-based industries and handicrafts are certainly needed to provide *additional* avenues of employment—but they should not be seen as *alternatives* to agricultural work. . . . Food, after all, will always remain the most important productive function and even though the labour is hard the life it promises to women is more satisfactory than most other productive fields" (Mazumdar, 1975, page 65).

Mazumdar's emphasis on rehabilitation rests on the startling observation that the number of Indian women employed in agriculture has not grown since the early twentieth century (with the exception of 1961, when the census definition of labor-force participation was particularly liberal), while the female population has doubled in size during this period (table 2-1). Although changing definitions and undercounting throw some doubt on the reliability of the figures, apparently six million fewer women found employment in agriculture in 1971 than in 1911.[7] As the number of female cultivators shrank, the number of agricultural laborers grew; by 1971,

Table 2-1. Women in Agricultural Occupations in India, 1911–71

	1911	1921	1931	1951[a]	1961	1971[b]
Total female population	123,898	122,749	136,075	173,549	212,467	263,900
Total no. female workers	41,802	40,095	37,600	40,539	59,402	31,298
Workers as percentage of female population	33.7	32.7	27.6	23.3	28.0	11.9
No. female agricultural workers	30,898	30,279	27,177	31,062	42,274	25,060
Female agricultural workers as percentage of:						
Female population	24.9	24.7	20.0	17.9	22.2	9.5
Female workers	73.9	75.5	72.3	76.8	79.6	80.1
No. female cultivators	18,090	20,276	12,180	18,368	33,103	9,266
No. female agricultural laborers	12,808	10,003	14,997	12,694	14,171	15,794
Percentage of female agricultural workers who are:						
Cultivators	58.5	67.0	44.8	59.1	70.0	37.0
Laborers	41.5	33.0	55.2	40.9	30.0	63.0

Source: Committee on the Status of Women in India (1974, pp. 153 and 158).
[a] Excluding Jammu and Kashmir.
[b] Provisional statistics.

[7] An additional 1.6 million women classified as nonworkers in 1971 were engaged in agriculture as a "secondary activity," 0.4 million as cultivators and 1.2 million as agricultural laborers (Committee on the Status of Women in India, 1974, p. 154).

half of the casual laborers, daily-wage workers, and contract and bonded laborers in agriculture were women, reflecting increasing landlessness and pauperization of the rural population in general (Committee on the Status of Women in India, 1974; and Chatterjee, 1975, page 31). In some tribal areas of India (among the Garo, for example) new crops, new farming techniques, and the biases of extension workers were pushing women out of their traditional agricultural roles in the transition from shifting cultivation to orchards and terraces.[8]

I would argue that where women's role in agricultural production is declining or already low, an alternative strategy should be considered for generating rural employment. To attempt to rehabilitate women workers in a sector in which there is little demand for their labor is to expose them to an especially vulnerable position. Where male unemployment and underemployment are high, women experience particular difficulty in finding work: the 1971 census of India defined 4.5 million unemployed rural women as compared with 3.2 million rural men, and national sample surveys counted more days of unemployment on the average for women than for men (Committee on the Status of Women in India, 1974, page 160).

Similarly, where agricultural wages are low, women are paid less than men, even for the same work. Figures available from the Committee on the Status of Women in India (1974, pages 165–166) for six Indian states show that legal minimum wages for male sowers, weeders, and reapers are approximately one-third higher than those for females, and even these wage minimums are notoriously difficult to enforce in rural areas where employment is geographically isolated and sporadic. Female agricultural workers are also far less likely than males to be paid for their work. For example, in 1961 approximately 14 percent of the rural male labor force in India consisted of unpaid family workers compared with 41 percent of the rural female labor force (Committee on the Status of Women in India, 1974, page 157); in Pakistan, the figures were 23 and 76 percent, respectively.[9] Even if they are paid, women may have no control over their earnings. Female cotton harvesters in Pakistan, for example, receive one-sixteenth of the cotton they pick through the season, but the men take it to market.

Women's agricultural labor in most developing countries has probably been consistently undercounted and undervalued. An economist in Pakistan remarked that men acknowledge the women's contribution "in their

[8] See Committee on the Status of Women in India (1974, p. 168); and for similar examples, see Boserup (1970, pp. 15–81).

[9] In addition, Youssef (1974a, tab. 4) reported that in seven North African and Middle Eastern Muslim societies, unpaid workers constituted from 39 to 74 percent of female agricultural workers and from 10 to 25 percent of male workers.

heart of hearts" but not in the sense that would permit female participation in institutions or decision making. In Bangladesh "a farmer is valued on the basis of the rice he grows, but his wife's part in processing it is not considered an economic activity. Nor is her role in poultry raising, growing vegetables, fruits, making household clay utensils, mats, fans, and preservation of seeds, pickles, dry fish, dehydrated rice, etc. ever taken into account" (Ahmad, 1976, page 25). Census definitions of economic activity usually exclude large numbers of women in agriculture, especially those who perform unpaid work in the family farm or who work seasonally or part-time.[10] When talking to census takers, male household heads are likely to exaggerate their own efforts, while deflating the contributions of female family members. Women themselves undervalue their own work, frequently omitting any mention of their labor in the fields when they are asked whether they work outside the home.

Perhaps this should tell us something about the potential of most agricultural work for raising the status of women or promoting rural development. As Youssef (1974a, page 18) concluded from an analysis of eight Muslim countries, "To promote women's inclusion into the agricultural sector will mean allowing women to continue dragging behind males; it will not add to the efficiency of labor productivity; it will only perpetuate the economic and psychological dependency of Muslim women on their men." As for its effect on the birthrate, there is no reason to believe that female participation in agriculture should induce women to marry later or to want or to have fewer children.[11] Alternatively, the creation of employment opportunities in small industries or organized services which can be monopolized by women could create an independent power base for women, provide a direct source of income, ensure more adequate scrutiny of earnings and working conditions, raise wages among women remaining in the agricultural sector, and, in the long run, create conditions favoring delayed marriage and controlled fertility among women workers.

[10] The number of economically active females of all ages reported for Morocco in 1960 excludes 1.2 "female family helpers in agriculture" by official count. Tunisia's 1966 census excludes 250,000 "female family helpers," and Algeria's 1966 census excludes 1.2 million "women in agriculture" (UN, Department of Economic and Social Affairs, 1975, p. 139).

[11] Chaudhury (1974) found a statistically significant, negative correlation between the percentage of the female population engaged in agriculture and the child:woman ratio in fifty-nine subdivisions of Bangladesh, in the 1961 census, and concluded that alternative roles for women, even in the traditional sector of the economy, may also lower fertility. Chaudhury's findings are an exception to the general observation that agricultural work and home-based handicrafts have either no effect on fertility or a pronatalist effect. See, for example, Jaffe and Azumi (1960); Bindary, Baxter, and Hollingsworth (1973); and Goldstein (1972).

SMALL-SCALE VILLAGE INDUSTRIES

India represents a classic example of displacement of women from agriculture without a concomitant absorption into the modern sector of the economy.[12] Although female workers—even those in secondary and tertiary occupations—are likely to be undercounted in the census because of the scattered and unorganized nature of most of their employment, the absolute number of women in nonagricultural jobs has dropped since 1911 in six of the seven employment categories shown in table 2-2. Particularly sharp declines appear in the economic activities traditionally

Table 2-2. Women in Nonagricultural Occupations in India, 1911–71

	1911	1921	1931	1951[c]	1961	1971[d]
No. female workers in industry						
Mining, plantations[a]	1,452	1,431	1,575	1,357	1,187	907
Household industry[b]	n.a.	n.a.	n.a.	n.a.	4,665	1,331
Manufacturing, other than household	4,391	3,689	3,281	2,906	789	865
Construction	294	289	291	291	243	204
Females in industry as percentage of:						
Female population	4.9	4.4	3.8	2.6	3.2	1.2
Female workers	14.7	13.5	13.7	11.2	11.6	10.5
No. female service workers						
Trade and commerce	2,266	2,189	1,914	1,153	815	556
Transport, storage, communications	79	67	49	123	65	146
Other service	2,422	2,151	3,313	3,647	4,364	2,229
Females in service as percentage of:						
Female population	3.8	3.6	3.9	2.8	2.5	1.1
Female workers	11.4	11.0	14.0	12.1	8.8	9.4

Source: Committee on the Status of Women in India (1974, pp. 153 and 158).
Abbreviation: n.a., not available.
[a] Also quarrying, livestock, forestry, fishing, hunting.
[b] Included in manufacturing from 1911 to 1951.
[c] Excluding Jammu and Kashmir.
[d] Provisional statistics.

[12] The assumption that rates of female participation in the nonagricultural labor force would automatically rise as poor nations became richer (Wilensky, 1968) has been effectively challenged by Youssef's (1974b) comparison of female labor-force participation in several Latin American and Middle Eastern countries at similar levels of development (per capita incomes, percentages of males in agriculture, percentage of urban population), and by Boserup's (1970) observations of Africa and Asia.

employing large numbers of rural women—cottage industries, including spinning and weaving; paper making; jute handicrafts; bidi (cigarette) making; rice processing and oil pressing; and trade and commerce. Women in these occupations have been increasingly forced into competition with factory producers in the expanding industrial sector and with wholesalers and intermediaries in marketing. The control over income that many women had derived from marketing their own food or handicrafts has largely been lost. In 1971, women accounted for 28 percent of rural workers engaged in household industries, for 14 percent of workers in industries outside the household, but for only 8 percent of those engaged in trade and commerce (Committee on the Status of Women in India, 1974, page 155). The number of women employed in mines and plantations (tea picking is traditionally defined as women's work) also dropped from 1.45 million in 1911 to under 1 million in 1971. Women construction workers declined in number, despite the growing utilization of female labor on public works projects. Although educated women have been entering clerical jobs, teaching, and the health professions in larger numbers, the general thrust of Indian development has also been to exclude more women from traditional service occupations than are absorbed into new tertiary jobs. Those displaced are disproportionately the illiterate and unskilled, as the demand for their labor shrinks and competition for scarce jobs intensifies. In short, a small minority of middle-class women are able to take advantage of new opportunities for employment in the modern sector of the economy, but the majority of women living in rural areas and among low-income groups in the cities are pushed into marginal economic activities or out of the labor force entirely.

Given this thrust, what are the possibilities for creating income-earning, nonagricultural employment for rural women? Recruitment into construction projects, such as government rural works, is one possibility. Large numbers of tribal and scheduled caste women in India are currently employed in construction work, and Muslim women in Bangladesh—mostly destitute women widowed in the 1971 war or wives of unskilled workers—have begun to turn to the Food for Work program for rural employment.[13] However, construction work, even on government projects, is usually highly exploitative. Its critics (Ranade and Sinha, n.d.) point to failures of protective legislation covering wages, working conditions, and hours worked. Given the undernourished condition of the workers, the work

---

[13] The term *scheduled caste* refers to those persons who have been given special treatment by the government because of their depressed status. For example, they have special representatives in legislatures and may be favored by so-called affirmative action policies in government employment.

tends to be exhausting. Women on construction projects are disproportionately concentrated in the lowest-skilled and lowest-paid jobs (generally, that of carrying earth or bricks) with no chance of learning new
skills.

Employing women in the rural service sector is another possibility.
With access to credit and with purchasing and marketing advice, some
could be productively employed in personal service occupations or in
trade and marketing. Again, this type of self-employment is economically
vulnerable. Unorganized service workers are unlikely to acquire the capital and skills necessary to ensure sustaining economic returns. Villages
require growing numbers of white-collar personnel as teachers, health
workers, community development officers, agricultural extension agents,
family-planning aides, and so on, but the extremely high levels of illiteracy
among rural women in India, Bangladesh, Pakistan, and Nepal effectively
preclude their participation in most of these occupations. In some cases
educational requirements could be lowered to recruit illiterate or semi-
literate village workers for on-the-job training, an approach that would
undoubtedly increase the representation of women in the service sector.

On the whole, however, the main avenue of nonagricultural employment for rural women would appear to be in small-scale industries and
agro-industries. Even a brief investigation of foodstuffs and commodities
available in rural markets in different seasons should suggest certain kinds
of economic production that would promote self-sufficiency of the local
community.[14] Ahmed (1975, page 29) suggests the decentralized manufacture of processed agricultural products, consumer goods, and light
engineering goods, that is, commodities that are labor-intensive, based on
local resources, and that require simple technology, small investment, and
cheap or little fuel. Logical possibilities include preserved foods, cloth
and ready-made clothing, soap, household and farm utensils, and small
manufactured items such as transistor radios assembled from imported
parts. (The advantages and disadvantages of particular products are discussed more fully in chapter 4.) In any case, if villages are strategically
placed in a transportation and communications network, production can
be aimed at supplying urban and export markets as well as (or instead of)
filling local needs either directly or by substituting domestic for imported
goods. Women recruited into small-scale, rural industries could simultaneously create an effective demand for labor-saving goods and services

[14] For a comprehensive evaluation of products appropriate to small-scale industries, see Staley and Morse (1965). Source materials on action programs, current
research, and publications relating to small-scale industries are cited in the American Council on Education's *Rural Development Network Bulletin.*

in order to reduce their own domestic burdens, thereby generating new jobs catering to the needs of families of employed women.

In their proposal for creating modern small industries in developing countries, Staley and Morse (1965) have created a typology of manufacturing based on the organization of work (table 2-3). *Small* industries range from those in which production is solely for family use to the small factory of, say, well under one hundred employees (fewer if production is highly mechanized). The *family-use system* consists of home-based production of commodities such as preserved food, clothing, pottery, and furniture for the household's own use, a type of production generally encouraged by community development programs. The *artisan system* includes workers who are family members or, in the case of artisan workshops, apprentices in crafts such as weaving, tailoring, shoemaking, goldsmithing, and so forth. The *putting-out or dispersed factory system* involves a more complex division of labor, with the work being dispersed through middlemen, such as merchants, factory managers, or agents, who deliver raw materials to the home or shop and buy the entire output. Whereas industrial homework employs family members (usually paid on a piecework basis), the dependent or quasi-independent small shop relies primarily on hired labor that is paid either by piecework or on an hourly or daily wage. Finally, the most centralized form of organization is the *factory system,* classified here into small, medium, and large factories on the basis of the number of employees and the power source used. Each of these organizational types may be located in either rural or urban areas, may be based on handwork or mechanization, and (with the exception of home consumption) may cater to either local or distant markets. What makes a small industry modern is its orientation to the needs of an emerging economy; its adaptability in the search for improved techniques, products, and design; its adoption of an appropriate physical technology and a more highly organized social technology; and a rationalized system of planning, budgeting, and marketing (Staley and Morse, 1965, page 4).

Table 2-3. Manufacturing Classified by Systems of Work Organization

Family-use system	Artisan system	Putting-out or dispersed factory system	Factory system
Own use manufacturing	Homework	Industrial homework (wage-paid)	Small
	Workshop		Medium
		Dependent or quasi-independent small shops	Large

Source: Staley and Morse (1965, p. 5).

Small-scale production units are particularly well suited to the manufacture of many consumer goods required by a rapidly growing population and to labor-intensive employment which utilizes intermediate
technology while reducing the need for high capital expenditures. Staley
and Morse (1965) warn against taking the ideology of labor-intensiveness
to extremes, for example, the employment of widows in India to make, by
hand, matches that are far more efficiently (and less dangerously) made
by machine. They argue, "Labor-intensiveness which achieves the saving
of some scarcer productive factor, such as capital, is a virtue . . . but labor-
intensiveness without saving of other factors is pure waste" (Staley and
Morse, 1965, page 294). It then becomes an unproductive form of work
relief rather than a genuine development effort.

THE CENTRAL WORKPLACE

Most government and private welfare programs aimed at raising the level
of living of rural women and their families have concentrated on encouraging greater productivity in the home through training in child care and
nutrition, cooking, vegetable and poultry raising, sewing, and other activities coming under the general rubric of home economics. If they have
addressed the issue of income-earning activities for women at all, they
have encouraged cottage industries such as weaving, basket making, or
embroidery, with the products being marketed through intermediaries,
local shops, or cooperatives. Frequently, programs are based on the desirability of raising consumption while leaving women's roles in the family
and community basically unchanged.

Although home-based production for the family's own use or for sale
undoubtedly improves the level of living of village women at least slightly,
and although under some conditions home-based industries may be a
necessary transitional stage to a higher form of economic organization,
locating economic production in a central workplace carries a number of
economic and social advantages. First, it permits closer supervision of
workers, control over the quality of goods, and more adequate protection
of working conditions and wages by regulating agencies.[15] Second, it
allows an economy of scale and division of labor that are impossible to

---

[15] A 1948 International Labour Organization study of home industries (garment-
making, spinning and weaving, and so forth) in Europe and North America, in
which workers were mostly women and children, concluded that ". . . industrial
homework is one of the least regulated, least supervised, and most hazardous systems of industrial production" (Staley and Morse, 1965, p. 76).

achieve in a dispersed system and encourages specialization and diversification of tasks. Third, it facilitates technological innovation and investment in capital equipment; and fourth, it draws women out of the isolation and conservatism of their domestic environments into social interaction with one another, capitalizing on their incentive to meet together. Fifth, it eases delivery of special training programs in vocational skills, literacy, nutrition, family planning, and other areas; and last, it encourages delayed marriage and fertility control by posing, among other contradictions, a degree of incompatibility between worker and family roles. Home-based industry, on the other hand, ". . . is almost always a barrier to improvements in production technology and managerial practices, is subject to grave abuses, and has psychological and social drawbacks that impinge on, among other things, the status of women and the control of population growth" (Staley and Morse, 1965, page 23).

Removing women physically from the pervasive influence of the domestic environment for at least a few hours each day may be essential to altering their situation substantially. Ahmed (1975, page 30) argues, "To be recognized as a person in her own right, to become an acting individual, she must build a link with the world outside her family. The strongest link is economic, one of contributing skill and energy to the social whole and earning the material and psychological rewards of this contribution. Individuality grows out of interaction." Removing production from the home can also ensure that women are paid for their economic activities directly rather than working as part of a labor unit in which the husband or father is the employer handling negotiations with the outside world, marketing the product, and controlling the household income.[16] This situation is typical of female workers in the khadi (homespun) industry concentrated in Rajasthan, Punjab, Haryana, Jammu, Kashmir, and Himachel Pradesh. Women usually spin and, with their children, "help" with the weaving, but they are not paid directly (Oza, 1975, page 27). Their productivity does not challenge the patriarchal structure of the village household. Similarly, women in a small village near Kathmandu spend all day squatting over a hot and smoky fire in the dark interior of their homes, making puffed rice which their husbands sell in the market. Their children play by the fire or in the dirt outside the door. If the women worked centrally, they could improve their equipment and techniques, save on expensive firewood, and take pleasure in one another's company. Someone could watch all the children together, and a division of labor could be instituted in which some women are free to do the marketing while others boil, husk, dry, puff, and package the rice. The women them-

---

[16] The idea of husband as employer is derived from Ahmed (1975).

selves would decide on the selling price of their product and receive the direct benefits of their income.

Drawing women outside the home should also create conditions likely to lead to delayed marriage and birth control. The powerless, physically isolated woman, entirely dependent on her husband and children for social status and economic survival, is an unlikely candidate for family planning. Home-based industries tend to encourage childbearing because they so frequently employ young children to weave rugs or saris, wrap bidis, shell prawns, make baskets, or help in other tasks. Locating production in a central workplace should devalue the economic contribution of young children and deter their exploitation as a cheap labor force.

EMPLOYING WOMEN IN THEIR EARLY REPRODUCTIVE YEARS

I would like to propose that special, small-scale industrial workshops be created for women only, and that workers should be recruited primarily from unmarried girls and married women in their early reproductive years.

The proposal to create special employment for women is bound to stimulate controversy, for strong arguments can be made on both sides. Its proponents argue that work in an all-female setting fits with the cultural values limiting contact between the sexes, which is characteristic of much of South Asia. It also encourages the development of decision-making and technical skills among women who might otherwise withdraw from direct competition with men; and it can create strong bonds of solidarity, cutting across family and caste boundaries, to provide an alternative social and economic power base in the community. Its opponents argue that the promotion of "women's work" in all-female settings is a regressive policy, perpetuating segregation rather than promoting equality between the sexes. Others argue more generally that women should not receive special attention for jobs at all so long as men are under- or unemployed.

Creating employment specifically for women makes sense in at least three situations: (1) when the tasks to be organized are traditionally performed by females; (2) when cultural values require that girls and women be sheltered from contact with men who are not family members; and (3) when men are otherwise likely to gain control over the income earned from women's labor, for example, by selling the goods that women produce.

First, opposition to women's gainful employment should be significantly reduced if the task is one traditionally performed by women or defined as *women's work.* I am not suggesting that jobs for women be restricted to these tasks, but the prevailing sex-typing of activities within each community can create a natural occupational base for women that does not threaten to take jobs away from men, but rather generates new employment. Women in South Asia care for milch animals and raise poultry and vegetables in subsistence activities that could be upgraded in many areas to commercial production; they process foods into salable items such as ghee, ground spices, husked and puffed rice, or pickles and chutneys, and then make household items such as mats, baskets, cloth, and sometimes pottery. In Bangladesh, some village women make fishnets; in Kerala, women manufacture palm gur and process vegetable fibers. All-women's industrial and artisanal enterprises would be logical outgrowths of these activities.

Employment can be successfully generated in fields not defined as *female,* however. Women's cooperatives in Poona operate a match factory and an industry for manufacturing radio transformers. In Kerala, an industrial scheme is being developed at Ernakulam to employ women only for galvanizing, anodizing, and manufacturing pins, hooks, and gem-clips and for operating a foundry. The Social Welfare Board of India has diversified its vocational training programs for women to include new occupations such as radio and television assembly, photography, and electroplating in addition to garment making, printing, handlooming and handicrafts, and dairy production (Varadappan, 1976). Ahmed (1975, page 29) argues strongly that the employment opportunities most likely to attract rural women are those that are "least rural and least womanish"—that is, small industries that would teach women to operate and repair machines and to supervise, manage, keep accounts, and sell their products. Since these tasks will also attract men, a quota may be required to ensure that women participate. One way of doing this is to design some workshops for women only.

The second condition under which an all-female work setting is desirable is where villagers fear that the chastity of the female and the honor of her family will be compromised if she mingles freely with men or is merely subject to their gaze or conversation. These fears are most elaborately symbolized by the institution of purdah, which regulates contact between the sexes by offering "separate worlds and symbolic shelter" to Muslim and Hindu women of certain social standing (Papanek, 1973). Women observing purdah must be assured of a protected working environment, at least initially, if they are to take advantage of employment opportunities outside the home. Among some tribes and lower castes of

India, where women move about more freely, and among Muslims forced by economic necessity to forgo the luxury of female seclusion, women may still prefer to work primarily with other women, even if the culture does not demand it.

Creating employment for women only is also effective in those instances where females are largely excluded from existing economic arrangements, especially where they perform much of the labor but acquire no control over the earned income. The National Cooperative Union of India (n.d.) provides one such example. Laws which, in the past, prevented Hindu women from inheriting property effectively blocked them from membership in agricultural cooperatives, most of which are based on land ownership, regardless of their participation in agricultural labor or their interest in the economic decisions of the household. Credit societies made up of male members similarly block women from direct access to loans for their own enterprises. Even in cooperatives such as the khadi or dairy industry, in which women play a major role in production, shareholders are usually male household heads who represent the family's economic interest. Virtually all of the societies' elected officials and permanent staff members are men.

Restricting employment totally or primarily to women not only ensures that economic rewards will accrue directly to female producers, but also promotes economic and social self-reliance by inducing women to take on a variety of tasks that men would ordinarily perform, such as buying raw materials, keeping accounts, supervising other workers, and marketing products. In a mixed group the women's initial shyness and inexperience are likely to cause them to defer to men in most decisions, thus negating much of the potential for individual development inherent in the new employment.

The proposition that jobs in these modern, small industries be reserved for women in their early reproductive years derives from the simple argument that little demographic impact will result from employing women who already have large numbers of children or who are beyond menopause or widowed. Yet, frequently it is the destitute widows and women abandoned by their husbands who are the first to come forth. These women would be good candidates for income-generating activities based in or around the home; such as growing vegetables or raising poultry or fish for the market, spinning and weaving, and other traditional tasks. But the new employment in central workplaces could more effectively be secured for girls of marriageable age and married women in the early stages of their childbearing years.

The employment of unmarried girls is perhaps the most important step in bringing about social and demographic change. The opportunity to learn skills and earn money before marriage should awaken a girl to the possibility of becoming economically self-reliant and, at the same time, allay her fear of destitution or her dependence on reluctant relatives if she should remain unmarried or become widowed or divorced in the future. More directly, income-generating employment outside the home should offer an economically attractive and (with careful planning) a culturally acceptable alternative to early marriage and childbearing, particularly if the girl contributes part of her income to her family.

The lower age limit for recruiting unmarried girls should not be set so young that parents are encouraged to take their daughters out of school (if, indeed, they are attending school at all) in order to put them to work, but it should be set low enough to offer gainful employment to girls at precisely the age at which their parents are most concerned to have them married. In many areas this will be as soon as the daughter reaches puberty. Almost half of the fifty-six mothers interviewed in a small village in the Pakistan Punjab said that girls should get married between the ages of twelve and fourteen (Anwar and Bilquees, 1976, page 34). In rural India, in 1971, at least 14 percent of girls between the ages of ten and fifteen were already married although the legal minimum age is fifteen (Committee on the Status of Women in India, 1974, pages 25–26); 18 percent of girls of this age (rural and urban) in Bangladesh in 1965; 16 percent in Nepal in 1971; and 1 percent in Pakistan in 1965 (Chesnais and Vallin, 1975, page 1089). Once the girls are working together, educational programs can deliberately promote postponement of marriage, at least until the age of eighteen or twenty. Direct financial incentives could also be incorporated into the work setting; some possibilities are suggested later in this chapter (see page 40).

A similar argument holds for married women: those most amenable to social and demographic change are still in their early childbearing years. Women could be recruited from among those with fewer than, say, three children, with special efforts being devoted to delaying additional pregnancies and preventing births past the second or third child. Forty-five percent of live births in rural India, in 1969, were fourth order or higher (Committee on the Status of Women in India, 1974, page 29).

An additional compelling reason for limiting employment to women in their early reproductive years is that younger women are likely to be more motivated to learn new skills and more open to acquiring new approaches to life. The National Board of Bangladesh Women's Rehabilitation Programme (1974, page 13) restricts recruitment for its vocational training programs to women under thirty years of age for exactly this reason. Older women, on the other hand, frequently admit their own lack of interest. For example, when women in a small village in the Pakistan

Punjab were asked whether they would like to learn new skills such as sewing, they replied, "We have passed our time. It is time for our daughters to learn things" (Anwar and Bilquees, 1976, page 41). Some constraints on the recruitment of unmarried girls and young married women, and how they might be overcome, are discussed in chapter 5.

THE PRODUCERS' COOPERATIVE

The concept of *cooperative* subsumes a number of organizational forms with a variety of functions—promoting group savings, obtaining credit and loans, buying raw materials or consumer goods, sharing agricultural services such as irrigation or fertilizers, manufacturing artisanal or industrial products, marketing, and organizing social services such as health care or housing, among others. In essence, a cooperative is a group of people who voluntarily form together, because of their common economic needs and interests, into an association in which decisions are made by members as a group or by elected representatives, and in which members share the costs and benefits of the enterprise. Cooperatives promote self-help through group action.

Although the suggestion is controversial, I would argue that organizing women's economic activities into small, industrial producers' cooperatives offers a number of economic and social advantages over the promotion of individual entrepreneurs or the provision of jobs by public agencies. First, workers acquire an economic stake in the success of the enterprise by contributing their own capital (however small) toward membership shares and by participating in the distribution of profits. Profit sharing disperses money over a large number of households rather than concentrating it in the hands of a few, thus raising the general level of living and encouraging expenditure in the local community. Second, members are generally required to save a portion of their earnings; the savings are credited to the individual member but pooled to provide loans to members or for group expenditures. Whereas private employers are unlikely to invest in public amenities, cooperatives generally allocate a portion of their profits to community projects such as schools or tubewells before distributing the balance as dividends. Third, registered cooperatives usually receive favorable economic concessions from governments in the form of easily obtained loans, lower interest rates, lower prices for raw materials, special marketing outlets, and technical assistance.[17]

[17] Government ministries in Bangladesh, Pakistan, India and Nepal have adopted rather elaborate criteria for registering and regulating cooperatives. Many women's

In addition, by involving workers in decisions about the conditions of their employment and their role in the community, and by teaching management skills, cooperatives can act as agents of social change by breaking down the psychology of female dependency, mobilizing women to act on their own behalf, and creating a sense of group consciousness that may be essential to the achievement of such community goals as environmental protection or the reduction of birthrates.[18]

Whether other forms of organization of the workplace can deal with these issues as effectively is open to question. Take the question of birth planning, for example. The immediate interests of the agrarian extended family are essentially pronatalist, while those of the wider community are likely to be antinatalist, especially where rapid population growth creates intense pressures upon available land or scarce educational facilities or jobs. Transcendence of immediate family interests requires that persons become aware of the socioeconomic costs to the community of their individual actions. Organizing women into cohesive associations could create competing loyalties between the family and the larger group, permitting new flexibility in reproductive ideals and behavior. Without an alternative base of information and support beyond the family, girls and women may be reluctant to resist pronatalist pressures from their kin.

In view of its many failures, critics are bound to question the promotion of a cooperative model. Its limitations are recognized, even by enthusiasts such as Ahmed (1973), who argues that for Pakistan the combination of collective efforts and individual freedom inherent in cooperatives offers an attractive and plausible alternative to pure capitalist or socialist models for rural development. No one could deny that the cooperative movement has confronted a multitude of social, economic, and political obstacles in its long history in South Asia as well as elsewhere. Stories abound of bureaucratic mismanagement, membership apathy, political interference, and financial collapse. A United Nations Research Institute for Social Development (1975, page ix) investigation of forty rural cooperatives of different types in Asia, Africa, and Latin America concluded that they rarely acted as agents of genuine social change for the rural masses because they were usually dominated by better-off inhabitants who were in

---

cooperatives do not register because they are unable or unwilling to fulfill government requirements for record keeping. I do not intend to imply here that cooperatives should be organized on the basis of government criteria, but only that the basic principles of cooperation, as outlined above, should underlie new forms of economic production among rural women.

[18] For an interesting discussion of group incentives for lowering birthrates, see McNicholl (1975).

a position to take advantage of their services and facilities. Staley and Morse (1965), too, dismiss the cooperative model for small-scale industry because of its history of failure and stagnation. They choose free enterprise instead:

> The best strategy yet found by which a development-minded government can bring into being a vigorous, progressive, modern small industry is not to try to set up government-operated units, nor to sponsor manufacturing cooperatives. It is, instead, to devote equivalent energies and funds to modifying the economic, social, and political environment in such a manner as to stimulate dozens, hundreds, or even thousands of private entrepreneurs to try their hands at organizing, modernizing, or expanding independently owned and managed small manufacturing enterprises. [page 326]

Finally, others argue that the idea of cooperation is alien to many villagers and is doomed to failure for this reason. Because of their mutual suspicion and mistrust, one group of Muslim women near Jalchatra in northern Bangladesh strongly resisted pooling income from their jute handicrafts, insisting instead on individual savings accounts, even after a year of working together. In other instances, imposing a too-rigid model of cooperation may overlook or even destroy indigenous informal networks that have grown naturally out of such activities as savings and loan associations, mutual assistance in farming, or exchanging information and personal services. Other forms of economic organization may be more appropriate. For example, several thousand self-employed cart pullers, sewers, street vendors, and ragpickers in Ahmedabad have been organized into a Self-Employed Women's Association (SEWA) which provides a number of credit and marketing services but is not technically a cooperative (Bhatt, 1976, and Jain, n.d.).

The critics' arguments are compelling. Nevertheless, I would argue that, on the whole, cooperatives offer the most promising model for organizing small-scale industries among village women; that many pitfalls can be avoided with proper planning and supervision; and that the potential for socioeconomic transformation inherent in the cooperative approach surpasses that which is possible in other modes of organization. Chapter 6 outlines an approach to cooperative organization for women that should circumvent, for a number of specified reasons, many of the problems of men's cooperatives such as the disparities in access to resources due to vastly unequal landholdings. Of course, the approach must be flexible, and under some conditions alternatives, such as private enterprise, will be preferable. But past failures should not necessarily lead us to abandon the principles of cooperation; rather, the principles could be adapted to current conditions in order to maximize their effectiveness.

The idea of women's producer cooperatives is certainly not new in South Asia, but no one knows how many there are.[19] Official registries are unreliable because many societies are not registered and because some that are registered are now dormant or defunct. Many of those registered are savings or thrift societies or consumers' groups rather than producers' cooperatives.

The Indian Cooperative Societies Act of 1904, stressing the development of agricultural credit societies, began what is now the oldest cooperative movement among developing countries (Chattopadhyay, 1976). Women's cooperatives have been gaining in popularity since the early 1960s; by 1970–71 there were approximately 3,300 registered women's societies in India, with a total membership of 138,000. Of these, 1,100 were industrial societies with a membership of 24,000 producing goods worth Rs. 5.7 million (well over $500,000), and the balance were consumers of thrift and savings (Chattopadhyay, 1976, page 48). Women's industrial societies have undertaken such activities as preparing pickles, jams, chutneys, and other foodstuffs, grinding and packaging spices, weaving and embroidery, rug making, knitting and doll making, and small-scale manufacturing and assembly of industrial components as ancillaries to larger firms.

Fifteen thousand women are members of registered all-women's cooperatives of various kinds in Bangladesh, but many of the societies are defunct (Ahmad, 1976, page 25). The Integrated Rural Development Program (IRDP) is specifically encouraging the formation of rural women's producer cooperatives in a program that is eventually to cover 1,900 villages of nineteen thanas, counties (Ahmad, 1976, pages 23–24). These will be organized primarily around poultry raising and vegetable and fruit gardening. The program is to train 20,000 women in cooperative organization, agricultural skills, literacy, and family planning. About 3,000 Bengali women make jute handicrafts in all-women's cooperatives, which market their goods locally and export them through the Jute Works, but most of these are not registered.[20]

Of the 30,000 registered cooperatives in Pakistan, with a total membership of almost 2 million, about 1,000 are women's societies, with a membership of 38,000 (Ali, 1976, page 102). It is not clear what type these

[19] See D'Cruz (1976) and other papers from the International Cooperative Alliance Conference (1976). Also, see the National Cooperative Union of India (1976a and 1976b) background paper prepared for the All-India Conference on Women and Cooperatives, as well as the proceedings of the Conference. On the role of women in the cooperative movement in Africa, see the International Cooperative Alliance (1974) report.

[20] A January 1976 interview with Vincent Jaydee, director of the Jute Works in Dacca.

are. A former registrar reports that no women's cooperatives exist in the Northwest Frontier Provinces, even though women there do beautiful embroidery, which is usually sold through middlemen or shop agents.[21]

In Nepal, there are no cooperatives composed exclusively of women (Lohani, 1976). The government is consolidating the many single-purpose societies into larger multipurpose units, one to a village, in order to provide a wide range of services to farmers in conjunction with the village panchayats (Nepal Ministry of Land Reform, 1975). It will probably be difficult for women to expand their membership or decision-making powers under these conditions despite the major role they play in agricultural and handicraft production. The Nepal Women's Organization (NWO) has not attempted to form cooperative societies in its training programs for rural women.

ADDITIONAL SERVICES AND INCENTIVES

If employment is to involve the worker in a genuinely developmental process, then additional services and incentives should be organized around the work situation. Among the most central of these are education in functional literacy, family planning, child care, and the establishment of living quarters for some workers. Financial incentives could also directly encourage delayed marriage and birth control.

Functional Literacy

The statistics on literacy in South Asia (with the exception of Sri Lanka) paint a dismal picture. According to the 1971 census, more than 89 percent of women workers in India were illiterate. In Pakistan (including Bangladesh), in 1961, 93 percent of adult women could neither read nor write; in Nepal, in 1971, 97 percent were illiterate. Although women's illiteracy may not be a major obstacle to their work performance except at managerial levels, it does symbolize a state of social and psychological dependency on men (frequently their own husbands or brothers or sons) and on the small elite of women in the community who *can* read and write.

The workplace presents an ideal setting for education in functional literacy by facilitating group instruction and by anchoring the learning firmly in the work experience.[22] Restricting employment to unmarried

[21] An April 1976 interview with Akbar Ahmed, former registrar of cooperatives in the Northwest Frontier Provinces, Rawalpindi, Pakistan.

[22] For an excellent review and evaluation of a variety of nonformal education programs for young people and adults, see Coombs and Ahmed (1974).

girls and young married women also creates an especially adaptable group who are more teachable than older or younger persons. One Indian study (Naik, n.d.) found that many students between the ages of fourteen and eighteen were able, after only two or three years' instruction, to pass the Primary School Leaving Certificate Examination, which is based on eight years of study for children beginning school at age six or seven. Young working women will learn especially quickly if the program's content is shaped by their immediate needs and experiences in their families, the community, and the workplace. One hour could be set aside each day for instruction.[23]

If women can perform simple work tasks without knowing how to read and write, why should instruction be offered at all? There are at least two reasons for doing so: functional education improves basic decision-making skills and raises the learner's consciousness of community issues.

At a minimum, all workers should know how to read and write simple instructions and to calculate wage rates by the hour or piece, simple interest rates on savings or loans, and prices for raw materials and marketed goods. These literacy skills are essential if workers are to protect themselves from exploitation by their own managers or outsiders and if they are to participate actively in cooperative activities. Some membership decisions require rather advanced mathematical concepts. A small, very poor fishermen's cooperative in Bangladesh, for example, had to agree on the terms for accepting men who wanted to join after the original members had been paying monthly dues of 2 takas each (14 cents) for over a year. Would new members be asked to pay the full amount of accumulated dues, in which case no one could afford to join, or would they receive proportionately fewer of the benefits (for example, leased fishing rights)? If the latter, how were these benefits to be distributed?

The second purpose is what Freire (1972a and 1972b) calls "conscientization," a process by which learners—not as passive recipients but as knowing subjects—achieve a deepening awareness of the sociocultural reality that shapes their lives and of their capacity to transform that reality. Education becomes a dialogue between teacher and learner, building on the concrete situation of the learner's life. It enables one to understand the origins of one's poverty, to cope with natural disasters such as floods and drought, to deal with community conflict, to expose the role of moneylenders, to develop improved agricultural techniques, and so on.

---

[23] Adult education programs conducted in women's vocational training centers in Bangladesh were apparently able to instill illiterate trainees with simple reading and writing skills in about three months. Intensive courses were offered for about one-third of the work day (National Board of Bangladesh Women's Rehabilitation Programme, 1974, p. 15).

Discussions exposing the oppressive aspects of early marriage, the dowry system, the sexual double standard, and constant childbearing would also be included. Women become genuinely involved in their own education as they learn to read and write what Freire (1972a) calls "generative words," while engaging in a critical analysis of the social framework in which they exist. Their education breaks through the "culture of silence" which results from the structural relations between dominant and dependent classes and from women's psychological and economic dependence on men. Freire's philosophy gave impetus to the Bangladesh Rural Advancement Committee's (BRAC's) functional education classes in the villages of Sulla. With materials developed by World Education, BRAC organized classes for village women in the afternoons and for men at night, using local people with only five or six years' schooling as teachers. Each student receives a certificate of graduation at the end of the seventy lessons. To keep villagers from quickly lapsing into illiteracy, BRAC started a newsletter, *Gonokendra* (Community Center), which is distributed through all of the villages in the area.

Family Planning

Women's isolation presents a major obstacle to community-level delivery of health and family-planning services. In contrast, the central workplace not only offers a convenient site for distributing family-planning information and supplies but also permits women to obtain birth control information and devices without the necessary knowledge or consent of other family members—a distinct advantage when husbands or mothers-in-law are most resistant.[24] Women also can derive social support from their co-workers for delaying marriage, postponing pregnancies, or forgoing additional births. The woman's identity as a worker begins to compete with her identity as a wife and mother; spacing and limiting pregnancies becomes a means of fulfilling her responsibilities as an employee and cooperative member. Birth planning takes on new meaning when it is offered in the context of raising the standard of living for the poorest sectors of the population through producers' cooperatives and alternative roles for women.[25]

[24] Many women from a village in the Mahtlab area of Bangladesh who enrolled in a pilot program testing contraceptive injections apparently did so without their husband's knowledge; this was seen as one of the advantages of injections over the pill.

[25] Similar points were emphasized by the National Cooperative Union of India (n.d., p. 7), and by the International Labour Office (1974, pp. 16–17).

Child Care

Child care on the job is controversial from a demographic viewpoint because the theory of role incompatibility specifies that women's work must clearly compete with childbearing and childrearing if fertility is to be reduced.[26] Providing child care for working women would thus negate the potential antinatalist effects of their employment by enabling women to choose *both* employment and children.

I would take a contrary point of view with respect to employment for rural women for several reasons. First, if women are to be directly exposed to an antinatalist environment at all, they must be encouraged to come out of their homes into a productive work setting in which they can learn new attitudes and behavior. Female employment must be *facilitated,* not impeded, if it is to have any effect on reproduction.

Second, rural women will bear at least two or three children in any case. The opportunity for gainful employment could influence (directly and indirectly) the timing of these births and the probability of having additional births. Direct exposure to family-planning information and services on the job will facilitate effective birth control.

Third, children already born need care if the mother is to work outside the home. If child care is not provided on the job, young children will be cared for by mothers-in-law, other relatives, older siblings, or simply neglected. Infant care on the job enables mothers to keep their babies close for prolonged breast-feeding, which not only has nutritional advantages for the child but also demographic advantages as a child-spacing mechanism. Older, preschool children will also benefit from group care.

Fourth, a working mother may otherwise take her eldest daughter out of school in order to care for younger children, sacrificing the daughter's future to the mother's immediate needs.

Finally, the object of creating income-generating employment for rural women is not solely to reduce birthrates. Women have an equal right with men to paid employment, regardless of its demographic consequences.

Living Quarters

The lack of hostels where women can live or stay overnight discourages many from participating in rural development programs as teachers, health and family-planning workers, cooperative inspectors, or in other

---

[26] See, for example, Weller (1968). For a critique of the implications of denying child care, see Piepmeier and Adkins (1973, pp. 515–516).

capacities requiring temporary or permanent lodging in the village.[27] But local unmarried girls could also benefit from living in a hostel at the work-site: they would be marginally removed from intense family pressures toward early marriage, which derive in part from the drain on limited financial and space resources when the girl lives at home; they would not be exposed to men's stares when walking through the streets to work; and they could create an environment of solidarity and self-reliance which would be bound to carry forward into other aspects of their lives. Costs would be reduced if the young women shared in growing vegetables and raising poultry for their own consumption and contributed part of their earnings for room and board.

The community might well find the idea initially shocking, however, since even the most respectable arrangements for single girls often meet with disapproval.[28] Cultural fears of public dishonor, deriving from the parents' loss of control over their daughters, could probably be overcome if living arrangements were chaperoned by a resident, older widow with a good name. And removing marriageable young women from the home could eliminate the prevalent fear of incestuous and privately dishonor-ing sexual relationships within the family itself. For keeping young girls confined to the home can also present a sexually volatile situation, one which propels parents toward arranging an early marriage for their daughters.[29]

Financial Incentives for Delayed Marriage and Birth Control

The producers' cooperative offers a number of opportunities for incorpo-rating specific financial incentives for delaying marriage and for spacing and limiting births.[30] Delayed marriage could be encouraged by offering

[27] It also poses a severe problem for single women working in towns and cities. The YWCA hostel in Dacca houses fifty working women, but many more are wait-ing for openings. Some single women in Islamabad, working in government posts, were illegally sharing rooms with students in the university dormitories.

[28] The Dacca YWCA, for example, was apparently looked on with considerable suspicion by its city neighbors in spite of its high standards of moral conduct and the high wall around the building.

[29] Although there are, of course, no indications of its prevalence, the theme of incest as a threat to premarital chastity was raised independently in several conversa-tions with development workers. Young girls are particularly vulnerable in societies in which it is commonly believed that men have little internal control over their sexual impulses. For a brief discussion of purdah as an institution for sexual control, see Papanek (1973, pp. 316–317).

[30] Pohlman (1971) discusses a variety of possible incentives; see also Ridker and Muscat (1973) and Simon (1968), among others.

a substantial bonus to girls who remain single to the age of twenty, perhaps splitting it between the girl herself and her parents. Married women could receive bonuses for each year that a child was not born, with higher bonuses going to younger women of low parity. Incentives could be offered for the adoption of family-planning practices, such as the sterilization of the woman or her husband. The woman's right to determine the size of her family should also be emphasized. These incentives would have to be tied to an educational program in which the benefits to the woman and to the community of altered reproductive behavior would be clearly specified, however.

CONCLUSIONS

The central, albeit largely a priori, argument has now been set forth. The goals of promoting rural development, raising the status of women, and encouraging delayed marriage and birth control in rural communities could be met by creating income-generating employment in small-scale industries, specifically for women in their early reproductive years, in cooperatively organized central workplaces that offer additional services such as functional literacy programs, family planning, child care, living quarters, and financial incentives.

Probably no rural development programs in India, Pakistan, Bangladesh, or Nepal meet all of these criteria. An Indian program encourages village women to grow vegetables for their own consumption, an activity which may be worthwhile for its nutritional value, but one that contributes little to rural development and probably nothing to advancing the status of women or altering their reproductive behavior. Programs in Nepal encourage women in making home-based handicrafts, which are sold for small amounts through middlemen or directly to urban shops. This activity might improve women's status slightly, if they controlled the income they earned, but would not generally motivate them to delay marriage or practice birth control. Some Pakistani projects do bring women out of their homes into workshops for weaving, sewing, or embroidery, but they usually offer little opportunity for development of skills, nor do they encourage women to participate fully in decisions about their work. The women's cooperatives organized in Bangladesh and India do not always adhere strictly to cooperative principles, such as democratic participation and regular membership meetings. Some offer programs such as functional literacy or family planning but only on a sporadic basis. Hostels are available in those training programs that require women to move to town temporarily, for example, in Dacca and Kathmandu, but are not utilized in conjunction with permanent local industries.

Nevertheless, a number of programs are promising, even though they do not meet all of the criteria specified above. Each has a lesson to teach about the problems of recruiting women, of creating a viable economic enterprise, and other issues. In chapter 3 I will attempt to evaluate five such programs, each providing income-earning employment for rural women. They include a series of small women's agricultural cooperatives for growing vegetables and raising fish and poultry in Bangladesh; village milk cooperatives in India; the jute handicrafts industry in Bangladesh; dispersed workshops for food processing in India; and carpet-weaving factories in Nepal.

3

EMPLOYMENT FOR RURAL WOMEN—
FIVE PROGRAMS

The five programs selected for discussion in this chapter represent a variety of types, none of which closely resembles the model described in chapter 2. They share the characteristics of being located in societies that place sometimes severe restrictions on the spatial mobility of females (varying in degree according to region, class, religion, and caste) and of generating new sources of income for rural women (see table 3-1). All but one are producers' cooperatives organized into federations with a potential for reaching tens of thousands of rural women. All but one are self-sufficient economic enterprises with marketable products. However, they differ considerably in the types of services they offer, the socio-economic and demographic characteristics of their workers, and the organization of the work setting.

The rural women's cooperatives of the Integrated Rural Development Program (IRDP) in Bangladesh and the Indian milk cooperatives of the Anand Milk Union Ltd. (AMUL) Dairy are agricultural and basically home-based; the jute handicraft cooperatives in Bangladesh are also home-based, although artisanal; the Indian food-processing cooperatives of Lijjat Papad constitute a dispersed factory (putting-out) system with some workers home-based and others located in central workshops. Only the Nepalese carpet factories fit the description of a true factory system, although their manufacturing techniques are simple and all work is done by hand.

The programs are described in some detail in order to convey a little of their flavor and to offer a basis for estimating their impact on rural development, the status of women, and reproductive behavior. In the absence of formal research findings, however, the preliminary evidence is largely impressionistic. (Ideas for future research are proposed in the appendix, page 190.) The reader should bear in mind that these programs, like others, are in a constant state of flux, so that characteristics attributed to them in this report may not hold true at some future date. The discussions which follow are intended not to present some static

Table 3-1. Characteristics of Five Programs for Rural Women's Employment in South Asia

Program characteristic	Agricultural co-ops in Bangladesh: IRDP federation	Milk co-ops in India: AMUL Dairy federation	Jute handicrafts in Bangladesh: two co-op federations[a]	Food processing in India: Lijjat Papad co-op federation	Carpet weaving in Nepal: two factories
Income-generating	Some (minor)	Yes	Yes	Yes	Yes
Rural	Yes	Yes	Some	Some	Near cities
Outside agriculture	No	Part	Yes	Yes	Yes
Small industry	No	No	Artisanal	Dispersed factory	Medium factory
Outside home	Occasional	Twice a day	Occasional	Some twice a day; some all day	Yes
Young women only	No, all ages	No, men and women, all ages	No, all ages	Some, yes; some, all ages	No, men and women; all ages
Cooperatives	Yes	Yes	Yes	Yes	No, but linked
Services					
literacy	Some	No	Some	No	No
family planning	Yes	No	Some	Some	No
child care	No	No	No	No	In one, yes; in one, no
hostel	Training only	No	Training only	No	No
Extra incentives					
delayed marriage	No	No	No	No	No
family planning	No	No	No	Yes	No

[a] Jagaroni/Jute Works and the Bangladesh Handicrafts Cooperative Federation (KARIKA)

formulation, but to offer examples of innovative attempts to stimulate a sense of social and economic self-reliance among rural women.[1] My critiques and suggestions are offered in the spirit of maximizing this contribution.

WOMEN'S AGRICULTURAL COOPERATIVES IN BANGLADESH

Rangunia Thana, interlaced with rivers and canals, is about a two-hour bus ride east of Chittagong.[2] The bluish mountains of the Chittagong Hill Tracts lie low across the horizon. The Thana is a lush rice-growing area, using available sources of irrigation water, but it has not always been so. Rangunia Thana had been a rice-deficient area, yielding only 1,360 pounds of paddy per year from its one crop of rain-fed Aman rice. For eight months of the year, the fields lay dry and cracked in the scorching sun.

A member of the Pakistan Foreign Service had recently resigned from the central government to assist his own Bengali people in discovering the resources of their land. As he said, "My people cannot be helped by begging in the world's capitals, they can be helped only in the mud of the rice fields." He settled in the area.

In 1967 severe flooding drowned the annual crop of Aman rice, causing famine conditions. The frantic farmers approached the retired official for relief arrangements. A self-help project was decided upon to turn the begging hands into rice-planting hands. In response to the challenge, a Liaison Committee was formed with the retired foreign service officer, a local businessman, a Baptist agricultural missionary, government officials, farmers, and students. Amid intense activity and without office, staff, or funds, over 1,000 farmers were organized into thirty pump groups or primary cooperatives. Canals were dug, cross dams built, pumps installed, and some 2,000 acres of mud planted in the next season with high-yielding varieties of IRRI rice. With the addition of credit, seed and fertilizer sup-

---

[1] Attributing low self-esteem to economically dependent rural women of South Asia is not simply a projection of Western values or biases. Field-workers frequently told me that the women's low opinion of the value of their work and of their own worth as persons required much patience and effort to overcome. Most women soon took enormous pleasure in their newly discovered capacity to earn their own money.

[2] Information in this section is drawn from Zeidenstein (1975); Zeidenstein and Zeidenstein (1974); Lindenbaum (1974); Mascarenhas (1975); and from interviews with Tahrunnessa Ahmed Abdullah, director of the Women's Programme of the IRDP in Dacca, and with David and Joyce Stockley at the Rangunia Thana Central Cooperative Federation in Rangunia. David Stockley kindly revised the first draft of this section.

plies, and instruction for participating farmers, a bumper crop of IRRI rice was harvested with yields of 6,000 pounds of paddy per acre. Farmers worked their own land individually but cooperated for training, credit, and water sources. The primary societies formed an association known as the Rangunia Thana Central Cooperative Association (RTCCA) Ltd. In 1971 the government decided to promote agricultural cooperatives for irrigation purposes and urged Rangunia to organize 200 new societies among families who would share pumps and canals. By 1975, over 200 cooperatives had been formed with about 9,000 members. The RTCCA now runs businesses in fertilizers, and has facilities for oil pressing, rice and flour milling and marketing of members' paddy. Seed experimentation and sales, a hostel and cafeteria, agricultural equipment sales, and poultry raising are also in the program.

At first there were no programs for women. But in 1972 the government began a national campaign to eradicate illiteracy, and about 300 people in Rangunia Thana volunteered as teachers, including nearly 100 women who asked why there were no women's cooperatives. They formed the first, with 47 members, and by December 1975, the number of societies had grown to thirteen, with a total membership of 412.

The women's cooperatives were modeled on the men's, which had been based on principles evolved at the Bangladesh Academy for Rural Development (BARD) at Comilla.[3] BARD did not permit all-women's groups, but changed its bylaws following the Rangunia experiment. The government's IRDP took over the administration of the RTCCA in 1973 and subsequently adopted a strong policy of advancing rural women's cooperatives in agriculture and crafts. The IRDP pays the salaries of the Thana project officer, the assistant, and the cooperative inspectors, of whom one inspector and one assistant are local women responsible for the thirteen women's societies. The inspectors help with the accounts, participate in training programs, and attend weekly membership meetings, among their other administrative tasks. The Rangunia women's groups engage in a wide range of activities which are determined by the women themselves, such as raising ducks and chickens, growing vegetables and fruit, culturing fish, making jute handicrafts, sewing, and manufacturing chicken-wire fencing. These are largely home-based activities for household consumption and for sale in the local community. Marketing has fallen to the cooperative federation because women do not yet have the required skills or the freedom to move about. The Bangladesh Handicrafts Cooperative

[3] The Comilla Academy, under the dynamic directorship of Akhter Hameed Khan, had long been considered a model training program for rural development. The literature on Comilla is voluminous; for a general description, see Raper (1970).

Federation (discussed later in this chapter) has agreed to buy crafts which meet its high-quality standards.

Of the thirteen women's cooperatives, the largest is Kodomtoli, with seventy-five members. It was formed in 1972 and registered with the government one year later. Members each purchased shares costing 10 taka (70 cents).[4] By December 1975 they had already accumulated savings of 10,000 taka (about $700), some of it loaned out to members at 15 percent interest, with the rest banked at 7 percent interest.

In a society in which few women earn money directly, how are the initial capital and subsequent savings to be raised? Organizers insisted that members could not simply take money from their husbands' pockets; they had to create it themselves. In order to do so, the women began a savings club in which each set aside every day (or every meal, if she could afford it) a handful of dry rice which would otherwise go into the pot for her family. By the end of a month even a daily handful amounts to two seers, worth about 6 taka (42 cents). With many women contributing to a common fund over several months, the rice can be marketed for $60 or $70. Each woman was also encouraged to grow vegetables, such as radishes and cauliflower, to eat and to sell. The profits went into an individually credited, but pooled, cooperative savings account.

In early 1975 the Kodomtoli cooperative borrowed 3,000 taka ($210) in order to excavate a silted pond in the village, stock it with fish, and plant its banks with one hundred banana plants and thirty lime trees. They used money from their own savings fund, losing the 7 percent bank interest but avoiding the 15 percent loan interest that the federation would charge. Originally the tank had been owned by fourteen men. The women obtained permission to excavate and plant from thirteen, but the fourteenth refused their request; he has since been suspected of trying to obstruct the whole project by stealing the first small crop of bananas. The venture has not yet earned income, but a good tank can produce fish worth 6,000 taka (over $400) in a year, and the harvested fruit will also bring in money.

Cooperative societies can borrow from the federation for projects if federation managers approve the loan; individual members can also borrow from their own cooperative fund or, with the sponsorship of their own society, from the federation. Loans are limited to 100 taka per 10-taka share ($21) per person. One enterprising woman, together with three friends, borrowed 1,200 taka to start a small store in her home; the

---

[4] The IRDP permits women to join cooperatives as provisional members with an initial payment of 2 takas (14 cents). They attain full membership rights after purchasing their 10-taka share, but may purchase up to three shares.

woman's friends in turn loaned her their shares. Another started her own poultry business; others borrow for rice seed or to buy harvested paddy for husking, which they resell as rice at a higher price. The elected management committee of the primary societies must agree to any request for withdrawal of members' savings.

Although most of Rangunia Thana's residents are Muslim, eleven of the thirteen women's cooperatives are Buddhist or Hindu. Local Hindu families were particularly hard hit by the 1971 war with Pakistan, and many Hindu women were left widowed with small farms to run. They were the first to seek agricultural training. Muslim women, afraid to come forward, asked the organizers to start with the Hindus so that their own husbands could see that no harm would follow. The Muslim men still resist the idea of their wives leaving their bari (household compound), even for weekly cooperative meetings or for tending gardens. Most cooperative members are illiterate, and the few who can read and write need further training in accounting and leadership skills in order to fulfill their managerial functions. One cooperative discovered it had been cheated by a member's husband who, being literate, had been asked to keep the books. The inspector took weeks to untangle the accounts.

Medina is an assistant inspector paid by IRDP. An unmarried Muslim of eighteen, she earns a basic monthly salary of 120 taka with a 30-taka traveling allowance—just over $10 altogether. Community social welfare workers, in contrast, earn 300 taka ($21) per month. By the time Medina pays for transportation from her village to the federation headquarters three or four days a week, she has nothing left. The cycle rickshaw from her village in which she rides over the rough mud road to the highway, where she catches the bus, costs 4 taka (28 cents) each way. It is not proper for a young woman to walk unaccompanied, and the jeep bus service which picks up men from her village will not take her. In any case, she refuses to ride in the jeep because the men tease her unmercifully.

Medina is an exceptional young woman. Her father—progressive enough to send her to primary school, where she was the only girl—nevertheless wanted to marry her off when she reached thirteen. She appealed to the school's headmaster, who told her father, "Your daughter is not your property to trade as you choose." Her father relented, and Medina went on through grade eleven on a government scholarship.

She has been working as a cooperative inspector now for one year. People ask her, "Why does a Muslim woman work? Why do you show yourself to men?" She tells them she is doing it for her country, that women cannot be of any use if they are to observe purdah. On one occasion, conservative village men came from the mosque to tell her father he would be damned for letting his daughter work. Medina said that her father replied, "You told me I was going to hell for sending her to school. So if I have already gone once, it won't matter if I go again." Medina is the only daughter in the family and has one brother. A suitor recently asked for her hand, but she told her father she was not ready to marry yet. She wants to become established in her work first.

Medina attended a training program in Dacca along with women inspectors and assistants from five other thanas where pilot projects are underway; they were instructed in the aims of the IRDP women's program, in cooperative organization and accounting, and in principles of health, family planning, and literacy programming. Back in Rangunia the managers of local cooperatives gather together one afternoon a week at federation headquarters to deposit their savings, discuss problems, and receive training in new agricultural methods, crafts, and family planning, which they are supposed to transmit to their own members at weekly meetings. Several local managers have been sent to Comilla for training in accounting, management, and horticulture. Some members, along with other village women, attend literacy classes held in one of their homes that are taught by paid workers drawn from among college students and the educated wives of male cooperative managers. Classes are held every afternoon in an effort to motivate women to continue their education, to take an interest in family planning, and to develop new economic activities.

The pilot projects in six thanas, including Rangunia, constitute the first stage of an IRDP three-year plan to promote income-generating programs with a strong family-planning component (funded by an international agency) for rural women in nineteen thanas within nineteen districts of Bangladesh. A deputy project officer and two inspectors in each thana are to organize and supervise ten women's cooperatives with about 120 members each, thus reaching almost 23,000 women overall. Members will have access to training and services in rural economic activities, family planning, functional literacy, and health care. Cooperatives are to recruit heavily from among the most needy women in the community and draw inspectors from the better-educated married women. The organizers believe that older married women will deliver services more effectively than unmarried girls because of their greater cultural acceptability. It is still considered shocking for unmarried girls to talk about contraception, and in any case, the village women ask, how can they know about married life and its problems?

The IRDP women's program is not yet economically self-sufficient: primary societies dependent for their initial capital on their members' small shares and savings are unable to support staff at the secondary level; federation officers and inspectors are paid by the IRDP, which in turn depends heavily on outside sources for funding. The program does emphasize economic self-reliance and birth planning, however, thus moving beyond the philosophy of "uplifting" rural women by simply improving their household productivity. And selling produce for cash, however little, does bring money into a new set of rural households and into the hands of the women themselves.

Whether women can use their agricultural productivity as a base for raising their status significantly may depend on whether they can obtain a monopoly over certain products and whether they can negotiate effectively for good market prices. Really efficient agricultural production and marketing would require considerable additional training at BARD, which would have to expand its services to cater more fully to the needs of rural women (Raper, 1970, chapter 6). And given the scarcity of land, how are women to acquire additional space beyond their small garden plots?

The IRDP's rural cooperatives will bring women out of their homes for meetings and for work on the land, but there appears to be little built-in incentive for delayed marriage and birth control beyond the women's exposure to family-planning propaganda and supplies. As a consequence, I would argue that while the agricultural program should continue to recruit from among needy widows and married women with many children who may be induced to limit additional births, alternative sources of employment should be offered to unmarried girls and married women in the earliest of their childbearing years.

One village group in Rangunia does draw primarily from among unmarried Hindu girls; although not a cooperative, the group sews clothing (mostly for children) from donated and recycled cloth and sells it at low prices to the Rangunia Thana cooperative store.[5] Two groups alternate at the center where the sewing machines are kept, one working the first three days of the week and the other the second three days. The women earn from 20 paise to 2 taka (2 to 14 cents) per garment, depending on its complexity. Most of the girls at the center are past marriageable age, that is, in their late teens or early twenties. Whether their income has induced them to delay marriage or whether they work because they are still unmarried cannot be easily established. One organizer remarked that the girls are unmarried because they come from very poor families who could not raise a dowry or because they are of dark complexion—a highly undesirable trait in a color-conscious society. On the other hand, their earn-

---

[5] The federation purchases the clothing regardless of quality or demand, however; thus many unsalable items are stockpiled in the store. It is doubtful that the sewing group could sell its garments competitively in the open market.

ings do reduce the economic burden and perhaps some of the shame that otherwise rests on their families for having an unmarried daughter at home. In any case, the non-Muslim minorities of Bangladesh tolerate later marriage for their daughters, and it is primarily these minorities who are recruited into the new work programs.

WOMEN IN THE DAIRY INDUSTRY: MILK COOPERATIVES IN INDIA

Almost everywhere in South Asia, women and children bear primary responsibility for caring for milch animals—buffaloes, cows, and goats. They collect fodder for the animals or take them to pasture, wash them or take them to a river or pond to bathe, bring them water to drink, tether them in the sun or under a tree by day and in shelters at night, collect dung to make into cakes for fuel, clean their stalls, and milk them twice a day. The tasks can be highly time-consuming: Pakistani women in one Punjab village spend on the average one hour and forty-five minutes every day caring for animals and an additional three hours and forty-five minutes collecting, carrying, and chopping their fodder (Anwar and Bilquees, 1976, page 51). The milk is consumed directly or made into ghee (butter oil) for cooking. Women may sometimes sell a little excess ghee for a few rupees; but if their husbands take it to market, they may not see the money at all.

Women who sell their buffalo milk to one of the 844 village cooperatives of the AMUL Dairy in India's Gujarat State earn cash every day, however, perhaps Rs. 5 or Rs. 6 (55 to 65 cents) on the average.[6] An ordinary buffalo gives about five liters of milk a day when it is not calving, although it can give up to ten and even more in the winter if it is fed the high-nutrient food that the cooperative encourages. Four liters of milk bring about Rs. 8, but special feed costs Rs. 2 or Rs. 3. A survey by the Department of Economics at Sardar Patel University in Anand found that milk money constitutes about half of the household income of families belonging to cooperatives, compared with about 20 percent where they do not. Unlike the sporadic incomes from crops or wage labor, the

---

[6] Information in this section was based upon a visit to the AMUL Dairy in Anand and upon interviews with R. P. Aneja and Narendra Trivedi at the National Dairy Development Board in Anand, Sam Thangaraj and Eve Steinhardt of OXFAM in New Delhi, and K. B. Kothari of CARE in New Delhi. Additional source material is found in the Kaira District Co-operative Milk Producers' Union publication (1971 and 1975).

reliable milk money is paid every day in cash. A woman may sell about two-thirds of what her buffalo produces during the morning milking and one-third of what it produces at night, using the rest for the family's own consumption. The poorest members sell a higher proportion of their milk for cash, however; thus, many children in the area continue to suffer from protein deficiency.

Any family owning a milch animal, if it promises not to sell to any other buyer, can join the cooperative by purchasing a share costing Rs. 5 (55 cents) for one household member or Rs. 10 for two, a man and a woman. Two men or two women from the same household cannot join. The primary village societies average about one to three hundred members, each with elected boards of nine, eleven, or thirteen, which meet monthly and three or six paid staff members for accounting, clerical work, testing and weighing the milk, and simple veterinarian services. Most member families are either landless laborers or small farmers owning an average of three acres. They own one or two buffaloes; more than two cannot be supported on such small holdings.

The first milk cooperatives were formed in 1946, when a deputation of farmers from the Kaira District, who were exploited by private milk merchants in the government-run Bombay Milk Scheme, went to Sardar Patel to seek his advice. Patel recommended that the farmers organize into producers' cooperatives in order to fight more effectively for fair prices. After a fifteen-day strike, in which farmers withheld all milk from the merchants, the government of Bombay acceded to the farmers' demands and permitted the formation of the first two village cooperatives in Anand, from which they purchased milk for Bombay. Ten years later there were 64 societies with 23,000 members; ten years after that, 567 societies with 120,000 members (table 3-2). By 1974–75, 844 cooperatives had been organized with 245,000 members. The Kaira District Cooperative Milk Producers Union of Anand, with assistance from several international agencies, built its own dairy in 1955 for pasteurized and powdered milk and butter, which was expanded in 1958 to manufacture condensed milk. In 1960 the factory again expanded to manufacture baby foods and cheese. In 1974–75 the AMUL Dairy sold milk and milk products worth almost $50 million through the Bombay market and throughout India. The share capital of the 844 cooperatives amounted to almost $500,000. All but a few cooperatives turn a net profit after the first (subsidized) year, averaging about $1,000 to $1,500; usually about one-third of the profits is distributed to members as dividends (perhaps $6), with the balance going to staff bonuses, dairy development, and social services or physical amenities in the village, such as libraries, schools, health centers, water troughs for cattle, and road construction.

Table 3-2. Production and Membership in the Anand Milk Union Ltd. (AMUL) Dairy in Gujarat, India, 1956–75

Fiscal year ending 31 March	No. of societies	No. of members	Union share capital		Kilograms of milk collected (thousands)	Sales of milk and products	
			Rs. (thousands)	$		Rs. (thousands)	$
1956[a]	64	22,828	317	35	11.1	7.4	818
1957[b]	107	26,795	362	40	14.2	8.9	984
1961[b]	195	40,500	741	82	23.9	19.8	2,184
1962[c]	219	46,400	749	82	35.4	31.5	3,468
1967[c]	567	120,000	1,651	182	71.6	117.6	12,941
1972[c]	744	215,000	3,857	424	133.2	336.0	36,964
1975[c]	844	245,000	4,418	486	130.9	446.5	49,111

Note: Rupees converted to dollars at rate of Re. 1 = 11 cents.

Source: Kaira District Co-operative Milk Producers' Union (1975, p. 3).

[a] Before the new dairy was built.
[b] After the new dairy was built.
[c] After dairy was expanded to produce baby food and cheese.

Although women care for and milk the animals, men constitute the majority of the 245,000 cooperative members (perhaps 60 percent); the vast majority of the over 9,000 directors of primary societies (only a handful of women are elected); and virtually all of the 4,500 or so paid staff members. Only a few office workers among the 2,000 employees at the AMUL Dairy itself are women. The absence of women among staff workers in the villages is said to be due to the low esteem in which such a position is held for women; those with sufficient education would prefer to go into teaching or the health occupations. Working at the center requires contact with men and women of different castes and backgrounds.

One cooperative forms an exception to the underrepresentation of women among members, however. In the village of Khadgodra an all-women's society was organized in 1962 by Mrs. Mehta, the leader of the village council. AMUL did not want to start a cooperative at Khadgodra because it lies near a town that already has a commercial milk buyer. The village men were apparently divided as to whether they should limit their sales to a cooperative, but the women were adamant and formed their own society. By 1975 they had recruited 231 members with an elected all-female board of nine (Mrs. Mehta being the only literate one) and five male staff members. The cooperative had a share capital of Rs. 1,275 ($140) and had made a profit during 1975 of almost Rs. 17,000, or about $1,900.

Things went smoothly until November 1975, when the women started to take their milk to a cooperative in a neighboring village instead of their own. They claimed angrily that the male staff workers were not weighing the milk properly and were withholding or delaying payment. The staff men, in turn, claimed they were being paid too little for their work, considering the hours worked and their education. The women avoided firing the wrongdoers because they feared repercussions from the men's relatives. In the confusion, a delegation of men wrote to AMUL, demanding that they should be permitted to join the cooperative, attend its meetings, and take over its management. AMUL sent a team to hold a village meeting at which the issues and charges were discussed. Two of the staff workers, whom all agreed were "making mischief," resigned. By February 1976 the cooperative had started up again, although the matter of whether men could join was still in dispute.

New cooperatives are organized by workers from the National Dairy Development Board (NDDB), who go into a village located in the network of transportation lines accessible to the dairy (milk is picked up by truck twice a day), address the assembled men, and choose two promising leaders, who are sent to the AMUL Dairy and to one of the existing village societies for a month's training. Women are not recruited directly; rather, the family is usually represented by the household head. The new leaders, with the help of NDDB, organize the families owning milch animals into a cooperative society, with AMUL contributing Rs. 10,000 ($1,100) toward the construction of a milk-collection center.

At first, the men typically do not want their wives to go out of the house: they wish AMUL to pick up the milk at their homes instead. When AMUL insists on the use of a collection center, the men often bring in the milk themselves for the first few weeks. But they soon tire of this task, and the women are sent out—at first for the morning deliveries—often covered from head to toe and accompanied by a young son. Eventually, they are sent for the evening deliveries too, when it is sometimes already dark. Women carry the milk in shining brass vessels balanced on their heads or hips. After a year, perhaps three-quarters of the deliveries are made by women and the rest by men and children. The importance attached to who brings the milk rests with the scheme of payment. Milk delivered in the evening is paid for the following morning in cash after its fat content has been weighed from a small test sample,[7] and milk delivered in the morning is paid for the same evening. Persons from different Hindu castes—some of them untouchables—and men and women alike mingle in the long queues while waiting for their milk to be weighed. AMUL's insistence on a single queue—challenging the established custom in public places of separate queues for men and women—derives from its Gandhian philosophy of eradicating differences among castes and equalizing the status of men and women. (The strategy does not always succeed, however; the women in one cooperative stopped coming to the center because the men teased and pinched them as they stood in line.) The assembly at the collection center often takes on the air of a community meeting, as villagers exchange news of the events of the day.

Women receive minimal training: by the end of 1975, about 125,000 had visited the AMUL Dairy's plant, cattle-feed factory, and animal husbandry center, in groups separated from men's training sessions, for one day's simple instruction in animal nutrition and in the benefits and techniques of artificial insemination. (AMUL maintains Surti buffalo bulls for upgrading members' stock.) But because women are not hired as staff workers, they do not receive training in accounting, management, or veterinarian services. Few women attend the yearly cooperative meetings. The societies offer no services beyond those connected with animal care. There is no savings and loan program, no literacy training, no health care for members or their families, and no family planning.

[7] Standardized payments across all cooperatives are scaled on the basis of fat content to encourage members to feed enriched food to their buffaloes and to discourage adulteration.

The greatest advantage of the AMUL Dairy scheme is that it reaches enormous numbers of rural families, for example, 250,000 in over 800 villages in the Kaira District of Gujarat alone. The National Dairy Development Board, with headquarters in Anand, offers a package of services for organizing new cooperatives and setting up dairy factories. At the beginning of 1978 it had established eighteen milk unions based on the Anand model. Together with ten similar projects assisted by the World Bank, the twenty-eight cooperative milk unions in twelve states supplied markets in Delhi, Madras, Calcutta, and Bombay. They included 5.5 million milk producers, of whom about 60 percent were landless laborers or marginal farmers (*Christian Science Monitor, 1978*). The second great advantage of this plan is that the cooperatives build on and create income from an activity in which villagers already engage. They require—at least at the primary level—little capital expenditure except for building a collection center.[8] The market for milk and milk products would appear to be infinitely expandable, at least in the near future.

AMUL also offers a lesson in what happens when men join cooperatives organized around women's work. Women are underrepresented at all levels, but particularly in the management and staff of village societies and at the dairy complex. They are not directly recruited as members in the initial organizational drives. Only in the single all-female cooperative are women managing their own affairs. The most effective solution to their underrepresentation may be to recruit women *only* in new societies. Or at the very least, the NDDB should hire and train females to join the organizing teams that NDDB sends into the villages. They would select trainees to be sent to AMUL from all-women's meetings to parallel the sessions for men.

Quotas could be set in every society for the presence of at least 50 percent women among elected managers and paid staff workers. (Quotas fit with national policies in India, Bangladesh, and Pakistan, where 10 percent of seats in the national and state legislatures are set aside for women. Nepal newly requires that at least one woman be selected as a member of every local and district panchayat; in India the quota is at least two.) The idea also fits in with the Gandhian philosophy of promoting fair representation of the "backward" classes in public positions. The cooperative unions could also encourage women's attendance at meetings. The BARD at Comilla, for example, consistently set aside a section of seats for

---

[8] Note that AMUL grants about 1,000 for construction of each new cooperative. Some societies pay more out of their own profits for a larger or more elaborate building, perhaps with meeting rooms and other amenities. The center may be the only pucca (brick, not mud) building in the village.

women at their public gatherings. If the seats remained empty, it was a constant reminder that half of the population was not represented.[9]

AMUL has undoubtedly advanced the economic development of the area by infusing regular cash incomes into the households of landless agricultural workers and small farmers who can afford a buffalo or two and by providing regular paid employment outside of agriculture in the village collection centers and in the dairy and feed plants at Anand (though not for females). Women who take milk to the centers do receive cash directly, and this is bound to affect their position in the home. Without careful research, it is not possible to say precisely how this money is spent or whether women actually control it. One AMUL employee announced that the money makes the women "very independent; they just spend it as they see fit." It is more likely to be spent on daily household needs, especially food. Although there is no cooperative savings scheme, some women are said to set aside a little every day—perhaps the small change—in a secret spot for a daughter's dowry or family emergency. Some men resent their wives earning money directly: stories prevail of husbands who have beaten their wives to get the cash, and of others who come to the center to find out exactly how much their wives have been paid in order to make sure that the women keep nothing back. Year-end dividends are distributed to formal members; if husbands belong to the cooperative, it is they who receive the bonus.

The cooperatives are bound to have a social impact in that women come out of their homes twice a day to gather at the center for conversations with persons from other streets in the village and from other castes—a type of exchange that generally is reserved for the men. Too, everyone's milk goes into the same pot, even that from buffaloes belonging to the scheduled castes (formerly referred to as outcastes, or untouchables). Women learn to orient themselves to a market and to report to the center at a specified time every day. The center would certainly be used as a base from which to offer literacy classes or basic lessons in health care or family planning, while the women wait to sell their milk, or at some other more convenient time of day. But it is unlikely that the work will induce women to marry later or to bear fewer children. On the contrary, children are especially useful in gathering fodder and taking the animals to bathe and to pasture.

[9] For additional suggestions on incorporating women more fully into cooperatives, see the International Cooperative Alliance (1974 and 1976) reports, and the National Board of Bangladesh Women's Rehabilitation Programme (1974, pp. 4–6); and National Cooperative Union of India (1976).

ARTISAN HOMEWORK: JUTE HANDICRAFTS
IN BANGLADESH

The artisan characteristically works as an independent entrepreneur at home, often with the help of children and adolescent family members. Shoemaking, pottery making, goldsmithing, brassware making, cabinet-making, and weaving are common artisanal household activities in South Asia. The artisan typically produces an entire product from beginning to end, often with individual variations tailored to specific requests. Products may be sold directly in the local market (for example, the shoe-makers of Agra) or to a single employer or buyer (for example, the sari weavers of Madras).

Although most artisans are boys and men, women in some areas of Bangladesh, Pakistan, India, and Nepal do engage in hand spinning and weaving, basketmaking, and fine embroidery (clothing, quilts, wall hangings, pillows, shawls, place mats). Women who produce handicrafts at home typically undervalue their work because they are not used to attaching a monetary value to time, and because they frequently define their handiwork—often interrupted by domestic chores—as an incidental, spare-time activity. The amount of profit is not important—any remuneration at all is better than none—so long as the raw materials are paid for. Retailers or export agents who come through the village to buy door-to-door easily take advantage of the women's ignorance of their product's worth and of the fact that alternative markets for their goods do not exist.

Nevertheless, if properly organized and remunerated, artisanal activities can provide a healthy source of income for rural women, while drawing on local materials and skills and requiring little capital investment. The organized sector of the jute handicrafts industry in Bangladesh is one such example: Sri Joni is one of its cooperatives.[10]

Akhtari Begum, the secretary of the Sri Joni Mohila Cooperative Society, lives in a stable, Muslim squatter community settled about ten years ago on low-lying land in the outskirts of Dacca. During the rainy season much of the area is flooded; even late in the dry season there is water in the ponds where the cattle and children bathe. She began making hand-

---

[10] Information in this section was gathered from direct observation of the programs described and from interviews with Sister Michael Francis and Sister Bruno of the Sisters of the Holy Cross; Vincent Jaydee, the director, and Louisa Brooke, the design consultant, of the Jute Works; Roberta McLaughlin, a volunteer worker at Jagaroni; Parveen Ahmed, the director of KARIKA, and others. Additional data are drawn from memos kindly provided by Adrienne Germain of The Ford Foundation.

bags from jute when the cooperative was organized in 1972 by a Dacca woman interested in providing income for destitute women.

As she talked, Akhtari Begum stood in a doorway, deftly knotting fine cord of dyed jute into an intricate pattern with only an occasional glance at her work. Hers is a success story. By working full time with her daughter, she earns approximately 3,000 taka per month—about $210—a small fortune compared with the average earnings of most Bengali male workers. Her husband quit his $40-a-month government job as a librarian to help his wife with the business. With her savings, Mrs. Begum bought land in her village, leased it to a tenant farmer, and with the profits from her share of the rice it produced, purchased land near Dacca, where she plans to build a house.

Mrs. Begum has four grown sons and an unmarried daughter. At age fourteen, her daughter was betrothed in traditional Muslim fashion, but when the cooperative was formed Mrs. Begum taught her daughter how to make handicrafts too. The girl's marriage was postponed, then canceled. Now she is eighteen, and her parents receive many offers of marriage as word of her value spreads, but neither she nor her parents are anxious to make any arrangements. In any case, Mrs. Begum's standards for a husband for her talented daughter have risen substantially: she now demands a well-educated man with a promising future, even though this will require a considerable dowry.[11]

Mrs. Begum is one of forty women in the Sri Joni cooperative who make jute handbags; an additional one hundred or so earn money from the members by cleaning and braiding the raw jute strands into fine cord. Members earn on the average about 100 taka ($7) per month by knotting bags in their spare time.

The women—most of them married, but some single or widowed—sell the bulk of their products through KARIKA, the Bangladesh Handicrafts Cooperative Federation, which has a shop in Dacca. Some also sell directly to exporters or to retailers in the city's New Market shopping center. That a few Muslim women are now taking their own wares to market to bargain over prices is truly revolutionary. In the cultural context of traditional codes of honor by which their mothers lived, a woman would never have dared to leave her home. Some, including Mrs. Begum, have even thrown away their burqas, a garment that completely covers their face

[11] As in many parts of Bangladesh, Pakistan, and India, the traditional Muslim bride price is gradually being replaced by a dowry system. Parents of brides in the Sri Joni cooperative usually give more than do parents of grooms. Expectations were escalating rapidly: husbands were said to demand not only the usual household furnishings but clothes for themselves, a watch, a radio or television, and a bicycle or scooter. The earnings of Mrs. Begum's daughter would go partly toward her dowry.

and body as they walk in the streets. At first, the women who began jute work were severely criticized by more traditional community members for their irreligious behavior, especially when they moved about outside their homes. Now, four years later, and during difficult financial times, the women are admired and envied for the money they earn.

In one member's house, five young women from Rangunia Thana were learning basic designs in a two-month training session sponsored by the women's program of the IRDP. After completing their training, they would return to organize cooperatives in their own villages and teach other women their skills. Four were married and had left their children at home; one was unmarried. Did their husbands or mothers-in-law object to their being here? Not at all, they replied, otherwise they would not have come! The women, never having been out of their villages before, were thrilled to have made the journey to Dacca.

KARIKA was founded in 1975 by several highly educated Dacca women who were interested in promoting Bangladesh handicrafts. They organized an exhibition that was widely acclaimed by the public, government, and craftsworkers alike. The women raised $14,000 in government funds, with additional help from an American foundation, in order to organize a permanent means for marketing handicrafts and stimulating new production. Approximately 650 women now sell their products through KARIKA, a few as individual craftsworkers, but most utilize the fifteen affiliated cooperatives. Aside from jute products, KARIKA sells wood carvings, lacquer work, pottery, leatherwork, and cane and bamboo products (most of which are made by men), and embroidered goods, woven articles, shell jewelry, dolls, baskets, and crochet work (most of which are made by women).

Federation members are permitted considerable leeway in their work. They are required to meet strict quality control at KARIKA before their goods are accepted for sale, but they can also seek their own markets as independent artisans. KARIKA's staff suggests designs, provides materials on credit where necessary, checks the finished products for quality, and sells the wares. The volume is as yet insufficient for export and does not even meet the local demand for high-quality handicrafts from the urban elite and from foreigners, many of whom are ensconced in an expensive hotel across the street. The federation has a small paid staff and a number of volunteers. A management committee of twelve persons, all shareholders in the cooperative federation, sets policy at monthly meetings.

Although 85 percent of the population of Bangladesh is Muslim, most income-generating projects for women have drawn disproportionately from the minority of Christian and non-Christian tribal groups, Buddhists, and Hindus. This was true for the Rangunia Thana agricultural cooperatives, and it is also true of the largest federation of jute handicrafts cooperatives in Bangladesh. Almost all of the 3,000 women marketing their jute crafts through Jagaroni, a Dacca training center and salesroom, and the Jute Works, its exporting arm, are non-Muslim. Distributed over forty or fifty villages, most within a few hours' travel from Dacca, the women produce finely wrought jute sikas (plant and basket hangers), wall hangings, handbags, mats, and other decorative objects. They are grouped into loose producers' cooperatives that usually start with from ten to thirty members but sometimes expand to three or four hundred as interest grows. (Unlike the IRDP cooperatives at Rangunia, few are registered with the government because of the strict accounting requirements.) The women work at home in their spare time or gather together in the afternoons with relatives or neighbors. Sometimes the whole family works, young children or old men braiding the jute into cord, women working the elaborate knots in the shape of pomegranate fruits or small blossoms suspended from the sikas.

Jagaroni, a training and sales center nestled among fruit-bearing trees and vegetable gardens behind high walls in sprawling Dacca, is run by the Sisters of the Holy Cross College located across the street. It is staffed by Bengalis and a few foreign volunteers. Up to fifteen women at a time can be accommodated in the center's living quarters for a training period of from two to six weeks (depending on the complexity of the task), where they learn to weave sikas and other goods to specified design standards. The trainees have been nominated by their own villages and will return to teach others. Many are tribal Christians. Women from nearby villages with established cooperatives come to the center by foot or by bus or train, loaded with large sacks of finished sikas to sell. Goods of unacceptable quality (those with loose knots, irregular sizes, poor coloring, or soiled) are returned without payment for correction.

The Jagaroni and the Jute Works staffs exercise final authority in setting design criteria, establishing prices, and instituting strict quality controls. Basic prices are determined by the number of hours that a reasonably skilled person would need to complete a given item if she worked uninterruptedly, based roughly on the daily wage rate of a rural laborer (about 50 cents). Since workers purchase their own jute, yearly and seasonal fluctuations in the price of jute can cut into the women's small profit margins. Because most women do not work full time at their craft, they earn considerably less on the average than their men; this discrepancy is a deliberate policy for avoiding possible conflict within the family. Profits from the sale of handicrafts through the Jagaroni shop and the Jute Works are distributed as annual dividends to primary cooperatives, being divided among the workers in proportion to their contribution.

The Jute Works, a women's handicraft marketing cooperative, was founded in 1973 to promote employment for destitute women and to provide an export outlet that would return profits directly to producers. Several foreign church-affiliated and secular voluntary agencies contributed approximately $60,000 during its first year of operation. In its brief existence the Jute Works has grown into a viable economic enterprise with sales of $125,000 in 1974, $260,000 in 1975, and approximately $500,000 for 1976. It has a paid staff of about twenty people, including a design consultant who adapts traditional patterns to Western markets. In 1975 the Jute Works exports accounted for half of all exported handicrafts from Bangladesh and perhaps two-thirds of jute crafts, with the remainder being exported by tradesmen who buy directly or through middlemen.

In spite of—or perhaps because of—the rapid growth of local and export demand for high-quality jute handicrafts from Bangladesh, Jagaroni and the Jute Works have had to cope with a number of problems (some of which are discussed more fully in chapters 4 and 5 as typical of a variety of enterprises). Briefly, they have not been able to maintain close ties with their affiliated cooperatives through regular visits; some cooperatives have been subverted by middle-class women who take advantage of illiterate members; orders are massive but sporadic, causing periods of overwork that alternate with underemployment in the primary societies; and most cooperatives have not provided regular training in functional literacy, cooperative education, and health care as the program intended. The growing pains have caused Jagaroni and the Jute Works to stop accepting new cooperatives temporarily, in spite of the demand for their products. It was a difficult decision to make, since village women come to Dacca from long distances to ask for help in starting new groups.

The jute handicrafts industry in Bangladesh uses plentiful indigenous materials and indigenous skills, for many women weave beautiful sikas for hanging baskets of stored food in their own homes. Others learn easily. It requires no capital investment at the primary level because women buy their own jute. The cooperative federation which handles marketing pays the expense of training two or three women from each village in standard designs for strict quality. Foreign markets are assured so long as Westerners maintain their taste for handiwork of this type. Administrative problems—not a lack of demand for goods nor a shortage of willing workers—form the main obstacle to more rapid expansion of an industry that could provide income for tens of thousands of rural women.

The underlying philosophy of Jagaroni and the Jute Works places a strong emphasis on democratic procedures among primary level societies, but tends to greater conservatism in the area of changing women's roles. Fixing piecework wages so that they fall below men's earnings—even though the jute work is highly skilled—is one example; not promoting central workshops because they are alien to the culture is another. The aim of the program appears to be to elevate women's self-respect, but not to alter their roles significantly in either the family or the community.

Women's participation in artisanal production could change their lives more fundamentally if they were to earn higher wages, work together, and receive regular training in literacy, health care, family planning, and other services. Although one organizer criticized the idea of a central workplace as being based on a "Western model of factory production," women might well find working together greatly rewarding. In at least two cooperatives women work together by choice. A program run by a Swedish group near Rajshahi in northern Bangladesh employs about one hundred Hindu and Muslim village women in jute handicrafts, which are sold to Jagaroni. The women are also employed in sewing, knitting, weaving, and embroidery, and these products are sold to KARIKA. Many women choose to work together in the village compound for six hours a day, six days a week, because they have fewer disturbances than when they work at home. Similarly, in the canteen on the highway in front of the People's Health Center at Savar, north of Dacca, young women (many unmarried, most Muslim) make sikas together in sight of the customers who come in for tea. They say they prefer to work in the center, even though it is not required, because they enjoy one another's company and the chance to learn new skills.

Some of the handicrafts cooperatives encourage family planning, but, again, so long as women work at home and their children can help, where is the strong incentive to space or limit births? The income alone may have some influence in delaying marriage in a few exceptional cases— such as Akhtari Begum's productive daughter at Sri Joni—but more radical steps, such as living in hostels at the workshop, may be necessary in order to effect a real change. Otherwise the strong cultural pressures toward early marriage, especially among Muslims, are likely to persist. The arrangement of daughters' marriages formed a popular topic among rural women trainees at Jagaroni. One frantic woman with a still-unmarried eighteen-year-old daughter was teased constantly by her companions; the daughter herself was apparently in no hurry to marry at all. Providing young women with an alternative source of social and economic support could begin to break the pattern of poverty, early marriage, and high fertility.

THE DISPERSED FACTORY SYSTEM: FOOD PROCESSING IN INDIA

The putting-out or dispersed factory system forms an intermediate stage between artisanal and factory production. Staley and Morse (1965, page 7) note, "In this system of manufacture a middleman (a merchant, a factory manager, or a specialized 'putter-out' who acts as agent) distributes materials to workers in their homes or small workplaces, prescribes the tasks to be done, and pays for work performed—usually by the piece." Or the work may be performed for a cooperative or association. Unlike artisans, who create a product from beginning to end and frequently sell it themselves, workers in a putting-out system perform part of a total process (for example, the women who shell the shrimps at home for canners in Karachi, or those women who roll bidis for cigarette manufacturers in India) or assemble one component of a product (for example, women who manufacture radio transformers in a Poona cooperative). These workers are usually paid by time or piecework. They may work at home, alone or with family helpers, or in dependent or quasi-dependent small shops with other employees. An obvious advantage of the putting-out system is the security of the market; a disadvantage is the existence of usually exploitative wages and unregulated working conditions, especially when the work is done at home.[12]

The Lijjat Papad Industry, with headquarters in Bombay and fifteen cooperatively organized production centers scattered throughout India, is a dispersed factory system for manufacturing papads—a light, tortilla-like flat cake made of flour, spices, oil, and water that is marketed in a soft state and fried by the consumer in hot oil to make a crispy snack food or meal accompaniment.[13] All of the 2,700 cooperative members are women, although some of the staff workers are men. The industry can properly be called a putting-out system because the women perform a single task on materials provided by the central employer: they roll the

[12] For an account of the depressed working conditions of bidi (cigarette) makers in India, see the report of the Committee on the Status of Women in India (1974, pp. 174–177).
[13] There are seven production centers in Bombay, three in Maharashtra State, two in Gujarat, and one each in Madhya Pradesh, Andhra Pradesh, and West Bengal.

prepared dough into flat cakes of specified size and weight, and dry them briefly in the sun. Their cooperatives buy all of the papads on a piece-work or time-paid basis.

In the middle of the hot afternoon, the women of Valod—a dusty town of about six thousand Muslim, Hindu, and tribal people near Surat in Gujarat State—come out-of-doors carrying stainless steel containers of papads that they have rolled out during the day.[14] They gather on the porch of their cooperative headquarters, which is housed in a solid brick building draped with crimson bougainvillea. Women and girls talk about the day's events as they queue up, waiting for their papads to be weighed and packaged. They will earn Rs. 4 or Rs. 5 (about 45 to 55 cents), paid daily in cash, for their work—an amount approximately equivalent to what their husbands earn laboring in the fields. Some may earn as much as Rs. 10 to Rs. 15 in a day during the busy season, when papads are in greatest demand for festivities. The minimum daily wage set by the Gujarat State government is Rs. 3.

The center is located at the edge of town in a complex of buildings that houses the training facilities of the Vedchhi Intensive Area Scheme, an indigenous development program that has been long active in this economically depressed area.[15] Young men learn spinning and weaving, cloth printing and dyeing, carpentry, machine repair, and typesetting. At least half the women in the Valod cooperative are Muslims, the rest Hindu (some, untouchables), and tribals. Drawing at first on destitute widows and the poorest of married women when it was formed in 1968, the cooperative now includes more than four hundred poor and working-class women, many of them wives of landless laborers. Most are illiterate; a few, however, are high-school graduates who roll papads because there is no other employment for them in the village. Cooperative members in Valod, as in all the branches of Lijjat Papad, elect a management committee from among the ranks of their own producers; none has outside members either as "sympathizers" or "well-wishers," as many Indian women's co-

[14] This section is based on visits to cooperatives in Valod and Golan, on written materials provided by the Vedchhi Intensive Area Scheme, and on interviews with Shikkhu Vyas, a founder of Vedchhi, and Sam Thangaraj of OXFAM in New Delhi.

[15] The Vedchhi scheme formulated its first five-year plan in 1961 under the leadership and inspiration of Gandhi follower, Jugatram Dave. Its organizers are dedicated workers drawn from the ranks of former student activists who have chosen to turn their energies to authentic rural development. It is a comprehensive program, incorporating elementary and high schools plus preschool care based on the methods of Montessori, health care, agricultural cooperatives and training, crafts training, and other activities. Its programs are aimed specifically at the "weakest" sections of the population: tribals, Muslims, Hindu untouchables, and women. See the report of the Vedchhi Intensive Area Scheme (n.d.) for a more complete description of the plan.

operatives do. Although the better-educated women tend to dominate decision making, all officeholders must continue to roll papads.

Every morning the women come to the center to collect the dough, which has been prepared during the early hours by paid staff. They carry it home in their containers, and spend four or five hours rolling out papads on tin plates and drying them for a few minutes in the sun, or over a stove when it rains. The women of Valod received no training because, as one organizer put it, "This skill is in the blood of the people." With 433 female cooperative members and 33 male and female staff members,[16] the papad industry of Valod and its small subcenter in neighboring Golan brought in the startling sum of $41,000 in cash wages to the village economy in its fiscal year 1974–75 (table 3-3). About two-thirds of the households of Valod are said to receive money from this source, with an average of perhaps one-third to half of their total household income contributed by the women workers.

Seven kilometers from Valod in an open field stands the new subcenter located at the Upasana Community Center of Golan. In a simple brick building, with a large central courtyard open to the sky, forty Adivasi (tribal) girls and women roll papads every day. The Adivasis had formerly been working through the Valod center but found the long walk to town twice a day exhausting, especially during the rainy season when the road was flooded. They asked the Valod management committee to provide a vehicle for transport, but the Muslim and Hindu women were apparently reluctant to spend so much of their cooperative funds on their tribal sisters. Organizers in the Vedchhi Intensive Area Scheme consequently sought help from British and Australian voluntary agencies in obtaining a vehicle and $2,400 in order to build a separate production center at Golan.

The Golan papad cooperative is technically a subcenter of Valod and is supervised by its management. Every morning a worker from Golan picks up the dough at Valod in the vehicles, and every afternoon he delivers the finished papads. But at Golan the women gather together to work in one location. The central workplace is not only a convenience but a necessity since tribal households are scattered widely through the fields, and most do not have proper facilities or space for food processing. Supervision for health purposes is difficult. In addition, the skill of papad rolling was not "in the blood" of the Adivasis, but had to be learned.

---

[16] The staff members prepare the dough every day for distribution to workers, weigh the rolled papads, package and label them in polythene bags weighing 250 and 400 gm, and prepare them for shipment. They also keep the accounts, pay the workers, drive and maintain the vehicles, sell papads to retailers in Baroda and Ahmedabad, and perform other tasks.

Table 3-3. Production and Membership in the Lijjat Papad Industry of Valod and Golan in Gujarat, India, from 1968–69 to 1974–75 (in thousands of rupees and dollars)

Fiscal year	No. of women members	No. of paid staff workers	Paid to members		Paid to staff		Papad sales	
			Rs.	$	Rs.	$	Rs.	$
1968–69	30	10	10.3	1.1	2.6	.3	42	5
1969–70	210	19	119.8	13.2	16.6	1.8	472	52
1970–71	210	19	189.9	20.9	15.2	1.7	776	85
1971–72	210	19	229.4	25.2	14.7	1.6	1,025	113
1972–73	245	18	270.5	29.8	16.2	1.8	1,257	138
1973–74	412	35	389.9	42.9	19.7	2.2	1,985	218
1974–75	433	33	343.6	37.8	28.2	3.1	1,575	173

Source: Figures provided by the Vedchhi Intensive Area Scheme, Valod.
Note: Rupees converted to dollars at rate of Re. 1 = 11 cents.

Most of the Golan workers are unmarried young women who earn the legal minimum wage of Rs. 3 per day. In the first eight months of 1975, when the cooperative was formed, forty-five tribal women earned a total of Rs. 23,659 ($2,600), or about $7 each per month.

Papads from Valod and Golan are marketed by salesmen located at depots in Baroda and Ahmedabad or are shipped to the Bombay headquarters of Mahila Griha Udyog Lijjat Papad (translated roughly as Women's Cottage Industry Tasty Papads). The Bombay office pays for the papads once a month. Once a year it distributes profits to its fifteen branch cooperatives. Each branch retains part of the profits for its own use, spends part on community projects approved by its board, and distributes the rest as dividends (one-third of the total profits at Valod) to its members. Women at Valod and Golan received their 1975 dividend in the form of lightweight cookware, worth about Rs. 100 ($11), which was distributed at a community feast for all of the members and their families. And with its 1975 profits the small subcenter at Golan has already repaid the loan for its vehicle, contributed $100 to the community center, and donated funds to the family-planning clinic.

The cooperatives have instituted a compulsory savings scheme in which 15 paise out of every rupee's earnings are deposited to members' accounts and matched with funds from the cooperative. The savings earn 15 percent yearly interest. Women cannot draw on their savings without the permission of the board, but loans are available to members in case of sickness or emergency.

The cooperative at Valod was founded in the late 1960s, when the Bombay company contacted Vedchhi workers to purchase locally grown pulses for flour. The workers asked for a production center as well in order to employ local women. The Bombay industry itself began on a very small scale, in the late 1950s, as a commercial enterprise designed to provide work for lower-middle-class women in the area. Sales have grown phenomenally from Rs. 7,000 ($770) in the first year to over Rs. 10 million ($1.2 million) in fiscal year 1974–75. About one-fifth of total production is exported to the United States, Canada, Europe, the Middle East, the Far East, and Africa, with the balance being sold through domestic markets. Its success is due in part to the uniformly high quality of its products. Most ingredients are distributed to the branches from Bombay in order to ensure that the seven varieties (based on the type of flour and spices) are consistent in quality and taste. Papads are identically packaged and labeled in all branches and sold at standardized wholesale and retail prices. The Mahila Griha Udyog Lijjat Papad, as a nonprofit cooperative organization, is eligible for special government concessions of various kinds. The state Khadi and Village Industry Commission has advanced loans of Rs. 865,000 ($95,000) for vehicles, buildings, raw materials, and other requirements. Over 2,700 women members worked during 1974–75 for wages totaling almost Rs. 3 million ($300,000). Sales of almost $1.5 million were anticipated for 1975–76, providing employment for 3,500 women plus associated staff.

The papad cooperatives, like the milk and jute cooperatives, work with local agricultural products (pulses, spices, oils) requiring little capital investment at the primary level other than for the production center. The industry organizes the women's existing skills into a marketable commodity, thus generating regular wages from an outside source. It recruits workers disproportionately from the poorest sectors of the population, with favorable consequences to the distribution of incomes within the community. The townspeople of Valod are installing water pumps, latrines, and electricity in their homes, although some improvements are a result of the Vedchhi Intensive Area Scheme as a whole, which integrates most households into agricultural cooperatives, marketing units, and other social and economic programs. The Vedchhi Scheme strongly emphasizes Gandhian ideals of narrowing income gaps by advancing the living standards of the "weaker sections" (including women) and narrowing social gaps by mixing religions and castes in economic activities and in cultural events, such as the yearly feast held for all papad workers and their families from Valod and Golan where Muslims, caste Hindus, scheduled castes, and tribals alike are in attendance.

When the Valod cooperative was first planned, organizers assumed that production would have to be based in the home if women workers were to be recruited. Now, conditions are quite different. After six years of successful operation, the once-conservative women of Valod move easily through the streets; indeed, when anti-Congress students attacked their cooperative building in 1974, both Hindu and Muslim women came out to defend it. Because Adivasi women were always freer to move about, their work at the production center in Golan is a less significant breakthrough. But their employment has expanded their alternatives and improved the bargaining power of landless tribal women remaining in the agricultural sector, who can now negotiate more effectively for higher wages—or, more accurately, for enforcement of the Rs. 3 minimum daily wage set by the state. Nonagricultural employment thus benefits the agricultural population by drawing off its excess workers. Three more papad centers are planned for the dispersed Adivasi population in the area.

The Adivasis have traditionally married at a later age than their Muslim or Hindu counterparts, in part perhaps because many unmarried girls were already earning money as farm laborers, in part because tribal norms place less emphasis on linking the family's honor so closely to the chastity of its womenfolk. Financial incentives to delay marriage would thus most likely attract the Adivasis disproportionately, as would hostels for unmarried workers (for example, a number of tribal children of both sexes already attend local boarding schools).

Certainly, the central workplace at Golan offers an ideal site for functional education classes dedicated to raising women's consciousness about the timing of marriage and the practice of family planning, among other issues. Valod and Golan both pay fifteen days' wages to a woman who undergoes sterilization, but few have taken advantage of this incentive. Almost all the Golan workers are unmarried; the Valod women continue to spend most of their days at home, where they are less likely to be exposed to antinatalist alternatives. A few have been sterilized after bearing four or five children, but it may be that incentives in this, as in other programs, could be tied more effectively to delaying the first birth and spacing additional births several years apart than to ending childbearing altogether.

CARPET WEAVING IN NEPAL

On the outskirts of Kathmandu, where the houses blend into rice fields that stretch to the edge of the valley and climb the terraced mountains, lies the village of Jawalakhel, the home of one of three Tibetan refugee camps set up in the early 1960s with assistance from several international agencies and the Swiss government.[17] The camp houses about two hundred families; each has paid Nepalese Rs. 50 ($4) for a membership in the Jawalakhel Multi-Purpose Cooperative Society, which runs a food store, a poultry farm, and a shop at the handicrafts center in which members can sell curios on commission. The government-registered cooperative earned profits of over Rs. 100,000 ($8,500) in 1975. Fifteen percent was distributed to members as dividends of about $5 each, 35 percent was kept in reserve, and the balance spent on cooperative development, education, staff bonuses, and a social fund. Profits formed a healthy share of the cooperative's 1975 gross income of Rs. 450,000 (about $36,000).

At the handicrafts center, across the road from the camp where some of the employees live, is a carpet-weaving factory employing about four hundred workers, most of them women. The factory is not a cooperative but is governed by the rules for commerce and industry in Nepal. Founded and originally owned by the Swiss government, the factory is now run by

---

[17] I am indebted to Tashi Dondupt, an accountant at the Jawalakhel Multi-Purpose Cooperative Society, for the statistics reported in this section.

the Tibetan government in exile (in India), as are carpet works at two other Tibetan camps at Pokhara and Chailsa in Nepal. All the carpets produced in the factories are sold to Switzerland, although both men and women weave smaller rugs at home. These are displayed in the factory sales shop for local purchase at a 15 percent commission, sold through retail shops in Kathmandu, or exported through other agents. The women weavers earn about Rs. 150 a month ($12) for a six-day work week and are paid on a piecework basis. Others clean, card, and spin the raw wool into yarn. Men do most of the heavy work, dyeing the yarn in large vats and spreading it out to dry. All work is done by hand: the women sit in threes or fours at the looms, talking and singing old Tibetan songs, as they knot the intricate designs of dragons and ancient symbols in deep reds or blues, ivories, or pale green jade.

The Jawalakhel Multi-Purpose Cooperative Society and the factory are managed by local people, most of them male, many of whom were sent by the Swiss government to school in Kathmandu for training in management, accounting, and English. But the ordinary worker in the carpet factory appears to receive little, if any, additional training. She does, however, earn a small pension on retirement. The Jawalakhel factory runs a child-care center, funded, along with the local primary school, by factory profits. At a second carpet factory in the rugged terrain north of Pokhara, younger children and infants often sleep or play near their mothers working at the looms. The management makes no attempt to teach the women about family planning; a spokesman at Jawalakhel claimed that the women express little interest in learning.

The Jawalakhel carpet-weaving factory is not technically a small industry because it employs several hundred workers. On the other hand, the level of capitalization and mechanization falls well below what one would expect of a workplace with so many employees, and its character is distinctly "small." A simple division of labor sets some workers to particular tasks, such as carding, spinning, or carrying wood for the fires, but the weavers are artisans who create—individually or in groups—a whole carpet in which they take great pride. The market for the factory output is assured so long as the demand for fine, hand-knotted rugs continues to grow in Europe and America, although whether the bold Tibetan designs can compete successfully with the subtler Kashmiri rugs or with expanding carpet industries in Iran, Syria, and elsewhere remains to be seen.

It is doubtful that the women's earning power has substantially altered their position in the family because the strong Tibetan women have always played an active role in production. The harsh environment of their homeland did not permit the luxury of such practices as female seclusion, nor did their Buddhist religion require it. In the crowded markets of Kathmandu the Tibetan women can be seen bartering, laughing, and talking with their menfolk, smoking cigarettes, and carrying their heavy loads, in sharp contrast to the more sedate behavior of the Hindu women or the virtual absence of Muslim women from the streets of neighboring Bangladesh. Thus, their gainful employment is as much an effect as a cause of their more egalitarian role in the family. Whether they use their power to space or limit pregnancies is another question; the possibilities of so doing might well be raised if family-planning education and services were provided at the worksite. Yet so long as the families also weave rugs at home, children will remain useful contributors to the household income.

CONCLUSIONS

In reviewing five programs in which rural women of South Asia are involved in income-producing activities, one is impressed that rural development appears to be more easily advanced than the status of women, and that reproductive behavior is the most resistant to change of the three.

Each of the programs has introduced into rural communities new opportunities for gainful employment, to which women from the poorest sectors of the population responded most immediately. Men were not displaced from jobs; instead new jobs were organized around activities in which many women already had engaged at a relatively unproductive level. The new income sometimes constituted a major portion of the household earnings: members of the AMUL Dairy cooperatives on the average earned half their household income from milk, compared with 20 percent among nonmember families with milch animals.

Four of the programs infused money into the community from urban or overseas markets; only the Bangladesh women's agricultural cooperatives depended on local markets. The tradeoff is that in the same four programs the villagers did not themselves benefit from the goods they produced. Families with buffaloes sold most of their milk for cash rather than consuming it, and they could ill-afford to buy prepared baby foods and cheeses. The jute handicrafts, papads, and carpets are all nonessential items shipped out of the community. Thus, the new employment did not necessarily make villages more self-sufficient in providing for their own consumption needs, but it did create a more effective demand for existing goods and services.

The extent to which new money has developmental consequences, of course, depends on how it is spent. Most women undoubtedly spend their small wages on food for their families or themselves; for, as one observer put it, many experience an "insatiable hunger" from years of deprivation, when as little girls, and then as daughters-in-law and wives, they were the last to eat. Some buy gold jewelry as a form of savings, and clothing, watches, or radios. Husbands sometimes spend the extra money on gambling, pan (betel), or alcohol, all prevalent pastimes, or they might work less themselves so long as the women are bringing in money. But a few women are able to make major purchases of land, a new home, or major home improvements.[18] In addition, all the cooperatives offer or invest in developmental programs of various types. The Bangladesh IRDP cooperatives organize literacy classes, encourage experimentation with new seeds, crops, and farming methods, and make loans available to individual members or groups for new economic enterprises. The AMUL Dairy cooperatives and the papad cooperatives spend part of their profits on community projects, such as roads, wells, and health centers. The Nepal carpet factory sponsors community schools with some of its earnings. The programs thus have a spin-off effect that can have far-reaching developmental consequences.

All five programs also appear to increase women's bargaining power in the family by providing a cash income over which they might have some control. At the very least, the employment provides concrete public and private recognition of the value of women's work. Members of all-female cooperatives elected to management positions also acquire decision-making skills that are likely to translate into a more active role in the family. But women in the mixed cooperatives of AMUL Dairy or at the carpet factories of Nepal do not participate in the decisions of the enterprise, even though they perform most of the primary labor. Recall that all but a handful of the approximately 9,000 managers of primary societies of the AMUL Dairy are men. And, with few exceptions, women play no part in marketing their wares. The exceptions are the jute workers in Bangladesh, who sell sikas and handbags directly to retailers, as well as through their cooperatives; the general rule is that the products—even the fruit and vegetables produced by women in Bangladesh—are marketed by male-dominated or solely male cooperative federations or employers. Most programs do not fully train women to exercise all of the functions of buying, selling, and production for which they could be prepared.

Partly as a consequence of their generally low representation among the main decision-making bodies at work, women appear as yet to play

[18] An agricultural and sewing cooperative of ten Garo tribeswomen in northern Bangladesh was able, in several years, to save enough money from their sweet potato and pineapple crops to obtain a loan, which enabled them to buy back fifteen acres of paddy land which had been lost to the moneylender eight years before. The village men had been working the land for wages of about 50 cents a day; once the women bought it, the men continued plowing and harvesting while women planted, weeded, and harvested the rice.

very little role in the affairs of the community at large. Village meetings, when they are held at all, cater almost entirely to a male audience and, except for legally required token representation of women, the villagers elect only men to the village panchayats. The women's political skills need to be further developed before they can share equally in community decisions. One of the major ways of encouraging these skills is through the workplace.

Finally, none of the programs appears to have altered fundamentally the marriage or birth patterns of its workers. Reproductive behavior remains highly resistant to change.

Among the Muslim community in particular, but among the Hindus and some tribals as well, cultural pressures continue to propel girls into early marriages in order to ensure their virginity and to avoid the possibility of their forming emotional attachments or developing a spirit of independence which would challenge parental control over the choice of a husband. In villages where girls are marrying later now than formerly, the delays appear to be stimulated by economic constraints rather than basic changes in cultural values. Marriages are put off if the family is too poor to raise a decent dowry for its daughter or if dowry demands are escalating beyond the family's ability to provide.[19] In the absence of strong propaganda to the contrary, it is possible, therefore, that introducing gainful employment for unmarried girls could initially result in *earlier* rather than later marriages, as they earn money for their own weddings. Indeed, saving for a dowry proved to be a major incentive for employment among girls and women in Pakistan, India, and Bangladesh. It will take more than an income for the marriages of young girls to be substantially delayed.

Nor was there any indication that women in these programs were choosing in large numbers to have fewer births, although they were frequently exposed to some elementary knowledge about family planning and sometimes to supplies as well (though delivery of contraceptives was often sporadic and unreliable). First, workers were often drawn from among women who were widowed or past their childbearing years. Second, women generally worked at home, where childbearing and child-rearing did not interfere in any fundamental way with their work tasks nor vice versa, and where children might even provide extra sets of helping hands for weeding vegetables, taking fodder to the cows, or twisting jute into

[19] In a Punjabi village in Pakistan, girls and women doing embroidery were earning from Rs. 50 to Rs. 200 ($5 to $20) a month depending on the amount of time they spent on their work. After some discussion, the assembled group agreed that they would have to pay Rs. 3,000 to Rs. 4,000 for a dowry and that the amount was rising.

cord. Only in the papad center at Golan and in the Nepalese carpet factories did women work outside the home on a regular basis. At Golan,
they were almost all unmarried girls; at Jawalakhel and Pokhara, they
were of all ages, the women with young children bringing them to
work. In neither setting was there a specific incentive to delay marriage
or to space or limit pregnancies, nor was there persistent propaganda to
do so, although both would be sensible in the context of the women's
working environment.

In the absence of all of the criteria listed in chapter 2, then, it is doubtful that rural women's employment, even outside agriculture, will have
a significant effect on delaying marriage or reducing birthrates, although
it may benefit village economies and the women themselves in other, important ways. In the next two chapters I will discuss major issues of production and recruitment as they affect the creation of nonagricultural
employment for rural women outside the home, isolating particularly
prevalent problems that might well be overcome if they are anticipated.

4

PRODUCT SELECTION AND FUNDING

If they are to promote genuine rural development, employment projects for rural women should be capable of becoming self-sustaining in the space of, say, three to five years. Although I do not want to belabor the obvious, there is little value in beginning a program that is likely to collapse as soon as the original organizers or funding sources pull out. It is probably better to attempt nothing rather than to raise women's hopes of earning a living only to abandon them later on to failure.

Disillusionment, unfortunately, is the outcome of a number of welfare-oriented training programs that teach rural women handicrafts, sewing, or weaving. After perhaps a year's training and production in a workshop, the women are turned out on their own, only to find that they frequently cannot make a living from their work.[1] Often they cannot afford to buy a loom or a sewing machine and are reduced to turning out handmade garments which cannot possibly compete in quality or quantity with those made by local tailors or manufacturers.[2] Many training programs are really only sheltered workshops, where women spend their days sewing or embroidering on products for which there is no real market, their work being subsidized by donations from well-meaning women's organizations, voluntary associations, or international agencies.[3] The women receive very low wages and little, if any, developmental training (for example, no

---

[1] Women in a large Bangladesh training program follow up nine months' training with nine months in a production workshop, a process that is intended to provide the intermediate step to self- or wage-employment. For a more detailed discussion, see the National Board of Bangladesh Women's Rehabilitation Programme study (1974, pp. 21–22).

[2] This situation appeared to be the characteristic result of the training programs for rural women sponsored by the Nepal Women's Organization, for example.

[3] The phrase *sheltered workshops* is derived from Adrienne Germain's observations of many crafts programs in South Asia. The following passage is quoted with permission from a memo to the Ford Foundation from Adrienne Germain (append. A, p. 3): "They are a source of employment for women who do not participate in their organization and management and who, usually, do not receive any other benefit (e.g., functional education). In some cases the programs are or can be exploitative in at least two ways: (a) products are given away to friends, relatives, etc. by program organizers; (b) women are not well enough trained to produce salable items on their own despite promises to the contrary."

75

functional education is offered) that could enable them to become truly self-reliant. Subsidies frequently do more harm than good. For example, one international agency distributed free sewing machines and cloth to women's groups in Bangladesh, but when the free supplies were discontinued, most groups were unable to survive. Indeed, their dependence on free materials prevented them from becoming competitive on the open market.

The issue of fair wages is crucial. An economically viable enterprise can pay wages high enough to act as a strong incentive for women to work. Skilled women workers should earn at least what men earn in agricultural day labor if their work is to acquire its proper value. Yet even this minimum requirement is unmet in many programs, where skilled women earn the equivalent of only 20 or 25 cents a day by making handicrafts that are exported to European and American markets. A government welfare program in India which encourages industries to employ women in small ancilliary workshops has been criticized on the grounds that it permits employers to pay lower wages to women workers while undercutting the unionization of male workers. The laudable goal of creating employment for women must not become a cover-up for the further exploitation of a cheap labor supply.

In this chapter I propose some criteria for selecting appropriate products and for financing small-scale industries employing rural women. Clearly, market-oriented production is not possible in all situations, for the extreme seasonal or year-round isolation of many villages severely impedes their access to outlets. The best that can be achieved in many areas is to enable villagers to provide for their own basic needs through increased production of basic foodstuffs, clothing, and household and farming utensils. Such is the case in many villages of Bangladesh that are heavily flooded during the monsoons and distant from major markets. In Nepal, too, perhaps half the population lives in villages that can be reached only by several hours or days of foot travel over narrow mountain paths and bridges.

Where villages and towns are on major transportation routes—on roads, rails, or rivers—the possibilities are greatly expanded for orienting production to neighboring urban markets or for export. It is toward these market-linked centers, and toward the goal of providing income-generating employment outside the home year round for young rural women, that the proposals in this chapter are directed. As noted previously, our interest lies in promoting labor-intensive, small-scale, rural industries with relatively low capital requirements and uncomplicated technologies.[4] The

---

[4] The search for intermediate technologies relevant to the needs and resources of developing countries is gaining momentum in the face of the disappointing performance of so many projects employing sophisticated imported equipment depen-

question is, What type of production is best suited to the small, rural industrial model?

As an overall strategy for encouraging modern small industries in developing countries, Staley and Morse (1965) urge policymakers to seek out projects that are:

(1) creative of real capital, in the form of physical improvements or human improvements; (2) high in labor intensity, so that a major portion of funds will go for labor or for materials produced by labor-intensive methods; (3) likely to bring a fairly quick increase in production, thereby minimizing inflationary dangers; (4) capable of using many different types of labor, with or without heavy equipment; (5) little dependent on materials or equipment requiring foreign exchange; (6) widespread in location, capable of bringing jobs and increased productivity to needy parts of the country; (7) capable of large-scale application, so as to make a real impact. [page 296]

Staley and Morse (1965, pages 112–127) also cite a number of conditions advantageous to the development of decentralized small industry:

1. *Locational influences* favoring factories processing a dispersed raw material (for example, butter or cheese); factories manufacturing products with local markets and relatively high transfer costs (for example, bottled and canned soft drinks); and service industries with individualized requirements (for example, printing)
2. *Process influences* favoring separable manufacturing operations with a high degree of specialization; crafts or precision handiwork; and simple assembly, mixing, or finishing operations
3. *Market influences* favoring differentiated products having low economies of scale (for example, ready-made garments); and industries serving small, total markets (for example, rice milling, glovemaking, making artificial flowers, and so forth).

In analyzing the role of small manufacturing in India's economic growth, Fisher (1968, pages 128–129) suggests expanding small-scale hand industries for the domestic mass market, small-scale hand industries for mass markets abroad, and small-scale powered industry. Clearly, it makes no sense to promote hand industries that are not competitive with larger manufacturers or ones that are likely to be displaced by them in the future. But small producers can complement large producers. Artisans,

---

dent on highly skilled service personnel, expensive or unavailable power sources, and imported replacement parts. An excellent overview of new developments in intermediate household and agricultural technology can be found in the journal, *Appropriate Technology* (9 King Street, London WC2E 8 HN); see also the annotated bibliography compiled by Carr (1976). A useful review of programs and research in the application of intermediate technologies to small-scale industries is found in the American Council on Education study (1977).

for example, can be encouraged to adapt to changing conditions by withdrawing from activities that compete with factory production or are otherwise becoming obsolete. By entering new lines—such as individualized installation, servicing, and repair of factory-made goods—that complement factory production and cater to new demands, they could continue to be self-supporting (Staley and Morse, 1965, page 52).

A number of sectors can probably hold their own, even in competition with advanced industrial methods; for example, those in which being small carries certain advantages, or, at least, is not disadvantageous. The manufacture of furniture, shoes, clothing, ceramics, cigars, and baskets, and metalworking and food processing, as well as almost all service activities, including retailing, fall in this category (Hirschman, 1958, page 129). Small firms can also be created to cater to the needs of larger industries, for example, manufacturing or assembling components or carrying out particular processes.

Staley and Morse (1965, page 56) classify economic activities into old-line trades marked for retreat, such as ordinary handweaving, shoemaking, manufacturing of glass bangles, and so forth; old-line trades for modernization, including artistic handweaving, artistic metalworking, basketry, and jewelry making; and new-line trades for immediate development, including precision toolmaking, electrical wiring, and bicycle, automobile, and radio repair, among others. They heavily emphasize modern, factory-oriented service trades relating to installation and repair.

In this chapter I will propose products particularly suited to the requirements of women workers that, at least initially, do not require extensive contact with the public as many service trades do. Our concern is with introducing small-scale industry that will fit within the prevailing cultural practices in South Asia, while at the same time creating conditions for the eventual breakdown of cultural constraints and the transformation of relations between the sexes. The goal is also to promote the acceptance of women's employment by selecting activities that are not seen as taking jobs away from men. That is why the suggestions in this chapter derive primarily from women's work in the home. Although I noted (see chapter 2) Wajihuddin Ahmed's insistence on industries that are "least rural and least womanish," I would propose initially that we build on the prevailing division of labor, skills, and interests, with the object of upgrading these skills and modernizing production.

PRODUCT SELECTION

The basic criteria for selecting a product are the raw materials and skills currently available in the community. Villagers themselves, and especially potential workers, should actively share in the preliminary discussions and decisions. Building on the available and the familiar is probably preferable to introducing an entirely new product that is dependent on outside supplies and requires considerable job training. Recall that the papad cooperatives in India and, to some extent, the jute cooperatives in Bangladesh and the Indian milk cooperatives were especially suited in this respect.

The following proposals offer several possible sources for new employment:

1. Finding new uses for local resources such as tree barks, leaf fibers, fruit and vegetable dyes, grass fabrics, drugs and herbal medicines. KARIKA (Bangladesh Handicrafts Cooperative Federation), for example, sent a trainee to the Philippines to learn the technique of weaving washable fabrics from the fibers of pineapple and banana leaves

2. Finding out what people want or need that cannot be obtained regularly, or at all, in local markets, for example, soap, candles, and other household utensils or food products

3. Finding new products that will not duplicate products already made in the country (Hirschman, 1958, page 130). Or, if there are similar products already on the market, making sure that the new products will be better or cheaper

4. Exploring the possibilities for import substitutions. What could be made locally that is now imported (for example, clothing, appliances, or cosmetics)? Hirschman (1958, pages 120–124) stresses the value of imports in creating a local demand for a product, but he acknowledges that it is sometimes difficult to shift to local substitutes once people have acquired a taste for the imported product

5. Establishing links with other industries in the area, as suppliers of component parts or as assemblers (Hirschman, 1958, page 134)

6. Choosing an enterprise that will generate new demands and create new possibilities for products and markets, for example, prepared foodstuffs.

The variety of possibilities is endless if one uses some imagination and carefully explores potential markets. The rather obvious proposals which follow are suggestions only, for the selection of an appropriate product and technology will depend primarily on a cluster of socioeconomic conditions unique to every region and probably to every village.

Food Processing

Food processing includes a variety of treatments: fish and meat canning, salting, smoking, and drying; fruit and vegetable canning and drying; the bottling of fruit juices and fermented juices; the making of jams, jellies, syrups, chutneys, and pickles; the making of cheese, butter, ghee, and yoghurt; the preparation of snack foods such as papads or puffed rice; the processing of macaroni, spaghetti, or noodles of various types; the bottling of soda water; baking; the shelling and roasting of seeds and nuts, and so on. The local cooperative could also supply partially processed pulp or juices for larger manufacturers.[5]

Fruit and vegetable preservation is uniquely suited to small-scale rural industry, although small- to medium-sized plants (that is, those with at least twenty employees and sales of over $20,000) generally hold some advantages over very small units by making possible the bulk purchase of fresh fruit or vegetables, more modern equipment, more storage space, and more effective marketing (Staley and Morse, 1965, page 152). A typical small unit in India in the late 1950s involved an initial investment and yearly output as shown in table 4-1.

A report (Staley and Morse, 1965) on fruit and vegetable preservation and canning in 1958 suggested that the outlook for small-scale fruit and vegetable processing in India was moderately good with rising (although low) domestic consumption. As many as 70 percent of employees in the industry were seasonal workers employed only four or five months a year, however, and many worked in their own households.

Employing women in the food-processing industry has a number of advantages. First, local agricultural produce is utilized, some of which might go to waste when heavy seasonal harvests are sold in the market at low prices. The government of Nepal, for example, is planting fruit trees on hillsides in order to stop erosion. Frequently, there is too much fruit to

Table 4-1. Initial Investment and Yearly Output of Four Typical Small-Scale Indian Industries
(in dollars)

No. of employees	Initial investment	Output	Principal products
10	10,000	6,000	Fruit and squashes (fruit drinks)
27	82,000	74,000	Canned and bottled fruits and vegetables
30	43,000	50,000	Canned fruits and vegetables, mango chutney, and squashes
50	65,000	90,000	Jams, and mango and vegetable canning

Source: Staley and Morse (1965).

[5] The technology of food preservation, although fairly simple, requires extreme care if spoilage and food poisoning are to be avoided. The U.S. Department of Agriculture issues the *Home and Garden Bulletin* and the *Farmers Bulletin* on home processing with information adaptable to small industries. One of the most helpful popular books is *Putting Food By,* by Hertzberg, Vaughan, and Greene (1975).

market, and it falls to the ground unused. Small-scale, dispersed processing plants could prevent such waste. Second, since food processing is typically women's work, the new industrial employment would not be seen as competitive with men's work. Third, food processing has important nutritional advantages by making available the surplus of one season for consumption during the rest of the year, when little fresh produce is grown. It also is appropriate to small-scale production, with intermediate technology, and at relatively low capital investment. Units of stainless steel and aluminum, with a daily capacity to produce 200 to 500 quarts per unit, can be manufactured to preserve fruits, vegetables, or fish. Utilizing small steam generators, fired by any fuel, the workers require only simple training for their operation.[6] Sun drying—a nutritious method of preservation that reduces problems of transporting goods in bulk—requires very little equipment and no power source unless it is necessary to substitute drying ovens during the rainy season. Additional investment is required for reusable glass containers or more expensive tin cans. Flexible units permit the industry to expand gradually in small segments in order to meet increasing demand without making heavy capital investment in the initial stages. And finally, processed foods appeal to a variety of local, urban, and export markets.

The basic drawbacks of food processing as an economic enterprise are its seasonal nature and its dependence on agricultural production, both of which are beyond the control of the cooperative. Prices may fluctuate drastically from year to year; a period of drought could throw everyone out of work. Both drawbacks could be controlled to some extent by diversifying agricultural production in the area and planning specifically for year-round use of equipment with a variety of fruits, vegetables, and fish. Some produce can be stored for processing at a later time. In addition, the cooperative might well extend its activities to the actual production of some, or all, of its own raw materials, or establish links with other women's cooperatives that raise tree crops, such as mangoes, jackfruit, date or tal palms; vegetables; fish in tanks; poultry (for dried eggs or canned chicken); milch animals (for cheese, butter, ghee, yoghurt); or other goods in sufficient quantity to supply the needs of the food-processing industry over and above the immediate demand for fresh produce.

Local markets for preserved foods, especially fruit and vegetables, may be quite limited when they compete with cheaper fresh produce, although some out-of-season canned or dried fruits, fruit juices, and canned or

---

[6] The League for International Food Education *Newsletter* of March 1974 describes such a unit manufactured in the United States by the Ball Corporation of Muncie, Indiana.

dried vegetables, as well as products such as jams, syrups, and some snack foods should find local buyers. Local demand is also likely to decline in bad years when people have little money to spend. In some rural areas villagers are beginning to grow a variety of vegetables, so that the pattern of consumption has not yet been set. The Bangladesh Rural Advancement Committee (BRAC) program introduced carrots, cauliflower, squash, broccoli, peas, tomatoes, onions, garlic, and potatoes to the Sulla villagers for their own consumption, but the gardens produce only in the winter before the monsoon floods the area. The villagers have dried fish and dal to eat all year round, plus green cooking bananas and spinach. But neither the supply nor the demand yet exists for market-oriented food processing.

Institutional buyers such as hospitals, restaurants, the armed forces, and factory canteens can provide a major market for processed foods. Two canning factories near Peshawar, in Pakistan, which employ several hundred women each during the busy seasons, sell most of their fruit, squash, and canned and machine-dried vegetables to the armed forces. Registered cooperatives in India are eligible to sell through such major urban outlets as the Super Bazaar stores in Delhi. It is doubtful whether one cooperative could produce in sufficient quantity to establish a steady supply, but federations of cooperatives producing the same product under standardized conditions—such as the fifteen papad producers in India—could supply bulk orders with some consistency.

Small food-processing industries do have special requirements, namely, transportation (for example, papads are picked up once a day and milk twice a day in Gujarat); plentiful fresh water; good storage facilities, free from pests, mold, and other spoilage, and theft; hygienic working conditions; fuel for boiling or steaming produce for the bottling and canning processes; and high seasonal needs for credit or loans to purchase produce in bulk. It is also necessary to observe strict quality controls and a good deal of technical assistance and planning is required, both at the initial stages and in the everyday and seasonal scheduling of production. At the same time, however, food preservation should stimulate agricultural productivity, while simultaneously providing for some of the nutritional needs of the local community.

Related Processing of Agricultural Products

Although there are regions of South Asia where women are rarely seen in the fields either planting, weeding, or harvesting (in the rice fields of Bengal, for example), virtually everywhere women are responsible for processing the harvested grains for their family's consumption. Their tasks include threshing, sometimes boiling, drying, pounding, winnowing, cleaning, and grinding of rice, wheat, corn, various millets (small-seeded cereal grasses), and pulses (seeds of leguminous crops such as peas, beans, and lentils). Oil is pressed from mustard or other seeds and nuts. They also dry, clean, and grind spices for everyday use and process nuts, such as the cashews of India and Bangladesh. In good weather women perform these tasks out-of-doors: in Bangladesh, they work in the center of the *bari,* a small cluster of inward-facing households; in parts of India and Pakistan, it is done in courtyards surrounded by high mud walls; and in Nepal, by the doorsteps of their homes scattered along the mountain paths. Some tasks are seasonal, while others—such as grinding flour or spices on heavy stone slabs—are done almost every day. Agricultural advances associated with the Green Revolution have added to women's (and men's) work in areas where irrigation now permits double- or triple-cropping. Not only are the crops more frequent and more abundant, but the larger heads of the high-yield rice varieties require additional parboiling and are more difficult to dry and husk.[7]

Technological advances are beginning to lift some of these heavy burdens from women's shoulders. Rice and oil mills, for example, do the work faster, cheaper, and in much greater quantity than women at home can do with their primitive methods. Women in some areas have consequently been increasingly displaced from their productive roles by the new technology.[8] The displacement would be welcome if it simply relieved women from a heavy and thankless chore, but such is not entirely the case. Some village women earned money (or, more usually, a share of the produce) by pounding rice or pressing oil at home for sale to their neighbors or others [Committee on the Status of Women in India (1974, page 169); Sattar (1975, page 60); and Von-Harder (1975, page 76)]. Yet the mills are run by men.

Rather than resisting the new technology, a more appropriate strategy would be to enable women to gain a monopoly over the new, as well as the old, processes, at least on the scale at which these functions are performed in small industries at the village or town level. The new technology need not be highly complex, labor displacing, or highly dependent on fuel. Rice processing offers a good example of time-consuming tasks that

---

[7] Von-Harder (1975) describes the impact of the high-yield varieties on women's role in rice processing in a village in the Comilla district of Bangladesh.

[8] In India, for example, many women suffered competition from the rice and oil mills which began operating in the 1950s; see Committee on the Status of Women in India (1974, p. 169).

could be performed more efficiently by a group using intermediate-level technology. Grain can be separated from the stalks in a pedal-driven thresher rather than by walking tethered bullocks round and round over the stalks or by hitting the stalks over a barrel. After threshing, the husks can be loosened by parboiling the rice in large metal cauldrons rather than in small earthenware pots, which sometimes are kept steaming all night over a low fire in order to supply only one or two days' food for the family. The rice can then be dried by a pedal-driven drying machine rather than by being spread out under the sun in the courtyard to dry.[9]

Simple rice-husking machines could replace the traditional heavy wooden beam (called a *dekhi* in Bangla) which seesaws rhythmically with a push of the foot at one end, while the wooden spike at the other end pounds the small amount of grain that has been placed in a hollow at its base. One or two women pump the dekhi by foot, while another pushes fresh grain into the hollow and clears out the husked rice (trying not to get her hands caught under the spike). Women in one Bengali village report that they spend at least half a morning or afternoon twice a week pounding rice (Sattar, 1975, page 47). Winnowing, sieving, cleaning, and milling the rice into flour could also be performed more efficiently with better equipment. Unhusked rice can be stored in quantity, protected by its hard husks from pests, and processed as time permits and the market demands.

A women's cooperative could not only process rice, wheat, corn, millet, pulses, and spices for village households in exchange for a cash fee or a portion of the produce, but could also purchase goods in bulk for processing and sale in local or more distant markets when prices rise. Nor do the centers need to be limited to processing; they can also manufacture mixed cereals, high-protein baby foods, and animal and poultry feeds, the last from the waste products of the refining process. With adequate storage facilities, proper planning, and some diversification of products, there is no reason why production could not become a year-round activity, employing a significant number of rural women. At the same time, the production would relieve them of some of their most time-consuming tasks in the home.

---

[9] Von-Harder (1975, p. 75) mentions a drying machine which costs about 1,000 taka ($70) in Bangladesh. This would certainly be worth its cost when one considers how the sun-drying process works. First, the courtyard must be swept clean and plastered with a wet mixture of mud and cow dung that is hardened to a smooth surface. The rice must be gathered up at night, or when it rains, and spread out again in the morning—all the while the women must turn the grains and chase away poultry and birds.

Garment Making

When village women are asked what skills they would like to learn, they almost invariably mention sewing or knitting first. Women dream of having a sewing machine of their own. Although men have monopolized the tailoring professions in India, Pakistan, and Bangladesh, in recent years women have been taught to sew by various welfare agencies, volunteer groups, and home economics classes throughout the region. Initially intended to make women better housewives, more recently the programs have emphasized sewing for self-employment. Toward this end, some groups have donated sewing machines to needy women. Unfortunately, most women find themselves with far too little capital and too little sales knowledge to earn a good living; many consequently turn to wage labor for contractors or retail shops, sewing at home on a piecework basis for very low wages. Eighty-six percent of 1,000 women contract sewers in Ahmedabad, India, who were surveyed by the Textile Labor Association in the early 1970s, were earning less than Rs. 50 a month, well under $6 (Committee on the Status of Women in India, 1974, page 178).

In spite of these problems, organized production of apparel for the domestic and, in some cases, overseas mass market in small-scale, light industries remains one of the most promising areas of employment in low-income countries (Staley and Morse, 1965, page 164). Although conditions vary across countries and regions, some garments are equally as suited to small as to larger manufacturers. Most items are made in short runs of one size and style so that economies of scale are limited.

The advantages of introducing garment making rest basically with the interest and skills that many village women already possess. With treadle or hand-operated sewing machines and hand-worked knitting machines, capital requirements are moderate and fuel requirements nil. As in food processing, production can grow incrementally with the addition of new equipment and can shift easily from one item to another. Among other possible goods are men's work clothes and shirts, children's clothing and nightwear, some women's wear (beyond the ubiquitous sari), underwear, knitwear (caps, sweaters, scarves, shawls), and uniforms (for nurses, armed forces, school children, or factory workers).

There are obstacles too. On the local level, women frequently encounter strong competition from male tailors—some of them already underemployed—who have trained since childhood and attained a high level of skill and community acceptance. (Organizers probably underestimate the time it takes for an untrained woman to become truly proficient at her task; Tahrunnessa Abdullah of the Bangladesh Integrated Rural

Development Program (IRDP) estimates five years.) The lack of supervision and appropriate training in many welfare-oriented programs has resulted in garments of nonstandard size, inappropriate design, or poor quality; sometimes elaborate embroidery is added on a basically unsalable item. The women also face competition from cheap imported clothing (although not in India) and from the secondhand clothing markets which spring up in most city bazaars.

The local demand is likely to be limited. Most villagers require few changes of clothing and have little spendable income. National mass markets, through department stores or other outlets, and export mass markets are probably more appropriate (consider, for example, the current popularity of handwoven Indian shirts and handprinted cotton skirts in the United States). Some women's cooperatives have produced for institutional buyers school uniforms, for example, or knitted sweaters for the armed forces. Large institutional orders tend to overwhelm workers temporarily, however, while leaving them long periods without any work.

Another major disadvantage facing small sewing and knitting groups and individual entrepreneurs has been the consistent or sporadic shortage or high cost of cotton or woolen yarns and fabrics. Of course, one advantage of a cooperative—and particularly a federation of cooperatives—is that it can buy wholesale, and, if registered with the government, frequently at more favorable concessions. Equipment needs are also moderately heavy: even small garment-making industries would require sewing or knitting machines for almost every worker since only a few additional hands are needed for such operations as cutting and finishing. As a consequence, needs are also fairly great for work space, as well as storage space, and security against theft. (The single sewing machine belonging to a cooperative of tribal women in northern Bangladesh was chained to the center post of the most solid house in the village.)

The industry also requires access to credit or loans in order to stockpile raw materials and finished products. This is particularly true if production is to be encouraged in villages that are not accessible year round. The seasons in which women have the most time free from household responsibilities often correspond to the times when the village is virtually cut off from contact with markets because of flooding (or, if Nepal, because of snow). If the cooperative had sufficient credit, it could purchase raw materials in large quantities, work throughout the season, and store the finished goods until the transport routes are reopened.

To draw an example from a very different region, an Egyptian apparel factory has been designed specifically to create employment for rural women in a village of about 1,000 Muslim families in the South Tahrir

Land Reclamation Zone.[10] The factory is unique in that it has an explicit family-planning component: the jobs for rural women are intended to create socioeconomic conditions favorable to smaller families. The direct objectives are (1) to determine the percentage of females that must be employed to make female labor acceptable in rural areas (Is there a "critical mass?"); (2) to determine the effect of the project on women's knowledge, attitudes, and practices of family planning; and (3) to form a group of motivators among the 200 women directly employed, who will be between the ages of sixteen and forty-four years. The factory is sponsored by the Supreme Council for Population and Family Planning and the Ministry of Land Reclamation, with funding from several international agencies.

As of early 1976, twenty-four industrial sewing machines had been installed, and twenty-six more were to be installed shortly, along with twenty-three other special purpose machines. Seventy-eight young women were training—ironically, all but four of them unmarried, even though the organizers hoped to recruit young married women.[11] Many more are on the waiting list for the time when the factory expands to its full complement of 200 workers.

The number of employees and the heavy capital investment classifies the industry as a medium-sized rather than a small factory. The building, which was purchased and remodeled for about 35,000 Egyptian pounds (£E35,000, or $45,000), is large enough to include a day-care center, a health and family-planning clinic, and living quarters for the factory directors and technicians.[12] Functional literacy classes will also be offered to the trainees. In addition to the building costs, machinery cost about £E28,500 ($37,050); vehicles, £E40,000 ($52,000), including two cars and three buses for transporting workers, and one truck for deliveries; furniture and other equipment, £E2,500 ($3,250); wages and salaries prior to opening, £E5,500 ($7,150). Operational costs for the first year of full operation were estimated at £E281,500 ($365,950), including

---

[10] Information in this section was obtained from UNICEF in Cairo, one of the funding agencies. The prime mover of the project is Aziz Bindary of the Supreme Council for Population and Family Planning, who has long promoted the idea of creating nonagricultural employment for rural women as an inducement to lower fertility.

[11] The recruitment of unmarried women offers an excellent opportunity for testing the effect of female employment on marriage age and thus the timing of the first birth. The project organizers, however, are more interested in how it influences the adoption of family planning so that they are eager to hire married women. Assured that almost all the unmarried girls were "engaged," their disappointment was somewhat abated.

[12] Egyptian pounds (£E) convert to dollars at the rate of £E1 = $1.30.

£E56,000 ($72,800) in wages for 232 persons, 188 of them female, working in two shifts.

The initial investment is clearly heavy. Smaller enterprises, employing perhaps twenty to fifty women, would have far lower overhead and equipment costs. On the other hand, the planners anticipated that production during the first year would amount to a healthy £E610,000 ($793,000). Although the plan was originally to produce ready-made clothing for laborers and school children (overalls, school smocks and pajamas) that were to be sold through cooperative societies in ten zones of the district, the factory currently has orders from department store chains, which will provide the cloth and pay on a piecework basis in order to cover additional raw materials, wages, and profits. The factory is not a cooperative.

The Textile Industry

Textile mills have been among the major employers of female workers during the early industrialization of Western Europe, the United States, and Japan (Leser, 1958, page 108). Few women are employed in the textile mills of India, Pakistan, and Bangladesh, but many do spinning and weaving at home in the extensive cottage industries of the region. It is exactly this home industry which is likely to meet increasing competition from the larger producers. Staley and Morse (1965, page 56) label ordinary handweaving an old-line trade which should be marked for retreat, whereas artistic handweaving is an old-line trade marked for modernization through improved technical assistance, designs, equipment, and marketing. In some regions, handweaving can still be a thriving industry.

One of the reasons that ordinary handweaving meets increasing competition from larger mills is that, in India for example, the largely rural industry has remained at a very simple level of technology with low productivity and, consequently, very poor economic returns. The introduction of power looms in some areas has been monopolized by a few entrepreneurs who set themselves up as employers of wage-laborers under rather exploitative conditions (Committee on the Status of Women in India, 1974, page 181).

In most parts of India, weaving is primarily a male prerogative. Even in the enlightened Vedchhi Intensive Area Scheme (a development program in Gujarat, at the site of the papad cooperatives), only tribal boys and men were enrolled in spinning, weaving, cloth-dyeing, and printing classes. In other regions of India, however, particularly in the northeastern hill areas, weaving is monopolized by women (Committee on the Status of Women in India, 1974, page 181). In the past most was done for the family's own consumption, but in recent years women have begun in some centers to market their own cloth. In Manipur, the women rent stalls in a women's market.

When women sell their cloth directly, they are able to earn considerably more than when they depend on intermediaries or contractors. The Committee on the Status of Women in India (1974, page 181) was told that "some women who could market their own products could earn an average income of about Rs. 400 per month from weaving. When they worked for others, however, this came down to between Rs. 50 and Rs. 80. Women complained of the rising prices of yarn and demanded that the State Government should take over the yarn trade to prevent black marketing. . . . The Government's efforts to market these handloom products outside the State has stimulated this industry," the committee report continues, "but the emergence of unscrupulous intermediaries between the producers, who are all women, and markets outside the State may affect the women's share of profits in the long run." Elsewhere, women may spin but not work the looms (as occurs in the silk industry in Banaras, for example), or they weave but do not receive a separate share of the earnings.

The government of India plans to encourage the handloom industry with an infusion of Rs. 3,000 million ($330 million) over the next five years.[13] There are allegedly more than 3 million handloom industries in the country, providing a livelihood to 10 million people and contributing more than 25 percent of the total cloth production of the country. The handloom industry earned Rs. 1,050 million ($115 million) in export in 1975. The investigating committee recommended expanding cooperative coverage of the industry from 30 to 60 percent of producers, thus bringing 70,000 more handlooms into the cooperative sector. Export production centers will be financed fully by the central government. Handweaving is also currently marketed locally through the All-India Handicrafts Board; technical advice and assistance are offered by the All-India Khadi and Village Industries Commission.

Unless productivity is greatly increased, handlooming cannot hope to compete with the larger mills and still pay a decent wage to its workers. Even an improved, six-spindle, Charkha hand-spinning machine introduced in the 1960s enables its operators to earn only Rs. 2.5 to Rs. 3 for a full day's work.[14] More recent machinery introduced for small-scale

[13] The information in this paragraph was reported in a newspaper article, "Handloom Industry to Get a Boost," *The Indian Express,* 29 March 1976.

[14] The equipment described in this and subsequent paragraphs is detailed in Bruce (1975, p. 9).

production includes prespinning machines that prepare the cleaned cotton; improved spinning machines; new, simplified winding and warping machines and sizers; and power- or pedal-operated looms with mechanized shuttle throws. Whereas the traditional handloom operator could produce about 1 or 1.5 meters of plain cloth per hour, the pedal-operated machine produces 2 meters, and the power-operated, 2.5 meters.

A packaged "mini mill," employing twenty-two workers in the spinning stages and twenty-eight workers in the weaving stages, would produce about 30 meters of cloth per hour. Even paying the relatively generous wage of Rs. 6 or Rs. 7 per day (agricultural laborers earn perhaps Rs. 4 or Rs. 5), the small-scale units can produce yarn at comparable cost to that of larger mills with double shifts, and only 10 to 15 percent higher cost with single shifts.

Whether the cost of building a large workshop for the mini mill is warranted remains an open question, however. Spinning and weaving components could be decentralized to individual artisans working at home, with a service center employing twenty people for buying raw materials, preparing the goods for weaving, and marketing the cloth. In this case, the weaving and spinning would be performed by older women at home, with the jobs at the center being reserved for unmarried girls and young married women. Home production does encourage child labor, however, and the working conditions are likely to be poor (for example, inadequate space and bad lighting).

Women's textile producer cooperatives need not limit themselves solely to the spinning and weaving processes. They could grow their own cotton (women in Pakistan and northern India commonly harvest cotton) or produce their own silk threads from sericulture (one Rangunia cooperative was experimenting with silkworms, and young women in Rajshahi, Bangladesh, work in the silk factories), or they could buy their raw materials from other women's cooperatives that do perform these functions. The group could also learn dyeing and printing, perhaps using natural dyes indigenous to the area. Among other outlets, weavers could establish links with women's garment-making cooperatives.

Nor do they need to limit themselves to the production of ordinary cotton (khadi), silk cloth, or saris, even given a more competitive technology. The possibilities for artistic handweaving and dyeing of specialty cloth are numerous. The women of Nepal weave beautiful soft blankets and shawls of goat's hair, for example, and weavers could produce fine cotton bedspreads, upholstery fabrics, and other unusual hand-crafted materials without the threat of competition from the larger mechanized mills. The central need, as most observers recognize, is for the upgrading of high-quality handweaving with improved techniques, established credit, design assistance, and secure marketing outlets.

Other Small-Industry Products

The list of possibilities is extensive.[15] If good markets can be found, producers' cooperatives might be organized around some of the following manufactures:

1. Items for household use, such as bathing and laundry soap (frequently expensive or in short supply in rural markets), candles, densely woven strong baskets for transport and storage, small portable cooking stoves to replace the frequently rebuilt mud *chulas*, lightweight metal or plastic pails and cooking utensils to replace heavy brass and pottery, mats for flooring and walls, cane and bamboo furniture, chicken wire fencing, fishnets (women in a Bangladesh village in Sulla make and lease nets to fishermen for a percentage of the catch), rope and twine, rope products, and other household and agricultural implements.

2. Crafts which benefit from a division of labor in a central workplace (unlike the individually made sikas, for instance), such as bookbinding and printing; the manufacture of other stationery supplies such as school workbooks and pens or pencils; costume jewelry, dolls and other toys, artificial flowers, and leather goods such as handbags, wallets, briefcases, or gloves. Bangladesh, for example, exports fine-quality goatskins which could instead be worked into finished products for local markets or for export.

3. Electrical or other appliances, such as radios, sewing machines, bicycles, lamps, electric fans, and other appliances, for which the cooperatives could produce component parts or assemble part or all of the product. Women could also be trained in the servicing and repair of appliances brought into the center.

4. Chemical products, such as herbal medicines or pharmaceuticals (making tablets or capsules and packaging them); cosmetics and

---

[15] The Japan Consulting Institute, in a series of pamphlets on how to start smaller industries, included 106 different categories as of October 1976. They range from fruit juice plants and rice-milling and rice oil plants to toilet soaps, plastic containers, ball-point pens, umbrellas, rope and twine, mosquito nets, men's dress shirts, dry cells, photoengraving, aluminum household goods, bicycle tires, and ninety-two others. The list can be obtained from the Japan Consulting Institute, Hibiya Park Building, No. 8-1, 1-Chome, Yuraku-Cho, Chiyoda-ku, Tokyo 100, Japan. Their plans require advanced machinery and worker training, however.

perfume, dyes and pigments, printing ink, cleaning and polishing preparations, and other chemicals (Staley and Morse, 1965, page 160).

A little ingenuity should suggest other possibilities as well. Any decision requires a great deal of preliminary research into the availability of skilled and interested workers, raw materials, credit or loans, and assured markets. Above all, the decision must be a flexible one tailored to the unique conditions of each village and involving the people themselves in the discussions. Activities already performed in the home may be upgraded and centralized for market-oriented production; existing small industries may be modernized; or entirely new manufacturing and agro-industrial processes may be introduced.

Two additional issues relating to the choice of products should be mentioned here. One is the exclusion of most handicrafts from the above list. Handicrafts are often the first to be suggested in proposals for rural women's employment. The seminar on Third World Craftswomen and Development at the 1975 International Women's Year Tribune in Mexico City, for example, concluded that handicrafts can be an excellent source of income for rural women because millions are already working in crafts. Crafts build easily on learned skills and are acceptable activities for rural women; they return some income whether little or a great deal of time is invested; they require little capital and use low-cost, native materials and available labor without displacing the already employed; they build up the country's exports; and they constitute an economic activity around which women can organize for other purposes (Major, 1975; Opondo, n.d.; and Dhamija, 1975). These are, indeed, appealing arguments. On the other hand, rural craftswomen are particularly vulnerable to exploitation;[16] quality controls are generally poor; and marketing is difficult (Hossain, 1975). Moreover, the products are purchased primarily by the elite within the country itself or abroad, and most handwork—being home-based—offers no real alternative for women's lives, nor does it create conditions favorable to lower fertility.

Although handicrafts can provide valuable *auxiliary* sources of income or employ women who cannot work outside the home (the aged, disabled, and so forth), it is important to place the highest priority on providing for

---

[16] Women in a West Punjab village, for example, having no concept of placing a value on their own time, reportedly would accept any amount of money for the baskets and embroidered pillow covers they did in their spare time. They sold the embroidered covers to middlemen for Rs. 20 ($2.00); they, in turn, sold them wholesale to shops in Rawalpindi for Rs. 55. The shops sold them for Rs. 85. This information was based on a conversation with Seemin Anwar and Faiz Bilquees of the Pakistan Institute of Development Economics, in Islamabad.

rural women full-time, year-round employment, which is located outside the home, pays a decent wage, and is capable of transforming their roles in the family and in the community. Some handicrafts are included in the small-industry list (weaving, for example), but with the intention of modernizing and centralizing production as has been proposed previously. Strong handicrafts traditions deserve support, but introducing new handicrafts to unskilled women may be more problematic, and ultimately less rewarding, than is at first perceived.

The second issue is whether production should be aimed primarily at local, urban, or export markets. Exports, of course, help the country's balance of payments, but the market is competitive, the products must please Western (or westernized) tastes, and the goods do not directly benefit the producers. Yet, on the other hand, local demand—and even urban demand—for some products may be limited or sporadic. If the self-sufficiency of communities and nations is to be encouraged, then we first might explore seriously the possibility of manufacturing locally those goods that are currently imported (India is following such a policy) and providing for basic consumer needs that remain unfulfilled. Raising import tariffs on new goods that are being produced locally would be one step in this direction.

RAISING CAPITAL

When Shalinitai Patil, a young social worker, returned to her native village in Maharashtra, the farmers' wives complained to her that no one would grant them a loan to enable them to stock a small dairy business. Mrs. Patil went on to found the first women's bank in India, a story to which we shall return. But the dilemma of the farmers' wives illustrates a basic fact of rural life: rural people in general—particularly landless peasants or small entrepreneurs, and more particularly women—find it almost impossible to borrow money on reasonable terms in order to start or to improve a business.

Even small entrepreneurs in urban centers have problems raising funds. A survey of almost 4,000 small manufacturing establishments in Moradabad, India, found that with restricted access to modern banking they depended mainly on noninstitutional sources of credit, such as traders and dealers in raw materials (brass, leather, cotton yarn, and so forth), relatives and friends, and moneylenders. Where interest was charged directly, the rate was often more than 20 percent per year (Staley and Morse, 1965, page 40).

In rural areas access to banks is even more limited. Few private or government banks are located in villages or other remote areas, so that rural people—unless they belong to an agricultural cooperative—are forced to rely primarily on relatives or moneylenders. Among the Pathans of the Northwest Frontier Province in Pakistan, for example, relatives (but not cousins) are the prime source of loans.[17] Even if banks were available, landless peasants, and certainly most women, would find it difficult to borrow money because they have little or no collateral to offer. The same holds for agricultural cooperative funds: landless peasants and women, being generally excluded from direct membership in cooperatives, are not eligible for loans (National Cooperative Union of India, n.d., page 2).

The ubiquitous moneylender—typically viewed by outsiders (and many insiders as well) as a greedy soul, living off the labors of the poor, and of their children, and of their children's children—has attracted much attention in South Asia. At one time in Connaught Circle, at the heart of New Delhi, an enormous billboard, illustrating the government's twenty-point economic program with folk paintings, pictured the moneylender (under the heading, "Liquidation of Rural Indebtedness") as a fat, pink-faced man in a green suit, sitting at a table stacked high with rupees. His villainous role having been exposed, the people were bypassing him on the way to the local bank for their loans.

Indeed, there is much evidence that moneylenders do exploit rural people, especially illiterate peasants. The field director of the BRAC program in Bangladesh, for example, told of a peasant he had met the day before who had borrowed 100 taka ($7) from a moneylender and was required to repay his loan after the harvest with paddy worth 240 taka on the market.[18] The moneylender had earned interest of 140 percent in three months. Interest on agricultural loans sometimes runs as high as 400 percent per year, with the capital debt being passed from generation to generation. The injunction against usury in Muslim religious law is avoided by requiring repayment in kind rather than cash. Among the Pathan tribesmen, for example, a lender may typically collect all the crops from a field until a loan is repaid. The amount of interest is, of course, concealed in this manner, requiring a good deal of sophistication on the part of the borrower to calculate it. In addition, farmers repay their

[17] Based on an interview with Akbar S. Ahmed of the Pakistan Academy for Rural Development, Peshawar, who was formerly the registrar of cooperatives in the Northwest Frontier Province. Ahmed, in April 1976, had just completed anthropological fieldwork on credit systems among the northern tribals. See also Ahmed (1976).

[18] Based on an interview with Abdur Rahman Chowdhury, of the Bangladesh Rural Advancement Committee, Markuli Camp.

loans in kind at harvest time, when the value of the crop is lowest, while lenders can store the crop and sell it later at higher prices. Thus, the borrower loses in both transactions.

Women in Ahmadebad, India, were paying interest to moneylenders of 10 percent per day for cash in order to rent the heavy wooden carts on which they pulled loads for a small delivery fee. They would repay the debt at the end of the day, using any leftover cash for food, beginning the next morning with a new loan (Jain, n.d., page 14).

In the absence of banks, however, middlemen and moneylenders have an important function. And many villagers continue to turn to moneylenders, even when banks are nearby, because they can obtain immediate loans for such expenditures as weddings and funerals that banks (or cooperatives) will not approve. As Hunter (1969, page 70) notes, "What is said of the Zamindar as landlord could also be said of the moneylender: he was a ravening wolf, but he lent, and the Co-operative, bound by its own regulations, will not always lend, or lend enough, or lend in time."[19] Similarly, suppliers and middlemen can play a valuable role in advancing loans or credit to artisans for raw materials and in buying up all their products. Although agents may pay poorly, they do pay immediately.

One of the prime advantages of cooperatives, of course, is that there is power in numbers. Where individual entrepreneurs have difficulty, cooperatives can turn to a variety of sources in order to avoid high interest rates. Indigenous sources include the share purchases and savings of the members themselves, loan funds of cooperative federations or cooperative banks, commercial and government banks, government agencies, and voluntary organizations. In addition, promising ventures may attract the attention of foreign donors such as voluntary groups, foundations, governments, and international agencies.

Women's cooperatives frequently start out with very little capital. Recall that one of the IRDP agricultural cooperatives in Rangunia, Bangladesh, began with a rice-savings scheme. The IRDP cooperative members are also required to purchase shares worth 10 taka (70 cents) for full membership. Capital grows with the addition of new members, from bank interest on share deposits, from required savings of a small fraction of each member's earnings, and from the retention of a portion of cooperative profits. These small beginnings are typical of women's agricultural and handicraft ventures. A major advantage of turning to the members themselves for capital is that women acquire a strong sense of

---

[19] Similar sentiments were expressed to me by Kamaladevi Chattopadhyay, chairman of the All-India Handicrafts Board and president of the Indian Cooperative Union in New Delhi.

accomplishment and involvement in the group enterprise. On the other hand, capital raised in this way is likely to be far too little to create a small industry with a central workplace that requires a building, equipment, and funds for training. Costs for such an undertaking are likely to run from $5,000 to $50,000.

However, even a fairly small capital fund from members' shares, savings, and cooperative profits can make the cooperative eligible for outside loans from a loan fund of a cooperative federation to which the society belongs (as in Rangunia), from commercial banks (some of which offer favorable concessions to government-registered cooperatives), or from government agencies. In deserving cases in India, for example, the state Cooperative Department will purchase cooperative shares, help the society to increase its volume of business, and grant interest-free working capital and a managerial subsidy, along with technical assistance from agencies such as the All-India Handicrafts Board, the All-India Handloom Board, and the Khadi and Village Industry Commission (Beniwal, 1976, page 34). Indian cooperatives that have already collected a certain amount of share capital may also be eligible to obtain a bank loan up to five times the amount of the capital (Beniwal, 1976, page 34). The Indian government's new economic policy encourages banks to make loans available to the formerly ineligible "weaker sections" of society by offering lower interest rates, easier repayment schedules, and lower collateral requirements.[20]

Registration is difficult for some of the smaller women's cooperatives, however, especially in rural societies with predominantly illiterate members. Complicated procedures often require repeated visits to different agencies in the city in order to register with the government, as well as strict accounting records and unnecessarily complex operating rules. The many women's cooperatives among the Garo tribe in Jalachatra in northern Bangladesh were not eligible for bank loans for this reason; instead, members relied on their own cooperative funds for personal or group loans. But because the funds were all extended during the growing season and repaid after the harvest, there was no money available during certain months, and several urgent requests for loans had to be turned down.

One innovative response to the dilemma of raising capital has been the creation in India of special banks for women. The Indira Mahila Cooperative Bank of Bombay, chaired by Shalinitai Patil, was founded in 1972 in

[20] To give one example: rickshaw drivers typically pay high daily rentals for their vehicles and are unable to accumulate enough capital to purchase their own. Formerly ineligible for loans as a poor risk, drivers who pledge themselves as a group of four persons are eligible for loans from some banks. In such cases, if one defaults, the other three are responsible for the total repayment.

order to help low and middle-income women in small businesses and to encourage women to save in banks rather than buying jewelry or other luxury items as investments.[21] The bank has four branches in Bombay and over thirty in villages scattered throughout the state of Maharashtra. Any woman over eighteen can join by buying a share worth Rs. 25 ($2.75) and may hold up to a maximum of forty shares. All shareholders and the entire bank staff, including the board of directors, are women. Within a year of its opening, the bank had attracted 10,000 shareholders contributing over Rs. 1 million in addition to Rs. 4 million in deposits, a total equivalent to more than $500,000 in working capital. Loans worth $300,000 had been distributed to about 1,000 women, ranging in amounts from Rs. 500 to buy a sewing machine to Rs. 50,000 to open a chemist's shop. The Indira Bank has organized credit and housing cooperatives, consumer stores, vocational guidance centers, and hospitals for rural and urban women.

In Ahmadebad, the Self-Employed Women's Association (SEWA), organized by Ela Bhatt in 1972, is a registered trade union of women garment workers, vendors of used clothing, cart pullers, vegetable vendors, junksmiths, and other low-income entrepreneurs.[22] Jain (n.d., page 25) reports that the vast majority of the over 7,000 members are illiterate, young married women, living in slums in families of seven or eight persons, with the families earning from Rs. 200 to Rs. 450 per month ($22 to $50). Most belong to the low-status Waghri community, and others are Harijans (outcastes), Muslims, or tribals from Rajisthan. The women earn between Rs. 3 and Rs. 15 per day on the average.

Almost all of the women were severely in debt to moneylenders or their suppliers and frequently borrowed on a daily basis. Bhatt (1976, page 3) remarks that "whatever little income they could eke out was eaten away in debt repayment. It permanently weakened their bargaining power." So the SEWA organized the Mahila Seva Sahakari Bank Ltd., with members purchasing Rs. 10 shares to launch the enterprise with a share capital of $5,500. After ten months the cooperative bank had also attracted more than 9,000 depositors who had deposited almost $33,000. Rather than using this capital for loans, the SEWA deposited the funds in several national banks which actually extend the loans to members; the women's bank provides information to borrowers, helps them fill out the necessary forms, advises them on their repayment obligations, and backs

---

[21] Information in this paragraph is drawn from a memo written by Torasker (n.d.).

[22] SEWA activities are described by Jain (n.d.) and by Bhatt (1976). Additional information was obtained from Adrienne Germain of the Ford Foundation.

the loan so that the banks are willing to cooperate.[23] By the end of 1974, 6,000 women had borrowed a total of Rs. 3 million ($330,000) at interest rates ranging from 9 to 13 percent, depending on the bank that actually granted the loan (Bhatt, 1976, page 3). All loans are to be repaid within twenty months.[24] The Mahila Seva Sahakari Bank intends to begin extending small loans directly to borrowers rather than going through the commercial banks. They will begin with weekly or fortnightly loans to replace the daily debts that many women incur from moneylenders or suppliers. In order to enable women to function better in their employment, the bank also provides low-cost housing to some of its members, a day-care center for the children of vegetable vendors, a social security scheme, and assistance in the buying of bulk materials, vocational training, and marketing.

The bank organized for the SEWA's members does not currently offer loans of sufficient size to enable one to begin a small industry with buildings and equipment, but the principle of using the members' share capital and savings as surety for obtaining larger loans from commercial banks could start a small-scale rural industry. This procedure is likely to be slow, however, depending as it does on members' deposits for building up the initial capital on which the larger loans are obtained.

Moving on from shares, savings, and bank loans as sources of credit, we enter the sphere of loans or outright grants from governments and voluntary agencies. Not surprisingly, women's programs are generally given low priority in national and state budgets in South Asia as well as elsewhere. Funds allocated for agricultural development or for small rural industries rarely find their way into the hands of women. Even money allocated specifically to women's projects is frequently diverted to other

[23] Although government policy now requires banks to help small borrowers, banks are reluctant to do so because of administrative problems and the strangeness of dealing with a "different" class of borrower. A SEWA report, quoted in Jain (n.d., pp. 12–13), colorfully describes the new borrowers:

"Being all women, accompanied by children, filthy in appearance, unaccustomed to manners and business talks, they were annoying to and not much welcome by the bank staff at their premises."

"Being illiterate, they would go to the wrong bank, go at wrong hours, could not fill the slips, were not consistent with their own addresses, names and surnames—sometimes suffixing father's name, sometimes husband's name—the bank staff has neither time nor understanding to deal with this class of borrowers and would start doubting their bonafides."

[24] Not surprisingly, many borrowers find it difficult to repay their loans on schedule because of heavy economic pressures (for example, illness, unemployment of husband, other indebtedness), lack of managerial skills (marketing, for example), and misunderstanding of the July 1975 government moratorium on the repayment of debts by the poor (Bhatt, 1976, pp. 4–5; and Jain, n.d., pp. 12–13).

sources (Chattopadhyay, 1976, page 50). When funds run out, women's programs are often the first to suffer. Within the cooperative movement, resources for industrial or handicrafts cooperatives, as compared with agricultural cooperatives, are scarce, a factor which further discriminates against women as recipients (Beniwal, 1976, page 37). India and Bangladesh have a mere handful of female educators or inspectors in the cooperative departments; Pakistan and Nepal apparently have none.

Yet income-generating programs for rural women must play a central role in government planning for development. Without it, as I argued in chapter 2, women impede rather than facilitate change. In addition, if they remain mired in their traditional roles, women are likely to want to marry early and to have many children as a form of social insurance. The creation of an integrated program to promote women's industries cannot be expected to survive on its own, at least in its initial phases. It will require strong government support through cooperative departments and small industry and handicrafts boards. Subsidies for small enterprises and for related training activities should "properly be assessed in terms of longer-range social and economic benefits, including contributions to employment generation and to bringing a whole area alive; they should not be judged simply in narrow terms of the short-range incremental earnings accruing to individual trainees and borrowers" (Hunter, 1969, page 154).

Of course, there are hundreds of competing demands for scarce government resources, all crying out for top-priority status. The argument here is only that where funds are allocated for rural development, conscious effort should be made to specify a healthy portion either for all-women's programs or for the incorporation of women into existing institutions and training classes. The Bangladesh IRDP is moving in this direction by creating a network of rural women's cooperatives, and the Indian government does offer support and training through its various state agencies. But the funds and personnel provided are insignificant in relation to the economic needs of rural women. Moreover, funds allocated for women tend to be directed into social welfare or home economics programs with few authentic developmental components.

Women's voluntary organizations are a common source of support for programs aimed at assisting destitute women with health care, literacy training, simple vocational skills, and sometimes employment. The All-Pakistan Women's Association (APWA), for example, runs a series of "industrial homes" throughout Pakistan in which poor women learn to sew or embroider or weave, with their handicrafts being sold primarily through APWA shops in urban centers. The Nepal Women's Organization (NWO) also runs training centers for rural women in homemaking, sewing, weaving, doll making, and other activities. Budgets depend primarily on members' fees plus donations from wealthy persons, with only very small profits, if any, accruing from the sale of handicrafts. As a consequence, most women's organizations are extremely limited in the amount of funds available for starting new projects unless they can draw heavily on wealthy individual donors. In addition, associations consisting primarily of educated and well-to-do urban women are, because of their class position, unlikely to encourage programs that stimulate the type of structural changes needed to enable poor rural women to become more powerful and self-reliant. They tend instead to favor a personalized type of charitable benevolence. There are exceptions, of course, but women's organizations on the whole are probably an unpromising source for strong programming or large-scale financing.

The most innovative projects involving rural women in income-generating activities with group participation are frequently those initiated by a handful of wealthy liberals acting alone who are willing to finance progressive social experiments, by small groups of dedicated but poor idealists who seek financial support from sympathetic, nongovernmental, local or foreign donors, and by local or foreign voluntary organizations, religious or secular. Coombs and Ahmad (1974) report that voluntary organizations have certain advantages as sponsors over government agencies:

> . . . They have greater operational flexibility; they can recruit abler and more dedicated people; and often they can get better results at lower cost. But they also have certain built-in handicaps. Because of financial constraints and uncertainties they are usually obliged to operate on a limited scale. Too often they decline sharply or disappear altogether when funds dry up or when their architects leave the scene. In some circumstances they are also vulnerable to changes in government policies toward voluntary organizations, but even when government takes a friendly attitude, ministries with programs of their own naturally prefer outside support funds to go into these. [page 74]

These words regarding nonformal education programs provide an apt description of employment-generating schemes as well. International voluntary agencies such as OXFAM, along with many religious groups, have supported a number of innovative small-scale projects in Bangladesh and India, as well as in other countries. OXFAM probably provides one of the best models of international assistance to small-scale, cooperative rural projects that create new employment for both men and women. With a large budget, low administrative costs, and a small number of highly dedicated workers (most indigenous to the recipient country), they manage to seek out and fund many promising ventures with long-range developmental prospects.[25] Smaller donor agencies are more likely to experience the difficulties that Coombs outlines, with religious groups in particular being vulnerable to changes in government receptiveness.

The major sources of large amounts of capital and technical assistance are, of course, the bilateral and multilateral aid agencies. Such UN agencies as the ILO, FAO, UNICEF, and UNESCO are turning their attention increasingly to the problems and prospects of rural women, focusing specifically on the need for vocational education and training in both agriculture and rural industries.[26] Whereas formerly these agencies tended either to pass over the role of rural women or to address themselves to issues such as maternal and child health, nutrition, and family planning, in the past few years they have begun to promote the employment of rural women in income-earning activities so that women can advance their status and establish economic cooperation with other women and their families.

Large donor agencies such as the World Bank and the U.S. Agency for International Development (AID) have, in the past, similarly neglected women in their emphasis on large projects requiring heavy investment in capital equipment. Small projects that might have benefited women have usually been overlooked because they were less visible and because they were potential consumers of too much administrative time; within a given budget it was logical in the organizational context to spend money on one large project rather than on many small ones (Tendler, 1975, pages 56 and 88–90). It may have been implicitly assumed that women would benefit along with men from the construction of roads or dams and from the new agricultural technology. In many cases, however, women's position has apparently worsened rather than improved under the impact of large-scale, agricultural development programs that introduce new techniques and equipment (Boserup, 1970; Tinker, 1976; and Van Allen, 1974).

With increased attention recently being paid to rural women, because of the timely intersection of World Population Year and International

---

[25] Among the projects discussed in this report, OXFAM assisted the Bangladesh Rural Advancement Committee, the AMUL Dairy in Gujarat, and the papad cooperatives in Gujarat. OXFAM has played a primary role in encouraging handicraft production, buying directly from Third World producer cooperatives for sale through its catalogues to European buyers.

[26] Among the many United Nations publications containing descriptions, analyses, and recommendations relating to the role of rural women in development, see the UN Department of Economic and Social Affairs (1973); United Nations (1975); UN Food and Agricultural Organization (1975); and UN Economic and Social Council (1973); International Labour Organisation (1973); UN Economic Commission for Africa (1975); and UN Children's Fund (n.d.).

Women's Year, the major bilateral and multilateral aid agencies are apparently also looking for fundable projects that would promote the integration of women in development while simultaneously leading to a reduction of births.[27] The World Bank in India, for example, is seeking to fund smaller projects that employ rural women in the production of goods with export potential. The IRDP in Bangladesh has received a large World Bank loan to build a family-planning component into the rural women's cooperative scheme, and the AID has invested in the Women's Rehabilitation Programme, partly for the same reason.

This new international enthusiasm, ironically enough, raises the possibility that another threat to the success and independence of some newly conceived development projects may be the infusion of too much capital rather than too little—or, more accurately, that such projects will become overly dependent on outside funding and neglect ways to generate capital locally through innovative means. This is especially true in Bangladesh, where several informants have reported that some programs are collapsing from the weight of too much outside funding being poured onto an administratively weak foundation. With heavy dependence on outside sources, priorities for expenditure often blur, and money is spent willy-nilly on pumps, and salaries, as well as on personal expenses such as wedding feasts. When the money runs out, the program stops because no local resources have been cultivated. The ease with which a few visible projects are able to raise money from large foundations and external donor agencies derives in part from the competition among the agencies in finding and funding promising ventures. Prestige accrues to the agency that initiates a new project, but not to one that maintains an ongoing one.

In any case, the funds for, and, increasingly, the interest in investing in women's projects at the international level are there. One solution to the overfunding of a few projects at the expense of neglecting other possibilities could be to create a local agency with a small, dedicated staff, familiar with rural needs, to act as a clearing house for large grants and loans from foreign donors. It is not so much the shortage of funds as the shortage of fundable projects that is currently impeding international investment in

[27] The focus on "integrating women in development" and on reducing births raises a certain amount of scepticism among some observers regarding the motives of the agencies. "Integration" is usually discussed in the context of exploiting the full potential of human resources, which translated into real programs, may mean the addition of a new burden of labor on already overburdened rural women. The family-planning component, too, raises questions because of its apparent centrality to so many aid programs. Overemphasis on family planning may alienate recipients and overshadow other aspects of women's status, such as their basic right to fair employment regardless of demographic considerations, and their rights to child care, education, health care, as well as other issues.

employment-generating schemes for rural women. The interest of donor agencies is matched by their uncertainty as to how such projects might get started.

CONCLUSIONS

In this chapter we have discussed a number of possibilities for introducing small-scale industries and agro-industries that would employ large numbers of rural women. Suggestions are limited basically to products that are suited to small-scale manufacturing, that are not in direct competition with large manufacturing, and that are amenable to a dispersed system of production and to labor-intensive methods using intermediate technology. Such industries are ideally located in those larger villages and small towns having access to transport and marketing outlets.

It was argued that it is essential to create an enterprise, or a network of enterprises, with a sound economic base that permits payment of at least a standard minimum wage to its workers and has the potential to become economically self-sustaining in less than five years. One method of creating new industries and expanding or diversifying existing ones is to establish what Hirschman (1958, pages 98–119) calls "forward and backward linkages" with other industries. *Forward linkages* refers to the utilization of products as inputs into some new activity, where the product does not "by its nature cater exclusively to final demands" (Hirschman, 1958, page 100). An example of forward linkages would be a food-processing plant that provides some partially processed pulps or juices to other manufacturers, or a weaving cooperative that seeks to expand into a garment-making factory. *Backward linkages* attempt to supply, through domestic production, all or part of the inputs needed in an economic activity as, for example, a food-processing plant growing its own vegetables or fruit or manufacturing its own containers, or a weaving cooperative growing its own cotton or building its own looms—or one that creates an ancillary firm to do so. In addition, larger-scale production can be established through *horizontal linkages* with other enterprises producing the same or similar products, as in the cooperative federations of jute-handicrafts workers or of papad producers. These horizontal linkages also provide excellent opportunities for training new members and for servicing individual cooperatives with technical, managerial, marketing, and credit advice.

New enterprises will need capital for buildings, equipment, and vehicles (where necessary); for training; for initial operating costs; and for routine operational purposes, such as seasonal loans to purchase large quantities of grains at harvest time for milling or oil-pressing. Unless they have already been engaging in economic ventures for several years, women's cooperatives will not be able to raise sufficient capital to start a new industry from members' shares or savings, nor will their share capital be large enough to attract bank loans. The very few women's banks have limited resources and necessarily favor small, individual entrepreneurs over large enterprises. Women's groups and other local voluntary agencies also have limited funds. Governments with scarce resources, regardless of their good intentions, are faced with numerous competing demands for high-priority expenditures and are unlikely to budget substantial funds for women's industries. As a consequence, the burden of funding new projects with either loans or outright grants would appear to fall on foreign voluntary agencies, on UN agencies, and on large government donors.

The danger inherent in this last situation is that governments will be encouraged in their benign neglect of women's programs in the sweet assurance that other people's money is at hand. One method of reducing this danger would be to rely on outside donors for the initially heavy investment in buildings and equipment, while allocating to the government the responsibility for training managers and providing ongoing technical and marketing services through existing (improved) agencies or boards. Local credit institutions—government or commercial banks or cooperative federations—should take the responsibility for providing additional credit and loans where necessary. Careful preliminary assessment of the economic potential of the industry would be encouraged if it were agreed that the initial capital investment were to be paid back interest-free over a period of years once the enterprise becomes viable. This obligation would also encourage a spirit of self-reliance among the workers.

The most central need is for someone to do the organizational work. Once a few enterprises become successful they are likely to spawn others. Governments should be encouraged to hire women organizers as part of their rural industry development programs. Indigenous voluntary organizations and committed individuals could also play a strong role in selecting geographic locales and initiating new ventures. Development projects already underway, having built up a sense of trust with the local people, could expand their activities to include the employment of women in small industries.

5

OVERCOMING CULTURAL AND STRUCTURAL OBSTACLES IN THE RECRUITMENT OF WOMEN WORKERS

Who among rural women will be willing—or able—to take advantage of new employment opportunities in the villages of India or Nepal, Pakistan or Bangladesh? Is it possible to overcome the major cultural and structural obstacles to women's work outside the home in those communities that advocate female seclusion, among other practices? Can cooperative work groups successfully transcend religious, caste, or class boundaries, or must the organizational structure inevitably reflect (or perhaps even intensify) the socioeconomic hierarchy of the community, and its pervasive factionalism?

In this chapter I will discuss conditions likely to influence young women's decisions to seek or not to seek employment in new rural industries, or those conditions likely to influence their families' decision regarding their employment. An a priori assumption that women will eagerly come forward may well prove false: at an Egyptian garment-making factory (discussed in chapter 4), which was designed to test the impact of female employment on fertility, organizers discovered that they had to shift their initial choice of site because they could not recruit women workers at the first location. At the second site, however, more women volunteered than could be trained, most of them unmarried girls and not the married women whose employment had been anticipated. The assumption that unmarried girls and young married women will *not* be willing or permitted to work may prove unwarranted, even in a conservative Muslim community. The central question is, Under what conditions will women and their families seek to participate in the new economic activities?

INCENTIVES FOR OUTSIDE EMPLOYMENT

Many rural women in the predominantly Hindu and Muslim countries of South Asia are already working outside the home, whether for wages in agriculture, as unpaid workers on their family's land, or in petty trade or service occupations. Among these women the incentive to work is apparently already strong enough to override cultural or structural constraints. Because official labor-force statistics generally exclude a range of economic activities among rural women (especially seasonal work), the following figures should be taken as minimal estimates of the labor pool. The Bangladesh (then East Pakistan) census of 1961 showed that 17.4 percent of females aged ten and over were in the labor force; of these, 92 percent were in agriculture. The (then West) Pakistan census reported that 9.3 percent of females aged ten and over were in the labor force; of these, 70 percent were in agriculture (Bean, 1968, pages 399–400). According to the 1971–72 national Labor Force Survey of Pakistan (Helbock, 1975a, page 32), females are more likely to be employed in rural areas (9.5 percent) than in urban centers (3.9 percent). Although female labor-force participation rates for Bangladesh and Pakistan are considerably lower than those for Muslim Indonesia and Malaysia, and far lower than those for non-Muslim Southeast Asian countries such as Thailand, where women work freely in the fields and the marketplace, they are considerably higher than those for most Muslim countries of North Africa and the Middle East, where fewer than 5 percent of women are generally reported as being economically active (table 5-1).[1]

With a rather liberal definition of economic activity, India's 1961 census reported that 31.4 percent of rural females were economically active (about half of them unpaid) compared with 13.1 percent under the more restrictive definitions of 1971 (Committee on the Status of Women in India, 1974, page 155). Rates of economic activity in the Indian states ranged from just over 1 percent of rural females in the Punjab to over 50 percent in Nagaland and Tripura (Committee on the Status of Women in India, 1974, page 156). In 1961, in the neighboring Hindu kingdom of Nepal, over one-third of females of all ages were reported as being economically active, almost all of them rural workers (see table 5-1). Although labor-force participation rates among rural women vary considerably across the four countries and among regions and districts within each country, it is probably fair to say that in all areas the girls and women defined as being economically active are drawn disproportionately from the non-Hindu and non-Muslim minorities (especially tribals, Christians, Buddhists), from low-caste and scheduled-caste groups in the Hindu community, and from the lowest socioeconomic ranks among the Muslims. Wives of marginal farmers and of landless agricultural workers are particularly likely to be employed.[2]

---

[1] See also Bean (1968); and Youssef (1974a).

[2] Boserup (1970, pp. 69–75) analyzes the bases of regional, caste, and class differences in women's agricultural participation in South Asia.

These introductory remarks suggest that in most villages and small towns of the countries under discussion here, there will be women who are already motivated to exchange an insecure, oppressive, and poorly paid job for one of higher status, better working conditions, and regular pay. Young tribal girls in the Vedchhi Intensive Area Scheme in Gujarat left their agricultural labor at below-minimum wages for papad production in the community center at Rs. 3 a day, and destitute wives and widows volunteering for heavy labor, carrying earth and bricks on Food for Work road-building projects in Bangladesh and India, would undoubtedly be happy to take a higher-skilled job in a small industry for a direct cash income. New rural production centers might attract women who are currently employed in less desirable circumstances.

Money as an Incentive

Among classes of women not currently working outside the home, one would undoubtedly discover a significant number with a strong economic incentive to work if the opportunity were offered. These women are most

Table 5-1. Percentages of Females and Males of All Ages Who Are Economically Active, and Ratio of Female to Male Rates in Selected Countries, 1961–71

Country	Year	Females	Males	Ratio F/M
Algeria[a]	1966	1.8	42.2	.04
Jordan	1971	2.6	43.1	.06
Libya	1964	2.7	46.6	.06
Tunisia[b]	1966	3.0	44.4	.07
Egypt	1966	4.0	48.4	.08
Pakistan[c]	1971	5.5	53.3	.10
Morocco	1971	8.0	44.5	.18
Iran	1966	8.3	50.7	.16
Sri Lanka	1969–70	13.1	45.2	.29
India	1971	13.2	52.4	.25
West Malaysia	1962	21.2	44.8	.47
Philippines	1970	21.3	46.0	.46
Indonesia	1971	22.0	46.0	.48
Republic of Korea	1970	23.2	42.8	.54
Turkey	1965	33.4	53.0	.63
Nepal	1961	36.5	55.3	.66
Khmer Republic	1962	36.7	50.6	.73
Thailand	1971	45.3	51.0	.89

Sources: United Nations, *Demographic Yearbook* (1964, 1972, tab. 8); and International Labour Office, *Yearbook of Labour Statistics* (1971, 1972, 1974, tab. 1).

[a] Excluding 1.2 million females in agriculture.
[b] Excluding 250,000 females in agriculture.
[c] Including Bangladesh.

likely to be widows or abandoned wives now solely responsible for their own support and that of their young children, if any, or wives and daughters living in households in which the male wage earners have low or sporadic incomes—usually landless laborers, marginal farmers, or unskilled rural workers. It is generally these women who first come forward when opportunities for work appear. The YWCA handicraft-training program and workshop in Dacca, for example, has a waiting list of women without husbands, or women with brothers or other relatives to support, who are driven to work by economic need. Because those who are taken on for training contribute so heavily to the family income, husbands soon find their initial objections appeased by the extra money.[3]

The financial motive, strongest among low-income groups, becomes more pressing in times of personal, community, or national crisis. Several informants remarked that Pakistani women turn increasingly to employment in order to cope with inflationary pressures in that country. The impoverishment of some segments of the population is intensified following major national crises such as wars, droughts, or floods. The violence and disruption accompanying the 1947 partition of India and the 1971–72 war between Bangladesh and Pakistan left a large population of widowed and abandoned women, many of them homeless, who were reduced to begging in the streets. A number of welfare programs were designed to assist these destitute women and to provide relief and rehabilitation through vocational training and employment. Poor harvests from droughts or floods also compound the problem of rural landlessness. As marginal farmers are forced to sell out or landless workers are unable to find employment, the whole family is left destitute and searching for work.

Even better-off village women may also have some financial incentive to work. Brahmin and Chetri women in one village located several miles from Kathmandu, for example, have said they would like to learn to knit or sew in order to earn their own money. They could buy a new sari or some jewelry, or new school shoes for the children, without having to ask the permission of their husband or father-in-law.[4] The concept of an independent income for personal use in the extended family is an alien one however. For in its ideal form, the family combines the income of all members and distributes it according to need, with the allocation decisions being made be the household head. It is not known whether the Brahmin and Chetri women would be willing to work full time outside their homes year round. Such employment could be seen as threatening to the ritual status of the family.

---

[3] January 1976 interview with Priscilla Padolina of the YWCA in Dacca.
[4] February 1976 interview with anthropologist Lynn Bennett in Kathmandu.

Noneconomic Incentives

Noneconomic motives can also play an important role in inducing women to work. In one small study in Delhi (Dubey, Bardhan, and Garg, 1975, page 27), 70 percent of one hundred middle-income women and 82 percent of fifty low-income women declared they would continue to work even if their husbands' incomes were increased by the amount of their earnings. The latter group consisted entirely of scheduled-caste women working as servants, vegetable vendors, sellers of lassi or cow dung, quilt-makers, and so forth.[5]

One major noneconomic incentive to outside employment is prestige. Obviously, most jobs available to largely unskilled and illiterate rural women—and men—carry little prestige. The few prestigious jobs, such as teachers, government agents, and other community officials, are generally closed to women, who lack the education, training, geographical mobility, and cultural acceptability that such jobs require. As a consequence, rural women who work outside the home are mostly engaged in farm labor, petty trading (for example, selling glass bangles door-to-door), or in menial service (as sweepers and household servants). It is thus not surprising that most work is viewed as "prestige-reducing" rather than "prestige-enhancing" both by the community at large and by the women themselves (Shah, 1975a, page 193). Indeed, the mark of a family's prestige is to keep their womenfolk at home, not to have them exposed to strangers or low-status people in a public place. Because in rural areas it is predominantly the low-caste, low-income women who work outside the home (the same can be said for towns and cities except for a small minority of educated women in admired professional positions), female employment becomes identified as a low-status activity. Even selling articles made at home may be considered demeaning by some. In one Punjabi village in Pakistan almost all the women were engaged in spinning, pickle making, straw weaving, embroidery, crocheting, and weaving elaborate belts, while a minority sewed, knitted, and made pottery or other handicraft objects for the family's use. But, according to Anwar and Bilquees (1976), "The women generally disapprove of selling something made with their own hands. When asked about this, the women replied, 'We do not sell our skills,' 'People who sell their skills are *Kammies* [low-caste]'."

Nevertheless, when there is good money to be made, women frequently become very proud of their ability to earn money from their skills. The

---

[5] The findings could also be interpreted as showing that the low-income women would have to continue to work even if their husbands earned more because their current combined incomes are insufficient to support a family.

Muslim women in the Sri Joni cooperative in Dacca who make jute hand-bags—although initially criticized for their behavior—came to be envied in the community when the value of their efforts became apparent. The young Muslim girls and women who have taken up embroidery in the village of Shah Jewana in the Punjab have gained considerable prestige, especially those who work full time and bring in a steady income. Their prestige is enhanced with every new addition to the household's appliances or to their clothing, jewelry, or dowries. Young Muslim girls working as paramedics in the People's Health Center at Savar, Bangladesh, overcame the initial disapproval of their actions, acquiring prestige when villagers realized that the paramedics can provide them with notes granting immediate hospital attention for severe illnesses (Lindenbaum, 1974, page 13). The female paramedics, many of them local unmarried girls about fifteen or sixteen years of age, earn a small monthly salary, live at the health center, and receive six months of training in health care and family planning. The jobs are considered so desirable that there is a waiting list of applicants who wish to join the program.

On the whole, employment in small industry may not initially be viewed as prestigious by the local community since, at first, it attracts primarily those driven by economic need. The community's initial reservations will most likely be transformed into admiration and pride as the skills and productivity of the workers increase. As women become literate and learn managerial skills, taking positions on boards and training in distant towns, they will be regarded in a new light as they, their families, and the community begin to benefit visibly from individual incomes and cooperative investments. A small, tentative venture will begin to attract additional applicants as the benefits become more clear. In the village of Shah Jewana only four women turned up when the announcement was first made in the mosque that Syeda Abida Hussein would buy their embroidery.[6] But when the word spread that she was paying good money, thirty or forty others quickly joined. Ten years later, over two hundred girls and women were registered as regular embroidery workers, and the villagers were clearly proud of their accomplishments.

A further motive which could be capitalized upon in recruitment is the women's desire to meet together outside the home. We noted that many rural women in South Asia already work outside the home either regularly or sporadically and seasonally, but others remain isolated in their homes

[6] Interview with Syeda Abida Hussein, member of the Provincial Assembly, Punjab. The first four were all "misfits" by traditional expectations—a widow financially dependent entirely on her brothers who mistreated her, two teenage girls without a father, and one unmarried woman in her thirties.

or family compounds with their daily social contacts limited to immediate kin. The usual meeting places for men—mosques or temples, tea shops, the "men's house" of the village, and the marketplace—are frequently closed to women. Rural women may pay occasional visits to their natal homes in another village, or gather together as passive observers of religious events, but, for many, opportunities for exchanges of information are few. Within the limited range of contacts, even an opportunity to meet other women for a few minutes at the river or well may be eagerly awaited. When women in one village of Nepal were asked which of their household tasks they found most onerous, for example, few mentioned having to go to the well several times a day to fill heavy clay or brass vessels with water. Apparently, this was one of the few occasions on which women could socialize with one another (Bennett, 1973). Brahmin and Chetri women in another village near Kathmandu work seasonally in their fields as a team, singing together and joking with the men as they plant the rice. But, except for the poorest households, this is the only time of year that women are out of their homes on a regular basis or interacting as a group.[7]

In parts of Bangladesh the women's lives are even more limited. In the Comilla District, for example, "the contacts the Bengali village mother has with the outside are extraordinarily limited. She may visit her kinspeople once or twice a year if they do not live too far away. Though the mosque is a weekly meeting place for the men and boys, as is also the local market, the village women do not go to either."[8] When the BARD in Comilla instituted literacy and vocational training courses for the rural women, the response was immediate. As Raper notes (1970, pages 165–166), "The benefits of the women's learning are clear in the villages, the courtyards, gardens, and households. But even more important is the fact that the women now leave their homes regularly and for a new purpose, that they meet with other women regularly in the villages, that they rarely, if ever, miss class, even during inclement weather."

How could the incentives be maximized for young women to work? The financial inducements are most straightforward: a steady income, at least equivalent to prevailing wage rates for male agricultural laborers. The woman herself should be able to set aside a part of her earnings for her own use rather than turning the entire amount over to the household as a whole. One way of accomplishing this without causing dissension in the family is to require that, say, one-tenth of her earnings be deposited in

---

[7] February 1976 interview with Lynn Bennett in Kathmandu.

[8] Based on research by Florence McCarthy, as reported in Raper (1970, p. 158). A similar situation is described by Sattar (1975) for a different village in the Comilla District.

a savings account managed by the cooperative. Several of the cooperatives described in chapter 3 consider that compulsory savings plans are an essential ingredient of their programs. Usually the elected management board decides whether a member may withdraw her savings for particular purposes or whether she should instead ask for a loan from cooperative funds. An appropriate withdrawal of savings might be the purchase of land that would ultimately provide a better income for the worker and her family in their old age; an inappropriate withdrawal would be one used to meet daily expenses for food and clothing.

Direct cash payments to the family might also be considered as an initial incentive. A gift, equivalent to one month's wages, given at the outset with the stipulation that the women would begin training and stay on the job for at least six months, could sensitize the family elders to the value of the woman's work. If the elders or the woman herself decided to withdraw her labor within the six-month period, the incentive payment would have to be returned, much like bridewealth at the time of divorce.

The prestige incentive could be maximized by providing a culturally acceptable environment (see pages 115–124), as well as opportunities on the job for women to gain competence in literacy and other valued skills. And the incentive to socialize with other women will be maximized by providing employment in a central workplace rather than in the home, by restricting employment to women, and by offering abundant opportunities for interaction on the job through functional literacy classes emphasizing discussion, or frequent meetings of cooperative members. Those who receive more advanced training in vocational skills and management will have the added opportunity to meet with women from other villages and to travel to distant towns or cities.

IMPEDIMENTS TO FEMALE EMPLOYMENT

On the basis of this brief review of positive incentives for rural women, at least those with low income, to seek paid employment outside the home, I would argue that the primary need is to overcome the major cultural and structural obstacles that prevent women who want to work from taking advantage of these opportunities. The first of these is the natural suspicion that villagers are likely to feel when confronted with organizers promoting a plan for their benefit; other obstacles relate to the cultural requirements for observing purdah among both Hindus and Muslims; and others, to the simple fact that many rural women—as motivated as they might be—simply do not have the time to take on a regular outside job. They are, if anything, not an "underutilized human resource," as the planners are fond of referring to them, but "overutilized" in a very basic way. They work hard, all day, with few visible benefits from their labors.

Reaction to the Project Organizers

Khushi Kabir, a young organizer of women's programs for the Bangladesh Rural Advancement Committee (BRAC), told of a village she had visited the day before in the Sulla area near Sylhet, where for several years BRAC has been working with the people to initiate health-care, adult literacy, housing, and agricultural programs.[9] A health worker had previously arranged for the Hindu and Muslim women to meet with her individually in order to decide whether they wanted to start a women's group and, if so, what they would like it to accomplish. When Kabir arrived in the village on the appointed day, in the company of a Dutch male anthropologist, none of the Muslim women came out to meet with her. A team of government family welfare workers who had visited the village a few days before had apparently broadcast their family-planning goals in a rather zealous fashion. When the city-bred Bengali woman and the bearded foreigner arrived a few days later, the Muslim women hid in their homes, fearing that the visitors were doctors who had come from Dacca to sterilize them. A number of Hindu women did show up, however, mostly wives past childbearing age and widows. They decided to start a rice-savings club and to plant potatoes for marketing during the next season.

The story highlights one of the major obstacles to organizing new programs: the villagers' suspicion of the organizers' motives. Their suspicion is, usually, a highly rational response to their concrete experiences of past victimization.[10] Among the impoverished Muslim families scattered through the national forest near Mymensing in northern Bangladesh, for example, fear of outsiders was pervasive. A stranger could be a government agent, levying new taxes or looking for bribes; a forest service agent, sent to evict them from their illegal dwellings;[11] or a spy for a band of thieves, who would steal everything they had right down to the last sack of rice. The Roman Catholic mission at Jalchatra had taken decades to build a sense of trust among the local population of predominantly Garo

[9] January 1976 interview with Khushi Kabir in Derai Camp, Sulla, Bangladesh.

[10] See, for example, the detailed account of exploitation at the hands of tax collectors, landlords, moneylenders, storekeepers, teachers, lawyers, policemen, creditors, politicians, relatives, and neighbors, as described by Wiser and Wiser (1971) in their account of the life of an Indian village.

[11] The national forest in the area was reserved for Garo tribespeople. Non-Garo were periodically evicted and their dwellings torn down, but they kept returning.

tribespeople through a comprehensive program of schooling, medical care, and agricultural assistance. One sister reconstructed the fears of the Muslim women this way: "What do these people want from me? What are they after? What is in it for them?"[12]

Mamdani (1972, page 145) tells of the reactions, in the mid-1950s, among the villagers of Manupur in northern India to family-planning workers who were trying to persuade them to use contraceptive foams: "The villagers searched for 'the clue' to what the Khanna Study was 'really doing.' Every detail of what the study members did was watched suspiciously. One report states: 'Serious difficulties sometimes have attended seemingly minor matters. Despite careful preparation of the village authorities, mapping of the village gave rise to uncontrollable rumors of a rise in taxes, another war, or that the village was to be moved.' " Other villagers speculated that the visitors were missionaries, or contractors come to straighten the streets. The family-planning workers in this case were Punjabis, not foreigners, but their educated urban background proved to be just as alien to the villagers (and vice versa) as that of someone from another land.[13]

And when missionaries/anthropologists William and Charlotte Wiser (1971, page 4) arrived in the Indian village of Karimpur, east of Agra, to do a brief statistical survey, "even the dogs yapped and the donkeys escaped as fast as their hobbles would allow."

The culture of suspicion and the structural conditions underlying it are aptly summed up in Banfield's (1958, page 97) behavioral principle, derived from his observations of a village in southern Italy, "No one will take the initiative in outlining a course of action and persuading others to embark upon it (except as it may be to his private advantage to do so), and, if one did offer leadership, the group would refuse it out of distrust." Although he centers his analysis on the phenomenon of *amoral familism* —acting to benefit one's own nuclear family over the short term in an economy of scarcity, while assuming that others will do likewise—the principle may also apply to a number of communities in which the extended family predominates. Any outsider may be suspect, as well as members of the community who belong to different kin groups, one's neighbors, or other household members who are assumed to be acting out of a motive for personal gain. If new industries are to be successfully introduced into rural communities, and if women and their families are

[12] January 1976 interview with Sister Bruno of the Corpus Christi Mission in Jalchatra, Bangladesh.
[13] For a discussion of the class bias of the original study, see Mamdani (1972, p. 48).

to cooperate actively in their planning and execution, the villagers' natural mistrust of the organizers must clearly be allayed.

Assuming that the organizers' motives *are* indeed honorable, the next step is to convince others that this is so. To this end, the central concern of the project should be with the whole development of the workers and not with the personal aggrandizement or enrichment of the organizers. It should also be designed so that workers will share in decision making, receive fair wages for their efforts, have a share of the profits, experience reasonable working conditions, and not be coerced into acting against their principles. Ultimately, the demonstration effect will do. But initially it will be necessary to identify and utilize as sponsors or intermediaries those local institutions (for example, successful male agricultural cooperatives or panchayats), groups, or individuals who have the trust and admiration of a substantial portion of the people from whom workers are most likely to be drawn. In addition, fears will be minimized if villagers are incorporated into the decision-making process from the beginning by the means of open meetings in which suggestions are elicited and proposals debated. In some villages meetings may have to be segregated by sex, but in others the men and women can meet together. In any case, it is essential that whole families participate and come to understand the nature of the projected scheme and its potential advantages or disadvantages if their womenfolk are to take on the new employment.

The Practice of Female Seclusion

In regions of Hindu and Muslim influence in South Asia, the ideal of female seclusion remains one of the major inhibitors of women's participation in public life. Institutionalized in the practice of *purdah,* the ideal is expressed in avoidance rules designed to regulate contact between the sexes and to segregate most male and female activities both socially and spatially. The manifestations of purdah most visible to the outsider are the virtual absence of women from the streets of towns and cities in some parts of Bangladesh and Pakistan; the segregation of those women who do appear in public into separate compartments in buses, trains, or waiting rooms, or their concealment by a curtain on the cycle rickshaws or scooter taxis to prevent strangers from seeing them (and vice versa); the form of dress which requires, at the very least, the covering of the head and shoulders with a sari or shawl, and, at the most, the covering of the entire body from head to toe with a *burqa,* out of which the woman peers through a small netting or thin cloth over the eyes; and, in many regions, the physical structure of dwellings, with high mud walls or bamboo or cane mats sheltering the region of household activities from view.

The practice of purdah is linked closely with other beliefs and practices relating to sexuality, honor, shame, and pollution; with the ideal arrangement of marriages for girls before, or as soon after, puberty as possible; and with structural conditions relating to kinship, the division of labor, and systems of social stratification in the society at large (Lindenbaum, 1968; and Papanek, 1973). In its most extreme form among Muslims, women remain totally secluded, leaving the home into which they were born or married only on rare occasions and then under the utmost protection.[14] If a woman must go out, she will make herself invisible in her burqa and will be accompanied by other women or children or by a close kinsman, but she will never go out alone. She will not gather with other women in public, or walk close to where men are gathered; and if she is accompanied by her husband or other kinsmen, she will walk a few steps behind. Within the home, if financial circumstances permit, she will share special territory with other women and children into which only the closest males are permitted. If someone who is not a close kinsman enters the house, women will be warned to hide, and not even their voices will be overheard. The women and children will eat apart from the men, and then only after the men have eaten their fill.

The degree to which purdah is practiced and the particular form of its observance varies considerably, depending on religion, caste, class, and region, among other factors. Although it is highly risky to try to sort out their independent effects, it is possible to make tentative generalizations.

Purdah is practiced among Muslims more than among Hindus, and among Hindus more than among Buddhist, Christian, or other religious minorities. Purdah appears to have originated as a Muslim institution that was adopted by Hindus, in somewhat different form, in a process of cultural diffusion that has permeated South Asia. Limiting the interaction between men and women outside certain well-defined categories, Muslim purdah restrictions "do not apply within the immediate kin unit, but only outside it," a rule that stresses "the unity of the kindred vis-à-vis the outside," whereas Hindu purdah regulates the interaction between a woman and the male members of the household into which she marries, but not

---

[14] The following description is drawn from Pastner (1971, pp. 187–197). Jahan (1975, p. 6) remarks that poor village women who wish to visit relatives in neighboring villages will usually go out at night, using umbrellas as veils. Because of previous restrictions on spatial mobility, caused by the need to remain invisible and the difficulty of doing so, many women apparently look on the burqa—a relatively new fashion in some villages—as a liberating garment, in that it enables them to move about far more freely than before (Papanek, 1973, p. 297).

of the household into which she was born (Papanek, 1973, pages 289 and 302).[15] For these reasons, one would expect that Hindus would be more liberal than Muslims in permitting women to work outside the home.

Purdah is practiced among high-caste more than low-caste families at similar levels of income and education.[16] Purdah in this sense becomes one aspect of the maintenance of the ritual purity of caste and subcaste, which, in Hindu tradition, is also bound up with rules for avoiding lower-caste persons and "polluting" objects touched by them. The practice of purdah among high-caste Hindus is linked with other conservative practices and values regarding the family, such as earlier arranged marriages, bans on divorce and the remarriage of widows, and a strong patriarchal structure of decision making. Indeed, among high-caste Hindus, women owe unquestioning obedience to their husbands—which in its extreme takes the form of religious worship—while husbands, in turn, owe unquestioning obedience to their fathers. Among lower-caste and scheduled-caste Hindus, fewer restrictions are likely to prevail. As von Furer-Haimendorf (1960, page 154) remarks of the Hindus in Nepal, "In this respect personal freedom and with it the right to moral choices increase as we descend the social ladder, and the women of lowly tenant farmers and agricultural labourers enjoy greater freedom in the choice of sexual partners than do the women of their high-caste landlords and masters." These so-called moral choices presumably also include the right (as well as the necessity) to move about more freely outside the home.

Female seclusion is also stronger among higher-caste than among lower-caste Muslims. Although caste is technically a Hindu custom, Muslims in some areas have adopted such Hindu practices as prohibitions on divorce and the remarriage of widows, the giving of dowry rather than bride price at the time of marriage, and the caste system.[17] The seclusion of women becomes firmly tied to the maintenance of caste status among Muslims adhering to traditional values.

Purdah is practiced more among well-to-do families than among poor families, within particular castes and levels of education. It is important to distinguish here between ritual status and economic status, the former

[15] The Committee on the Status of Women in India (1974, pp. 410–413) reports, on the basis of a national survey of over 5,000 respondents, a higher incidence of purdah observance for Muslims than Hindus within the family in the presence of father-in-law, mother-in-law, and husband's elder brother, as well as outside it. The sample is not representative, and there are many nonresponses.

[16] Ibid. However, high-caste Hindus in the Indian study observed purdah within and outside the home less frequently than did middle- and low-caste Hindus, although rural-urban residence and education are not controlled.

[17] Muslim castes in India are described by Bhatty (1975). See also Ahmad (1973).

being associated with caste purity, the latter with the material conditions in which the family or subcaste currently finds itself. Some villages of Nepal, for example, are heavily settled by Brahmins of high ritual status (by definition) but low economic status, most of whom engage in manual labor tilling the soil (von Furer-Haimendorf, 1960). The tension between low economic status, which requires that women must engage at least seasonally in some economically productive activity outside the home, and high ritual status, which calls for their seclusion, leads to a number of compromises in the ideal. In times of severe economic need women will enter the labor force as agricultural laborers or in other capacities, but when conditions improve, they withdraw to their homes.

One explanation of the relationship between income and purdah within castes may be that the wealthy can well afford to keep their women in purdah while the poor cannot (Jahan, 1975, page 6). Not only does an upper-class woman not have to work, but she can remain in separate quarters in the household and send servants or children on errands to the bazaar. Few among the village poor can afford to observe such restrictions regardless of their caste status. But several studies from India, Pakistan, and Bangladesh (Papanek, 1973, page 322; and Husain, 1958, page 15) have suggested that in some situations purdah is more prevalent among lower-income than higher-income families. No doubt education is a strong factor here: women in well-to-do families are likely not only to have a higher education, but, if they are employed, to be working in white-collar occupations, such as teaching in girls' schools or colleges, which protect them from contact with men. Lower-income women must wear the burqa for protection and status maintenance and, being little schooled or illiterate, may hold to more conservative values (Jahan, 1975, page 10). In looking at the relationship between class and purdah, then, one must distinguish between upper-class families that are highly *traditional* in their adherence to religious norms and family customs and those *liberal* upper-class families that increasingly reject restrictive attitudes and practices (Bhatty, 1975, pages 34–35).

The bases of class stratification in rural South Asia are closely related to inequalities in the distribution of land, which in turn are related to inequalities in the distribution of income.[18] Although the variations are complex, one can distinguish roughly among large landowners who employ hired labor or lease land to tenants in order to release themselves and their families from manual labor; small landowners who rely primarily on fam-

---

[18] They are also, of course, tied closely to caste distinctions, thus concentrating property, income, privilege, and power in the hands of the same elite rather than dispersing them across different groups. Béteille (1974) discusses the concepts of class and caste, especially on pp. 35–55 and 69–70.

ily labor (including that of women), with perhaps occasional hired labor, but who may abstain from manual labor if their status maintenance requires it; sharecroppers and other tenant farmers, among whom women engage in manual labor at least occasionally; and landless laborers, among whom the women may frequently find employment as hired laborers alongside their men (Boserup, 1970, page 70). The relation of people to the land may be more useful than income in distinguishing life-styles of agrarian social groups, although the two are certainly related.

Purdah is practiced more by upwardly mobile families and subcastes than among nonmobile families or subcastes, especially among lower-income groups. The adoption of elite norms of ritual behavior, encouraging the seclusion of wives and daughters in the home and their withdrawal from the labor force, is a common manifestation of upward mobility among both Hindu and Muslim low-income and low-caste families. Among Hindus, this is one aspect of the process of Sanskritization.[19] Its effects are clearly visible among peasants in some of the more prosperous regions of northern India. As reported by Mazumdar (1975, page 6), "Recent studies on the changing pattern of village life indicate that improvement in prosperity, the spread of education, or acquisition of white-collar jobs by the lower castes invariably leads to a withdrawal of women from active employment outside their homes. This has been particularly noticed in the green revolution districts, where agricultural prosperity has led to a sharp drop in women's participation in agriculture."[20]

The status of the entire kin group becomes tied to its ability to keep its womenfolk secluded in the home, much in the nature of the "conspicuous consumption" of nonproductive women among the upper classes that was identified by Veblen (1934, pages 179–180) in the West. The more tentative the newly acquired social position, the more important the correct observances become. As Papanek (1971, page 522) remarks, "Observance of purdah in the lower middle class may function as a signal of status, especially for persons who have just achieved this class level."[21] Even slight improvements in agricultural prosperity may permit peasant families to hire (sometimes female) paid labor when it is needed in their fields as a replacement for the work done previously by female family members.

[19] Srinivas (1970) describes the Sanskritization process as one in which lower-caste groups or individuals emulate the religious purity of higher-caste groups as a means of upward social mobility. For ways in which women's freedom of movement and employment status are influenced by upward mobility, see Béteille (1975) and D'Souza (1975), among others.

[20] See also the Committee on the Status of Women in India (1974, p. 75). For an example from southern India, see Epstein (1973, pp. 191–200).

[21] See also Pastner (1971, p. 196).

Among Muslims, too, upward mobility is commonly associated with a strengthening of the practice of female seclusion in emulation of the traditional practices of higher castes. In Uttar Pradesh, for example, "There is a marked tendency among those non-Ashraf families [lower-caste Muslims] who have done relatively well to put their women in purdah and to withdraw them from the family work force. It is now said in praise of a husband that he is able to give his wife leisure to 'stay on bed,' instead of forcing her to work in the field" (Bhatty, 1975, page 34). Bhatty also tells of a newly prosperous family of the oil-presser caste in Uttar Pradesh in which the women of the household had previously helped to work the oil press and sell the mustard oil in the village streets. Now that the family has built a partly *pucca* (brick) house, the young daughter-in-law has taken to purdah, while the mother-in-law continues to work.[22] Pastner (1971, page 200), observing the same process in Baluchistan, calls the increased traditionalization of women in the face of the upward mobility of males an example of "negative modernization."

Observers have noted that the adoption of modern amenities, such as tubewells and latrines, by newly prosperous rural households also intensifies the seclusion of women by undermining two major excuses for leaving the home: to use the fields for elimination, and to gather water from the wells or the river. As a consequence, even these opportunities for visiting with other women are closed.

The withdrawal of women from the labor force, while heightening the family's ritual status, has an additional financial disadvantage beyond the direct loss of income. As girls and women become economic liabilities, the pattern of exchange at the time of marriage frequently shifts from bridewealth—a system generally practiced by tribal and low-caste groups, whose women are more frequently economically productive, and by Muslims—to the dowry.[23] The family must now worry about how to raise money to find their daughter a husband of suitable status.

Purdah is practiced in towns (but not in cities) more than in villages.[24] The difference between town and village is, of course, confounded by

[22] Similar incidents are reported in Muslim villages of the Comilla District in Bangladesh (Abdullah, 1974, pp. 25–26) and in a Punjabi village near Lyallpur (Anwar and Bilquees, 1976, p. 51).

[23] For discussions of the relation between female economic productivity and marital exchange, and the shift from one form of exchange to another, see, among others, Boserup (1970, pp. 48–50); the Committee on the Status of Women in India (1974, p. 70); Epstein (1973, pp. 194–200); and Lindenbaum (1974, p. 3).

[24] In the Pakistan National Impact Survey of 1968–69, 82 percent of currently married urban women said they were observing purdah, as compared with 37 percent of rural women (Shah, 1975b, p. 479). The unrepresentative survey by the Committee on the Status of Women in India (1974, pp. 410–414) reports more frequent purdah observance in rural areas than in cities.

caste and class differences, for town dwellers on the whole are likely to be of somewhat higher economic and caste status than those living in villages or scattered in rural districts. Villagers, being poorer, are more likely to require that their women work in the fields, at least seasonally if not full time. Women who plant and weed and harvest cannot keep themselves covered from head to toe. They must forego the veil (although they will usually keep their heads covered) and may even tuck their clothing up around their legs to permit greater freedom of movement.

The observance of purdah in small towns is associated not only with the higher economic and ritual status of many town dwellers, but also with the greater likelihood of encountering strangers, or at least unrelated males, in the streets. For Muslims, this necessitates either the strict seclusion of women or the wearing of the burqa in public. Wherever there is an influx of outsiders into the area, one would expect an intensified concern with protecting the honor of females, not only in towns but in border regions or other newly prosperous areas as well.[25]

Cultural variations across regions affect the practice of purdah. Within India, for example, norms regarding women's work outside the home appear to differ strongly by region, with far greater restrictions generally placed on women's freedom in the north (a region of strong Muslim influence) than in the south. Mazumdar (1975, page 6) goes so far as to call purdah a strictly northern phenomenon, reporting that participation rates of women in agriculture are generally high in the south, low in the north, and particularly low in West Bengal, where "the taboo on women in field work has penetrated even among the scheduled castes." (See also the report by the Committee on the Status of Women in India, 1974, page 61.)

The caste system in general and the restrictions on high-caste activities are said to be less rigid in the Hindu kingdom of Nepal than in India (von Furer-Haimendorf, 1960, pages 18–19). Within Nepal, Hindus in the Muslim-influenced southern Terai are more conservative than are Hindus in the north, where there is a strong Tibetan and Buddhist current. Among the latter, von Furer-Haimendorf (1967, page 172) argues that the relationship between husband and wife conveys "a relaxed and cheerful atmosphere" of closeness and warmth. The Nepalese Buddhists have simultaneously been influenced by Hindu tradition, however; the Newar people of the Kathmandu valley, about half of whom are Buddhist, have

---

[25] Pastner (1971, pp. 187–197) reports an increase in purdah during the past twenty years among the women of Panjgur, Baluchistan, as more outsiders are attracted to the area.

apparently adopted the caste system of their Hindu neighbors (von Furer-Haimendorf, 1960).

Although the impressions are difficult to verify, observers have also suggested that Muslim observances of purdah are stricter in Pakistan than in Bangladesh; within Bangladesh, they are stricter in the south (near Chittagong) than in the north; and within Pakistan, they are stricter in the north (near Peshawar) than in the south. There is little systematic research to substantiate these observations, however.

Purdah is practiced among women in their prime reproductive years more so than among younger girls or older women. Whereas the seclusion of Muslim girls begins at puberty, Hindu seclusion, strictly speaking, begins with marriage (Papenek, 1973, pages 289 and 302). Because the practice is so closely linked with the maintenance of family honor through protecting the sexual purity of its womenfolk, restrictions on interaction between the sexes should be greatest during those years when women are viewed as sexually most attractive, and, thus, vulnerable to possible illegitimate sexual intercourse and pregnancy. The notion of the woman's sexual–reproductive value is quite explicit in the rules relating to unmarried girls, among whom a dishonoring sexual union could not only cause great shame to the family but could greatly reduce the girl's economic value in the marriage market (or, among groups practicing the dowry, greatly increase her cost). Even worse, the girl could become potentially unmarriageable and thus a permanent economic drain on the family's resources.

Once the sexual value of the woman declines, either through aging (and the loss of reproductive capacity) or through widowhood, greater freedom of movement is generally tolerated. She no longer poses a major risk. A widow's behavior may remain somewhat circumscribed, however, for widows are frequently expected to dress in a distinctive and unattractive manner (among traditional Hindus, by shaving their heads, wearing plain white saris, and walking barefoot) and to avoid certain ceremonies on auspicious occasions where their presence could bring bad luck. On the whole, though, widows and older wives are relatively free to move about outside the home.

This brief summary of purdah observances, which may well be contradicted in specific instances, obscures many important variations and complexities, including the consequences of cross-cutting influences. A high-caste married Hindu woman may experience more restrictions than a low-caste married Muslim woman, for example, and a low-caste Hindu woman of northern India leads a more restricted life than does a higher-caste Hindu woman in the south. In some areas, certain religious minorities (although not Buddhists or Christians) may practice purdah to the same extent or to a greater degree than do Hindus and Muslims.

The discussion perhaps also obscures the distinction between purdah practiced within the home in the presence of family elders, and purdah practiced outside the home. The latter is more important with respect to recruiting women for rural industry, for we need to know the circumstances under which women are actually permitted to move about outside the home. Purdah observance within the home does have some bearing on these issues, however. To the extent that conversation between a young wife and her father-in-law or husband's older brother is considered a breach of proper conduct, it will be difficult for a woman to try to persuade reluctant elders directly to agree to a new form of social behavior.[26] She may well work through other sympathetic family members, however— her husband, perhaps, or her mother-in-law—to effect a change of heart. It is probably a major misconception to view the joint family as a solidary or impermeable institution which resists adoption of social change. Even if the family values the idea of female seclusion, the potential monetary advantages of permitting an unmarried daughter or young daughter-in-law to work outside the home may well outweigh the cultural resistance to the idea in the minds of the family's decision makers. And there may well be disagreement among these same decision makers which can be used to advantage. The points of fission in the extended family—the time when brothers decide to break up the joint household and establish independent residences with their wives and children, for example—can provide an opportunity for the adoption of new practices as well as a major financial incentive for female labor.

We must not gloss over the fact that in many instances it will be not just her husband, the elders in the household, or the community at large, but the woman herself who resists the idea of working outside the home. Bennett reports of the Brahmin and Chetri women in a village near Kathmandu that those who were forced by economic necessity to work in the fields looked forward eagerly to the time when they could stay home. This is not at all surprising in view of the onerous and unreward-

---

[26] The Committee on the Status of Women in India (1974, p. 415) found that almost half the respondents in their large survey said they were not supposed to talk to their husband's father or older brother, with the proportions varying only slightly among upper-, middle-, lower-, and scheduled-caste Hindus. Only 16 percent of adult women in Gore's study (1968, pp. 153–170) of rural and urban communities of Agarwals in India said they felt free to discuss important decisions with the person in authority in the household, and most observed purdah in the presence of older males (including their husbands) by keeping to separate quarters, standing while males were present, and eating only after the men had finished.

ing labor in which most employed rural women find themselves. In addition, because their work in the fields is generally considered a normal part of their domestic role, it does not translate into economic independence or greater power within the household. If we take the view of the woman herself, then, it is clear that unless she *must* work for economic reasons she is likely to weigh the potential gains and losses of her employment quite carefully, in some cases deciding that the security of the home and what she perceives at her more privileged position there are not worth risking for some unknown quantity in the workplace.

The obstacle of female seclusion could undoubtedly be more easily overcome if certain protections were offered to women and their families. The most basic is an all-female work environment, including female supervisors, where this is considered a necessary precondition for women to work outside the home. Sentiment may initially require that the workplace be secluded from view by walls or bamboo shades, although experience is likely to show that these barriers become less necessary once the enterprise has gained legitimacy. In locales where it is still considered wrong for women to walk in the streets, even in burqas, or where they must travel some distance to work, some form of transport will be required, such as curtained cycles or scooter rickshaws.[27] Hostels may be required for some employees, such as unmarried girls whose parents are anxious to marry them early, workers from neighboring villages, or visiting trainers and supervisors. And the type of work itself must be considered respectable. In deciding on a product it is important to take into account local beliefs and practices; for example, caste restrictions among higher-caste groups on performing certain "lowly" tasks such as leatherworking or pottery making. This latter consideration is unlikely to pose real problems, since it is lower-caste Hindus, low-income Muslims, and religious minorities who are most likely to seek employment.

Farming and Domestic Responsibilities

A typical village of the rice-growing regions of Bangladesh is built on high ground in the midst of watery fields that stretch flat toward the horizon. Villages are joined by high roads or by paths through fields that are flooded during the monsoons. The houses, clustered together in compounds (bari) containing several households of a joint family and sepa-

---

[27] The Bangladesh Academy of Rural Development in Comilla paid cycle rickshaw fares in order for women from surrounding villages to come for training sessions (Raper, 1970, pp. 161–63).

rated from other bari, are typically built of mud with a thatched roof, although sometimes the walls are of woven cane matting tied to bamboo frames and the roofs are tin. The houses must be repaired frequently. Surrounding the houses are smaller structures for sheltering animals and storing straw, a few fruit trees, and sometimes a small vegetable garden. The bari usually centers on a large pond or "tank" in which people bathe themselves and their buffaloes, women wash dishes and clothes, and ducks dabble for food.

The houses contain two or three small, dark rooms with, perhaps, one tiny window in each and a mud floor which is periodically coated with a mixture of mud and cow dung to give it a hard, clean surface. The house contains several *charpoys* (wooden frames strung with cord) for sleeping, some rolled-up bedding, and perhaps a chair or small table. The walls are decorated with pictures from old calendars, photographs of family members, and framed samples of embroidery. There is a separate cooking area with a mud *chula* for cooking built into the floor, a few brass bowls and containers stacked on the floor or on shelves, and large earthenware jars to store water. Rice and other staples are suspended from the ceiling in baskets or jars hung in woven jute sikas. The chula burns leaves, sticks, or dried cakes of cow dung mixed with straw; smoke fills the dark room. When the weather is good, the women do most of their cooking and washing out-of-doors in the courtyard, where a few skinny chickens peck in the dust and the children play. The goats and buffaloes have been taken to pasture, but at night they are tethered in shelters near the house. During the day the men of working age are all off in the fields; only young children and old men remain at home with the women. When a stranger approaches, the women hurry indoors to hide or quickly cover their heads and faces. When the rice fields are bright green and the sun glints off the patterned water, the village looks beautiful and prosperous, but during the monsoons everything is flooded—perhaps even the house itself—and the cattle stand knee-deep in water. Access to other villages is cut off except by boat. It is within this setting that the women carry on their domestic activities.

Our knowledge of how rural women actually spend their time is extremely limited. Pilot studies by Sattar (1975) in the Comilla District of Bangladesh and by Anwar and Bilquees (1976) in the Lyallpur District of Pakistan contain helpful descriptions of the daily and seasonal round of activities among women in those villages,[28] but systematic time-budget data which could throw light on regional, class, and caste variations in

[28] See also Abdullah (1974); Von-Harder (1975); Ellickson (1975); and Saeed (1976).

women's work have yet to be gathered. What is clear from the few available studies is that the time spent on different activities varies dramatically among different groups within the same village and among villages within the same region.

The daily round of domestic chores, combined with seasonal fluctuations in the demand for labor in the fields or for crop processing, appear to leave little time in the lives of most women for taking on additional activities. In spite of the low percentage (under 10 percent) of women counted as part of the rural labor force in Pakistan, for example, interviews with village women reveal extremely high rates of mostly unpaid labor in the fields or nearer home in crop processing. In four villages of the Lyallpur District in the wheat-growing Punjab at least 20 percent of women in the five major castes cut wheat during harvest, at least 40 percent thresh wheat, at least 27 percent pick cotton, at least 60 percent cut fodder for animals, and so on (table 5-2). The general pattern is for higher-caste women (Rajput and Jat) to participate less in farm activities than do lower-caste women (Gujar and Baluch), although the relationship does not hold for all activities. Given the subsistence agricultural conditions that prevail in most regions, the question thus arises as to whether it is foolish to propose full-time, year-round nonagricultural employment for rural women in South Asia. Even if cultural values did

Table 5-2. Percentage of Women Participating in Farm and Domestic Activities by Caste in Four Villages of the Lyallpur District, Pakistan

	Rajput	Jat	Arian	Gujar	Baluch
Sowing season					
Hoeing	—	6	46	3	4
Harvesting season					
Wheat cutting	40	20	42	31	65
Wheat threshing	40	51	53	86	84
Cotton picking	40	40	64	33	27
Sugarcane processing	20	14	27	76	24
Fodder cutting	60	80	74	80	78
Cleaning grains	78	95	68	91	95
Animal care					
Milking animals	91	88	92	91	74
Cleaning shed	52	82	89	88	81
Other activities					
Preparation of farm meals[a]	39	95	88	76	95
Leisure work[b]	96	88	88	76	78

Source: From Kishwar Saeed, Rural Women's Participation in Farm Operations, reproduced in Helbock (1975, p. 40).

[a] Preparation of meals for workers in the fields.

[b] Includes spinning, weaving, sewing, knitting, and other handicrafts made in spare time for home consumption.

not restrict so many women to the home, would they have time to take on new activities? This section addresses briefly some of the major domestic responsibilities of rural women and suggests a few possibilities for circumventing these obstacles.

The major domestic tasks in which women engage, aside from their regular or seasonal participation in agricultural labor, include the processing of food and other crops for household consumption or for sale (rice, wheat, other grains and pulses, cotton, fruits and vegetables, nuts, oil, and so forth); collecting water, animal fodder, and cooking fuel; cooking, cleaning, and washing; and caring for children. In addition, women often fill their so-called leisure time with spinning, weaving, embroidery, mat or quiltmaking, or other production primarily for home use. In almost all these activities, both scarcity of raw materials and primitive technology require that women spend many hours every day on tasks of very low productivity. If women are to be free to engage in more productive labor, or if work outside the home is not simply to add to their already heavy burdens in the home, then clearly one of the first priorities is to reduce their domestic chores.

Let us take the major activities in turn. Even if women do not toil directly in the fields, almost everywhere they are primarily responsible for handling the harvest. Women's work begins where their husbands' ends. The time-consuming nature of traditional techniques of rice and grain processing has been described in chapter 4 (see page 83). Extracting oil from seeds; cleaning cotton; drying mango pulp; washing and cleaning jute; drying and husking corn; grinding corn, wheat, pulses, or rice into flour; peeling the tops of sugarcane for animal fodder—all take time. Wives and daughters of small farmers are generally more involved in crop processing than are the wives and daughters of landless peasants who instead hire themselves out as agricultural laborers or as daily wage-labor in processing (Sattar, 1975). Processing time has increased significantly in areas where irrigation now permits multiple-cropping and where new high-yield varieties offer more abundant crops (von Harder, 1975). Far more attention should be paid to innovative means for reducing the work load associated with increased agricultural productivity through the introduction of more efficient intermediate technology in household-centered processing and storage activities.

Collecting water from a distant river or well for cooking, drinking, bathing, washing clothes and dishes, and watering poultry and animals frequently requires that women walk miles each day carrying heavy jars. Bennett (1973) calculates that an average household of ten members in a village in Nepal, with its own convenient well, uses about forty gallons of water a day, whereas households farther away from a water supply may use about twenty. Households owning livestock need considerably more water because a buffalo consumes eight gallons a day, a cow three or four, and a goat about a half-gallon. The water is carried by women and children in narrow-necked, copper, brass, or clay vessels holding from three to eight gallons each. The brass vessels are cleaned daily by rubbing them with ashes; the clay vessels are cleaned less frequently with sand. The Nepalese women wrap long cloths around their hips to support the vessels or else carry them, supported by a headband, in baskets on their backs.

Improved water supplies are a high-priority item in most rural development programs. Gravity-flow, piped water systems in the hills and tube-wells in the plains will reduce women's work load significantly. It should be noted, though, that the insistence of public health workers on using boiled water adds to women's work, not only in time but also in the search for additional fuel. Other methods for sterilizing water should thus be encouraged.

Village women who also care for poultry and animals can spend hours every day collecting fodder, washing and watering the animals, taking them to pasture, cleaning their stalls, and milking. In the arid, rocky regions of the Khyber Pass one can see tribal women leaving their villages at dawn to search for grass for their animals. Returning from the distant mountain valleys at noon, they carry tremendous loads on their heads. In one village located in a wheat-growing area of the Punjab women spend, on the average, over six hours every day finding fodder for their buffaloes and goats, caring for and milking the animals, and churning the milk (table 5-3). Gathering time could be reduced by encouraging the planting of fast-growing fodder, such as protein-rich lucerne, on banks and idle fields close to the villages; by introducing more efficient techniques of chopping the fodder; and by using prepared animal feeds. The AMUL Dairy in Gujarat makes a highly nutritious feed by mixing oilseed by-products, such as groundnut cake or cottonseed cake, with damaged cereals and cereal by-products, such as rice or wheat bran, and adding mineral supplements.[29] AMUL's prepared feeds are cheaper and more nutritionally balanced and produce richer milk than the sometimes expen-

---

[29] In the United States a grass machine, requiring little energy, has been invented that grows fodder hydroponically in water-filled and lighted trays inside a boxlike structure. According to the *Christian Science Monitor,* "The smallest unit (4 feet by 4 feet by 8 feet) produces up to 200 pounds of barley grass from 24 pounds of seed in just one week." Operated continuously, the unit can produce 1 ton of grass in ten days. Manufactured by Agricultural Growth Industries in Concord, California, the largest model yields up to 800 pounds of grass a day. Although the initial investment is high, women organizing agricultural cooperatives for raising chickens, pigs, goats, or cows could greatly reduce their labors and increase their yields through a version of the machine modified to fit local conditions and fuel sources.

sive cottonseed that farmers formerly fed their cattle. Prepared feeds could be manufactured locally by women's cooperatives.

The search for cooking fuel is another time-consuming task. Women of Nepal walk for miles in search of wood from the once-forested hillsides; now many hills are denuded, and they must go farther afield to find fuel. Even small saplings are pulled up for kindling. Elsewhere, women gather twigs and leaves for fuel, or collect dung, which is mixed with straw, formed into patties, dried on the mud walls of the house, and stored for later use. The dung cakes give off a low and smoky heat. More efficient sources of fuel would include electricity, kerosine, butane, compacted sawdust, or crop by-products, solar heat, or methane gas produced in Gobar tanks from animal and human wastes and other biodegradable products. Methane gas produces a hotter, cleaner heat than does cow dung, while the remaining sludge is a richer fertilizer.

Cooking time varies considerably by region, caste, and class. Women in south India, for example, are more likely to engage in lengthy meal preparations two or three times a day, cooking afresh for each meal, than are women in the north, who frequently prepare their staple foods (wheat chapatis and vegetables) only once a day, warming them up for other meals (Singh, 1976, page 73). A typical midday meal in Bangladesh of rice, dahl, and vegetable requires that the husked rice be cleaned and cooked, the dahl cleaned, the vegetables peeled and cut, onions sliced, and all *masalas* (spices) cleaned, dried, and ground on a special stone grinder or between two stones, with water added to make a paste. The

Table 5-3. Hours Spent on Daily Domestic Activities by Women in a Muslim Village near Lyallpur, Pakistan

Activity	Hours:minutes	Percentage of waking time
Collecting, carrying, and preparing fodder for animals	3:45	24
Animal care	1:45	11
Milking and churning	1:00	7
Cooking	1:45	11
Carrying food to fields, and feeding children	1:30	10
House cleaning, and making dung cakes for fuel	:45	5
Carrying water	:30	3
Child care	:30	3
Other domestic chores (includes food processing, crafts)	3:00	19
Afternoon rest	1:00	7
Total waking hours	15:30	

Source: Anwar and Bilquees (1976, p. 51), but using corrected percentages.

food is cooked over a wood fire on one or two chulas. The chula itself is rebuilt about twice a month. After the meal, the dishes and saucepans are taken to the pond to wash; the whole process may easily take several hours (Sattar, 1975, pages 41–49). More efficient stoves, cooking utensils, and facilities for food preparation (for example, spice grinders and oil presses) and storage would reduce considerably the time spent on cooking.

Child care as a specific activity tends to take up little of a woman's time (see table 4-3) because either she keeps her young children with her while she works, or she delegates their care to their older siblings (usually girls) or to other relatives in the household, perhaps a mother-in-law. But lack of alternative child care will interfere with some women's work outside the home. If women are not to neglect their children or to try to work with toddlers beside them, facilities for child care will have to be provided at the place of employment.

Factors Influencing Women's Domestic Responsibilities

The extent to which women are tied to domestic and agricultural chores will depend, not only on the family's economic status and on the regional differences discussed above (themselves related to differences in agricultural productivity and in the division of labor by sex), but also on the structure of the household in which the woman lives and on her position in it.

The Committee on the Status of Women in India (1974, pages 61–62) argues that the joint family imposes greater constraints on women's freedom of movement than does the nuclear family, although to the degree that the joint family is correlated with higher caste or economic status, the relation may be spurious.[30] One could argue that the joint family is not only more culturally conservative, on the whole, but also that the economic vulnerability that pushes a woman into the labor force is mitigated by the joint responsibility of several male workers for the family's support. It is assumed, on the other hand, that the nuclear family permits a more egalitarian relationship between the husband and wife which would facilitate her employment outside the home; it is also more vulnerable to financial stress requiring an additional income. The 1968–69 National Impact Survey in Pakistan of 2,910 currently married women of reproductive age living with their husbands found that 25.1 percent of rural

---

[30] Kolenda (1967, pp. 147–148) finds no support for caste or landowning status as a major determinant of regional variations in family structures in India however.

women in nuclear households (about half of all rural households) were currently employed as compared with 19.2 percent in joint households (Karim, 1974, page 134). Corresponding percentages for urban women were 11.4 percent and 7.8 percent, respectively). The nuclear structure was apparently more conducive to female employment (in this case almost entirely agricultural) despite the fact that women in the sample nuclear households had an average of 3.5 living children as compared with 2.4 for those in joint households.

The common assumption that the joint or extended family is not only the ideal but the typical family form in South Asia is challenged by Kolenda (1967, page 148), who notes that in India, although the majority of people live in joint or "supplemented nuclear" families, the majority of households are nuclear or "subnuclear," that is, incomplete. Nuclear households are more common in the south than in the north. The incidence of joint families in a community can be largely explained by the timing of their dissolution. Joint families are least frequent in communities in which brothers commonly set up a separate household at, or soon after, their marriage; more frequent where brothers commonly wait until the father's death to divide the property; and most frequent where brothers continue living together with their wives and children, even after the father's death.

In trying to explain regional variations in the Indian family structure, Kolenda argues that these different patterns of fission in the joint household are shaped in large part by the bargaining power of women who, being "outsiders" and thus less committed to the maintenance of the extended unit, are assumed to have a stronger incentive to break up the household.[31] A woman's bargaining power, in turn, is derived from the relative amount of resources that the couple (particularly the husband) obtains from her or his own kin.[32] In brief, couples are most likely to set up a separate household after marriage in communities that permit initiation of divorce by the wife, that emphasizes bridewealth rather than dowry, and that provide close linkages between the husband and his wife's natal family or linkage through her family's economic or social support to the couple. Couples are most likely to remain in a joint family, even after the father's death, in communities in which the wife's family provides relatively few resources compared with those provided by the husband's. This

[31] The theme of quarreling women is a common explanation for the breaking up of extended households in South Asia. New daughters-in-law are particularly vulnerable to accusations of dishonesty or trickery if something is missing from the household.

[32] For a summary of seventeen resources and their relationship to family structure, see Kolenda (1967, pp. 204–205).

analysis suggests that the bargaining power of women in the household may be more *cause* than consequence of nuclear family living, and that a woman who has successfully negotiated the transition from living in her father-in-law's home to living in her own home could, in turn, more successfully negotiate the right to work outside the home.

It is a mistake to consider the joint household an insurmountable obstacle to female employment, however. For one reason, the differences in employment rates in the Pakistan survey are not great. For another, the joint household may provide considerable advantages for female employment in that it permits adjustments in the division of labor. A mother-in-law or sister-in-law may well be willing to take on additional domestic responsibilities in order to permit an unmarried daughter or a young bride of the household to earn money, especially if the whole family will benefit from the earnings. In this sense the availability of other family members provides a supportive environment, freeing women who would otherwise be tied to the home.

This brings us to the question of the woman's position in the family. Most village studies suggest that it is the older mother-in-law who, having achieved her life goal of retiring from domestic chores while her daughters-in-law take over, is most free both culturally and structurally to take on employment outside the home. I argued earlier that this group of older wives and widows could be usefully employed in income-generating activities centered in or around the home, such as handicrafts or market gardening.

The primary goal in this scheme for creating employment outside the home, however, is to recruit unmarried girls and young married women in their early childbearing years so that their new status can have a maximum potential impact on delaying marriage, delaying the first birth, and spacing and limiting additional births. Unmarried girls are likely to be relatively free of domestic responsibilities as compared with older married women if others in the household are willing to take over some of their tasks, and if they do not have younger siblings to look after. If they do have to care for younger children, then child-care facilities may also be necessary in order for unmarried girls to work. So, too, new brides who have not yet borne children may have more free time than after childbearing begins. The most difficult group to recruit would be married women with rapidly growing families, but as we have argued, the demographic impact of their employment will probably be limited in any case.

Recruitment of unmarried girls will have to be timed so that parents will have maximum incentive to delay their daughter's marriage. Among traditional Muslims, female employment may have to begin when the girl reaches twelve or fourteen in order for it to serve as an alternative to marriage; among Hindus, the most extreme pressures appear somewhat later; and among religious minorities, such as Christians, Buddhists, and some tribals, even later. Hardly any rural teenage girls will be enrolled in school. In Pakistan, in 1961, only 2.5 percent of all females (rural and urban) aged fifteen through nineteen were enrolled, and the proportions were probably only slightly higher in India and much lower in Nepal. Having never attended school, having attended only sporadically, or having been withdrawn from school by the age of ten or twelve because schooling was not seen as a good investment for daughters, the girls are at a critical juncture with respect to their futures.

The nature of this critical juncture is revealed in table 5-4. In Bangladesh, in 1965, only 13 percent of girls between the ages of fifteen and nineteen were still unmarried, and virtually none remained single past twenty. Pakistan presents a far more favorable picture, with over two-thirds still unmarried in their late teens, while India and Nepal range between these extremes. Although all four countries show a notable tendency for the marriages of females to be increasingly delayed, only in Pakistan is the marital timing even approaching the point where it could begin to have a significant impact on lowering fertility.[33]

Table 5-4. Percentage of Females Still Unmarried at Younger Ages, and Average Age at First Marriage, in India, Bangladesh, Pakistan, and Nepal, 1961–71

Country	Year	Age			Age at Marriage[a]
		10–14	15–19	20–24	
Pakistan[b]	1961	89.4	46.6	12.0	17.5
	1965	98.7	69.1	16.2	19.3
Nepal	1961	84.9	25.7	5.5	15.8
	1971	84.1	39.3	7.9	16.6
India	1961	80.4	29.2	6.0	15.8
	1971	88.1	42.9	9.1	17.2
Bangladesh[c]	1961	67.4	8.3	1.3	13.9
	1965	82.0	13.0	1.6	14.9

Source: Chesnais and Vallin (1975, p. 1089).
[a] Singulate mean age at first marriage, as calculated from proportions still single within five-year age groups for a given census year.
[b] Then West Pakistan.
[c] Then East Pakistan.

[33] On the other hand, age-specific, marital fertility rates in Pakistan were far higher than in Bangladesh or India in the mid-1960s. Cumulative fertility rates for women married at age twenty (based on age-specific rates) were 8.0 children for women in Pakistan (1963–65), 6.5 in Bangladesh (1963–65), and 5.2 in India (1964–65); for women marrying at age fifteen, the corresponding figures were 10.2, 8.1, and 5.8, respectively (Chesnais and Vallin, 1975, p. 1090).

Offering supervised hostels as living quarters for unmarried female workers could, as I argued in chapter 2, relieve space pressures in rural households as well as minimizing the threat of dishonoring sexual unions within the family. It could also permit unmarried girls from neighboring villages to take advantage of employment that would otherwise be denied them because of the difficulties in traveling over long distances.

CONCLUSIONS

In this chapter it has been argued that at least three incentives could motivate rural women to seek employment outside the home—money, prestige, and social contact. These inducements could be strengthened by ensuring that the rural industries pay wages at least equal to prevailing rates for male agricultural workers; provide an opportunity for the acquisition of vocational and literacy skills; and encourage the formation of strong bonds of social solidarity in a central workplace. Against these incentives must be weighed several major impediments to the employment of girls and women outside the home: suspicion of the motives of the employer, cultural values favoring the practice of female seclusion, and a generally arduous round of domestic responsibilities that leaves women little free time to take on additional work.

In response to the question, Under what conditions could women and their families be induced to take advantage of new employment opportunities, we could suggest the following criteria:

1. The potential workers and their families must perceive the concrete and immediate material benefits to be gained. In this sense, recruiting for paid employment differs from projects with deferred or less tangible rewards, such as literacy classes or nutrition or health-care training, in that it has a clear and immediate payoff. It has been suggested that family heads might even be offered some initial financial incentive to encourage them to permit an unmarried daughter or young daughter-in-law to work, if she is willing, and that care should be taken to ensure that both the family as a whole and the individual worker benefit from the new income. Saving a fixed portion of earnings should be mandatory.

2. Certain protections can be offered to workers within the framework of prevailing cultural restrictions on contact between the sexes. This would include providing for secure travel between home and the place of work, a protected work environment under all-female supervision, and in some cases hostels or other acceptable living arrangements (for example, sharing the house of a respectable fam-

ily) for workers, visiting female inspectors, training agents, and so forth.

3. The type of work must be acceptable to the woman herself and to her family. It is assumed that most of the proposals in chapter 4 for small rural industries would be culturally approved, but certain caste-specific tasks such as leatherworking or fish canning may be unacceptable in some areas for some groups.

4. The motives of the employer must be considered trustworthy. New employment schemes for rural women would best be introduced under the auspices of an already known and trusted community group or institution, such as an integrated rural development scheme. The cooperative nature of the venture must be fully understood. To this end, villagers should be incorporated into the planning process from the beginning.

5. Major time-consuming domestic chores can be reduced. It could be argued that when women have no opportunity to earn income their household tasks expand to fill the time available. This is not intended to belittle the arduous nature of their work, but only to suggest that women might well shift their priorities if new opportunities for earning a direct cash income were introduced. Most families can absorb some cutbacks and make adjustments in the division of labor by age and sex to accommodate women's work outside the home. In addition, the introduction of recommended labor-saving technology, such as oil presses, prepared foods, or centralized grain processing, can free women to use their time in more productive ways. Women are more likely to adopt the new technology if more productive and status-maintaining alternatives are available. Without new alternatives, women may resist rather than seek displacement from their former tasks.

6. Children can receive proper care. Child-care facilities at the place of work will permit young married women to keep their children nearby and to breast-feed infants, an important nutritional advantage. Child care may also be required so that unmarried girls, who otherwise look after their younger siblings, can be employed.

7. Hours and days of work can be somewhat flexible, where necessary, to accommodate demands for seasonal agricultural labor. It is an open question as to the extent to which the new employment should compete, rather than integrate, with current patterns of agricultural labor among women. Some forms of industrial production will require year-round operation, whereas others are more adaptable. Decisions on flexibility of employment should be geared to the conditions of each village. If a severe labor shortage during planting or

harvesting seasons threatens to interfere with agricultural productivity, then it may be necessary to close the industry for several weeks. But if seasonal demands for female agricultural labor are not compelling, then the industry should probably remain in operation year-round. Indeed, removing some young women from the agricultural labor force will often improve the bargaining power over wages of those remaining.

The tension between the incentives and obstacles to working outside the home shapes the characteristics of women drawn into the rural labor force. In India, Bangladesh, Pakistan, and Nepal these workers include women who are experiencing the most intense economic need (women in families of landless laborers; the unskilled and illiterate; groups discriminated against by the dominant society, such as tribals, scheduled castes, and the Muslim minority in Hindu areas); women who are most free of the restrictions of purdah (religious minorities, scheduled-caste Hindus, and low-caste Muslims); and those with fewest domestic responsibilities (frequently also the poorest segments of the population, such as women in families of landless laborers without their own crops to process). Within each of these groups one generally finds an overrepresentation of destitute widows without families to support them who are simultaneously freer from the restrictions of purdah and relatively free of domestic responsibilities. Two canning factories near Peshawar in Pakistan, each with several hundred women workers in the busiest seasons, employ mostly widows or older married women. Unmarried girls are also overrepresented in some employment schemes. Most of the tribal girls working in the papad center at Vedchhi are unmarried, as are the young Muslim women at the People's Health Center in Savar, Bangladesh; predominantly scheduled-caste Hindu volunteers for the rural women's training program of the Nepal Women's Organization at Jawalakhel, Kathmandu; and recruits for the garment-making factory in the village of Salah-el-Din, Egypt (despite the organizer's interest in recruiting young married women).

A combination of natural forces and deliberate policy would suggest that unmarried girls and, to a lesser extent, young married women with one or two children could be induced (if they are not already compelled) to take up employment in small rural industries, which would simultaneously expose them to new ways of looking at themselves, their role in the family, and their role in the community. These young women are most likely to be drawn from the poorest segments of the population, from groups of low ritual status in the caste hierarchy (both Hindu and Muslim), and from religious minorities.

The naturally preselected economic homogeneity of the group is particularly helpful in avoiding the tendency for privileged members of the community to accrue most of the benefits of the new enterprise for themselves, a phenomenon characteristic of programs, such as agricultural cooperatives, that include members with landholdings of widely divergent size. As Béteille (1974, page 70) remarks of agrarian societies placing a high value on hereditary privilege, ". . . Reforms directed towards greater equalization confront a number of challenging problems. Those who seek to implement such reforms find it particularly difficult to bypass the groups at the top and to reach down to those for whose benefit the reforms are primarily designed. In the absence of countervailing forces the privileged themselves become the principal beneficiaries of every type of innovation." If women from the landless classes are most likely to be attracted to employment opportunities, a factor that would frequently discourage higher-status women from participating, then the chances are reduced of creating cooperatives that structurally reflect or exacerbate, rather than challenge, prevailing class distinctions within the community. In chapter 6 it will be argued that a policy of class homogeneity should be deliberately pursued in order to concentrate benefits in the hands of the most exploited groups. Economic homogeneity builds on common experiences and aspirations to form a more cohesive group, while simultaneously encouraging the full development of the talents of all participants through on-the-job training.

6

THE SOCIAL STRUCTURE OF THE
WORKPLACE

This chapter addresses three issues relating to the structure and functioning of small-scale rural industries for women. Can cooperative work groups be recruited from towns and villages marked by class, caste, religious, kinship, and political divisions? Is the cooperative form of organization appropriate, and, if so, how should it be structured? What types of vocational and managerial training can be designed for rural industries drawing workers primarily from illiterate and economically deprived segments of the population?

The question of cooperation among women generally unused to working together in a group that transcends the boundaries of the immediate or extended family relates to the balance of incentives and disincentives for female employment discussed in chapter 5. I contend that it is possible to build successfully on the natural inclination of certain types of women to seek employment in the new industries and that the self-selected economic and religious homogeneity of the group can facilitate a spirit of cooperation based on shared interests. Indeed, one method of overcoming mutual suspicion would be to recruit workers largely from existing social networks of women who have already built a sense of trust and cooperation through informal exchanges of information and services. But cooperation does not come easily; there must be visible benefits accruing to the group before women and their families can be convinced not to take advantage of one another for personal gain.

Whether a producers' cooperative is the most appropriate organizational structure depends on the nature of the current or proposed economic activity in which women engage. Jain suggests that the Indian government's policy on cooperatives has been misplaced in that it emphasizes the setting up of cooperatives before enlisting support for them and finding membership. "Unless we shed ourselves of this misconstruction of the basic principles of cooperation," she remarks, "we will always be burdened with cooperatives that do not function or cooperative societies which are nothing more than Government departments . . ." (Jain, 1976, page 2).

The organizing strategy should instead begin with identifying the basic economic activities of the group to be assisted in a particular area, then deciding what kind of institutional arrangement would help the group best (for example, trade associations, unions, and so forth), and only then deciding whether the people should be organized into a cooperative (Jain, 1976, page 3). The strategy she proposes is people-oriented rather than product-oriented or structure-oriented, with products and structures evolving naturally out of people's goals and interests. In this chapter I will discuss some of the structural aspects of producers' cooperatives, such as membership obligations, decision-making processes, and the formation of producers' networks, occurring in situations where cooperatives appear to offer a promising organizational base for industrial production.

Vocational and managerial training for workers and staff forms the third major issue. In most cases training will have to begin with teaching basic functional literacy in conjunction with production and administrative skills. A strong argument is made for training young village women in techniques of self-management rather than relying on outsiders for managing and staffing their enterprises. This spirit of self-reliance forms the core of the entire approach to promoting rural development, raising the status of women, and creating conditions favorable to delayed marriage and fewer births through female employment.

CREATING A COOPERATIVE ETHIC

Economic development, according to Hirschman (1958, pages 11–20), is impeded by two contrasting images of change that are common to static societies with scarce material resources. The "group-focused" image discourages or penalizes individual initiative in a society that is communal, cooperative, and cohesive. Change is feared if it will alter people's relations with one another. The "ego-focused" image values individual advancement while recognizing that the community as a whole, which is loosely integrated, cannot improve its lot. As Hirschman (1958, page 6) perceives it, success in this system is seen "not as a result of the systematic application of effort and energy, combined perhaps with a little bit of luck, but as due either to sheer luck or to the outwitting of others through careful scheming." Whereas the former image impedes the more dynamic and individualistic patterns of change, the latter impedes cooperative action in its adherence to the principle that, in any agreement, one party must always profit at the expense of the other. No one is to be trusted outside the inner family circle, not even one's neighbors. Consider this paraphrase of an Indian villager's world view, as reported by Wiser and Wiser (1971):

> We do not trust the outside world, and we are suspicious of each other. Our lives are oppressed by mean fears. We fear the rent collector, we fear the police watchman, we fear everyone who looks as though he might claim some authority over us; we fear our creditors, we fear our patrons, we fear too much rain, we fear locusts, we fear thieves, we fear the evil spirits which threaten our children and our animals, and we fear the strength of our neighbor. Do you wonder that we unite the strength of brothers and sons? [page 122]

One question to be raised in this chapter is whether a women's cooperative can successfully challenge strong kinship loyalties, factionalism within the village, the monopoly of traditional class elites, and religious and caste prejudices. The question becomes particularly relevant because these four categories of social stratification are hereditary and cumulative rather than fluid and transversal. Would it be possible to create new bonds of solidarity in the work group that will compete with traditional loyalties and put to rest old fears?

Let us begin with the question of loyalty to the extended family. In chapter 5 I noted Banfield's analysis of the ethos of amoral familism underlying the inability of southern Italian villagers in nuclear households to act together for their common good or for any end transcending the immediate material interests of the nuclear family. Banfield (1958, pages 143–144) argues that northern Italian peasants were more willing than southerners to participate in farmers' associations and cooperatives because of their experience in working together cooperatively within extended families under the authority of the eldest male. The contrast in the prevalent family forms of north and south was traced to land tenure conditions and their resulting insecurities.

The notion of amoral familism can be applied to the extended family system, however, if we suggest that a commitment to group action will be difficult to maintain in a society in which the major organizing principle and set of loyalties center on extended kinship relations. Not only the immediate material interests, but the relative status and honor of the family within the community, are at issue in this case. Nepotism pervades government, business, and industry; why should it not also pervade village institutions? A man would not dream of testifying in a court of law against his cousin accused of bribery, for example, even if the charges were known to be true. For how could such a man arrange a good match for his daughter once his disloyalty to his own relatives became known?

Who would marry into such a family? Clearly, there will be instances in which cooperative principles are sacrificed to family concerns.

Factionalism within the community—what Hunter (1969, page 61) terms that "curse to village life"—poses a second problem. Can women drawn from families competing for power and material resources be expected to work together, or will they carry their husbands' and brothers' arguments into the workplace with them? Factions are characterized by patronage and cohesiveness within groups and conflict among them. Must women be chosen from one side or the other?

The third question is whether a women's cooperative can resist the tendency for the traditional elite to monopolize the benefits of social change. Here we refer to the inherent contradiction between the concept of cooperation within a formal democratic structure and a social hierarchy with its supportive value system based on inherited rights and obligations. According to the UN Research Institute for Social Development (1975, page ix), agricultural cooperatives, as reflections of the prevailing landholding structure, appear far more frequently to have served as a mechanism for further entrenching the elite than for promoting progressive change.

Finally, the question arises as to whether religious and caste distinctions can be overcome within a women's work group. This is particularly relevant in those traditional Hindu communities adhering to strict avoidance rules. The AMUL Dairy and the Vedchhi Intensive Area Scheme in Gujarat both made a deliberate effort to integrate cooperative members from different religions and castes, but their joint participation usually involved little beyond queuing at the collection centers. (The papad cooperative in which women worked together in a center was entirely tribal.) Convinced that caste barriers pose a grave obstacle to the development of community life, the 1972 Aurangabad Experiment among rural workers of Maharashtra State also tried to integrate religions and castes in housing, at meals, and in training programs during their intensive two-week sessions. According to the International Confederation of Free Trade Unions (n.d., page 27), "Without community life there cannot be any joint effort by all the villagers in cooperative and collective work. Community life is a prerequisite for the social transformation of the rural society of India."

The general conclusion drawn by most observers is that class homogeneity, and probably also religious and caste homogeneity, are essential for the creation of a viable cooperative group. A UN Research Institute for Social Development survey (1975, page 17) of forty agricultural cooperatives found that "in communities with a more flexible socioeconomic structure and in cooperatives with a more homogeneous membership, there was greater effectiveness in introducing technical changes, and the cooperatives were also better able to create a cohesive group oriented to local improvement." Those conflicts that did persist were based on kinship, not on class or caste. In contrast, the survey noted (page 105), "Heterogeneity of membership may mean not only the existence of divisive forces, group barriers, and divergent interests, but also the absence of democracy and equality within the rural cooperative. This is especially the case where some members are dependent upon other members in their daily lives outside the cooperative. Béteille, too, suggests that the effectiveness of a separate panchayat of Harijans (outcastes) in a Brahmin-dominated Indian village followed from its social homogeneity and the pervasive nature of the moral bonds that united its members (Hunter, 1969, page 63).

The experience with women's cooperatives in South Asia appears to bear out these assertions. Organizers of the Bangladesh Rural Advancement Committee (BRAC) report that egalitarian cooperatives were much easier to create in economically homogeneous villages of the Sulla area in Bangladesh than in more stratified villages; within communities, women were more effectively organized when they came from similar occupational backgrounds—for example, wives of fishermen or landless peasants—than from mixed groups.[1] Religious homogeneity was also important. Hindu and Muslim women did not generally believe that they shared common interests. Most of BRAC's women's literacy groups reflected the natural spatial segregation of Hindus and Muslims in their own territory of each mixed village.

The experience of a number of sika cooperatives in the Jagaroni/Jute Works federation in Bangladesh also supports the desirability of economic homogeneity within work groups.[2] Members of cooperatives that included different social classes tended to elect the highest-status women as their officers, even if they did not trust the women to handle their affairs or represent their interests. Members apparently felt they had no option but to behave in this way because their families depended on the elite for various goods and services. The high-status women, in turn, tended to dominate decision making, to disdain the work of actual handicraft production, and to exploit the members economically and socially. Jain (1976, page 10) concludes from her analysis of the women's cooperative movement in India that "one principle . . . which seems fundamental for a cooperative to be a genuine one is for those members to belong to the same trade

[1] January 1976 interview with Khushi Kabir, Derai Camp, Sulla Project.
[2] January 1976 interview with Sister Michael Francis of the Sisters of the Holy Cross in Dacca.

or class. Self-interest seems the most binding force and therefore there is more democracy within such institutions which are bound by common interests, common caste, and economic background than those institutions which try to represent a locality like a village or a mohalla [neighborhood]." Once homogeneity of class, caste, and religion is established, it may be possible to transcend kinship loyalties and factionalism within the base of common interests.

The idea of perpetuating occupational segregation by class, caste, and religion will undoubtedly raise objections similar to those brought against perpetuating segregation by sex. But the creation of an economically and socially viable enterprise will depend deeply on the ability of the group to work together as a cohesive unit. Homogeneous groups admittedly reflect, rather than challenge, prevailing distinctions, but I would argue that they will ultimately compete more effectively for an equitable share of material and social resources in the community than if low-ranking women were prematurely integrated with higher-ranking women in mixed-status groups. This argument is strengthened by the observation that the most disadvantaged women in the community are most likely to volunteer for the new employment. Segregation, in this case, would exclude higher-status persons rather than the powerless. The material and social benefits of women's producers' cooperatives would thus be concentrated precisely in the hands of those who are most in need of them. There is no reason why several cooperatives—each relatively homogeneous by caste or religion within its own structure—could not coexist in a single village or cluster of villages, as elements in a larger federation.

Encouraging a cooperative ethic can be problematic, even in a relatively homogeneous group. Much depends on the past experience of the women themselves. A group of destitute Muslim women from one village in northern Bangladesh, who were coming together for the first time in functional literacy classes, allegedly made so much noise yelling and arguing on their way to class that the village headman fined them 200 taka ($14) for disturbing the peace after his previous attempt to have the classes canceled had failed.[3] The women—argumentative, envious, and intolerant of one another—had no experience or skills in social interaction within a group. After a year of working together, Sister Bruno reported that they were "less noisy, but no more cooperative or trusting" than they had been at the beginning.

Their mutual distrust may have derived not only from the women's previously restricted social contacts, but also from patterns of private

[3] January 1976 interview with Sister Bruno of the Corpus Christi Mission, Jalchatra, Bangladesh.

ownership characterizing their extended families. Because every item in the bari was individually owned by someone—plants, chickens, and household utensils alike—conflict over inheritance rights gave rise to family dissension. Given the concern with ownership in a context of poverty, it is not surprising that women working together for the first time would be distrustful. In contrast, women of the Garo tribe in the same area worked together easily in cooperatives. With a matrilineal and matrilocal tradition, Garo women frequently farmed their land together as a group and extended their activities into more formal cooperative arrangements quite naturally. Bennett reports that much mutual suspicion existed among the Brahmin and Chetri women in a village near Kathmandu, where a neighbor's unexpected appearance in the family compound would elicit fear of thievery or witchcraft;[4] such women might well resist communal organization and the pooling of money. Yet many of the tribal groups in Nepal, as in Bangladesh, form natural cooperative units.

One method of creating a cohesive work group would be to recruit from existing social networks. Village women's networks of kinship, caste, class, and religion will generally form tightly overlapping, closed circuits in contrast to the more open, fluid networks characteristic of cities (Kerri, 1974, page 11). Informal associations include indigenous savings clubs, visiting patterns centering on the exchange of information and assistance, and other alliances. In Panjgur, Pakistan, for example, women observing purdah are excluded from important public institutions, but they maintain linkages with female friends based on the principle of reciprocity that encompasses "obligations to visit one another's household at frequent intervals, gift exchange on important occasions such as weddings, material aid in the form of goods and services, and long-term support of non-material nature" (Pastner, 1974).

Park and coauthors (1976, page 275) report that the highly successful rural Korean Mothers' Clubs were often founded on traditional women's associations called *kae,* or money clubs, with an established "common experience, collective spirit and achievement of mutual aid." This is a rotating credit association, common to many parts of Asia and Africa, in which each woman contributes a specified amount of money at regular intervals.[5] The accumulated sum is dispersed in whole or in part to each member of the association in turn. The cooperative ethic and leadership training in these clubs formed a natural base on which to build the

---

[4] February 1976 interview with anthropologist Lynn Bennett in Kathmandu.

[5] In Bangladesh they are called *mushti* (Kabir, Abed, and Chen, 1976, p. 15); in Nepal, *dhikuri* (Lohani, 1976, p. 91); in Indonesia, *arisan* (Papanek, 1975, p. 199); in Malaysia, *kutu* (Meng, 1976, p. 85).

Mothers' Club program for the spread of family planning. In fact, according to Park and coauthors (1976), many of the Korean clubs go far beyond family planning to include:

1. Cooperative agricultural projects: fruit and vegetable gardens, greenhouses, small-livestock projects, mulberry plants for silkworms, and pine tree projects.
2. Community construction projects: special buildings for club meetings, weddings, and other village activities; concrete bridges; street pavement; playgrounds; replacement of thatched roofs with tile, and so on.
3. Income-producing projects: cooperative stores, ropemaking and noodle factories, clothes-making in the home, and so forth. [page 278]

In addition, most clubs continue their traditional banking and credit functions.

Papanek (1975, page 199) points out that both the well-structured and the less formal women's associations may sometimes act as "counter-institutions" to the more dominant institutions run by men in many social settings. They may, for example, "provide the anchorage for women newly married into a village, through the solidarities developed in informal neighborhood groups of women . . .; or these associations may be the locus for the actual power exerted by women in societies that give them no overt authority and no public source of power" (Papanek, 1975, page 199; and Nelson, 1974, page 559). As an organizing strategy one might fruitfully identify indigenous social networks of women and recruit members from within these groups. Women could select their own co-workers (of appropriate age) from among relatives and neighbors whom they already trust. These smaller, more cohesive units might later align themselves with others around larger goals. True, many members will be related to one another by blood or marriage, but they will form a naturally integrated base. As one critic of the Western model of cooperation commented, "Why is it that when ten strangers work together it is called a cooperative, but when ten brothers work together it is called nepotism?"[6]

ORGANIZATIONAL STRUCTURE

One cannot propose a single, ideal model of organization for cooperative small industries in the abstract, for each will be tailored to the unique conditions of its village locale. The following discussion outlines several of the issues that typically arise in determining an organizational structure appropriate to the industry.

[6] Reported by Larissa Lomnitz at the June 1976 Wellesley College Conference on Women and Development, Wellesley, Massachusetts.

Size and Membership Criteria

The size of the cooperative depends on its function. Credit and consumers' societies benefit from very large memberships, but producers' societies are naturally restricted by the type of product and the mode of manufacture. Associations of artisans producing at home or of industrial homeworkers in a putting-out system have few limits on their growth except the marketability of their products. The primary village societies affiliated with the AMUL Dairy average several hundred members each; the home-based papad producers' cooperative in Valod includes about four hundred women; the jute-handicrafts cooperatives in Bangladesh usually begin with ten to thirty members, but some have grown to three or four hundred. BRAC's cooperatives for both men and women set a goal of fifteen members as a minimum and one hundred maximum because they are concerned with maintaining face-to-face interaction and facilitating group meetings. For employment in a central workplace, the appropriate size of the producing unit naturally follows from the economies of scale inherent in production. The papad makers in the Golan center number about forty, with future expansion to be located in additional subcenters close to the homes of other tribal girls in the area. The Tibetan carpet factories employ several hundred workers, but these centers go beyond the type of small rural industry generally proposed here; their scale is more appropriate to larger towns and cities.

In general, one could conceive of small rural industries employing from twenty to fifty women. If a market develops for additional output, new centers could be organized in the same or neighboring villages, or a pattern of shift work could be introduced (say, two six-hour shifts from six in the morning to noon, and noon to six in the evening). Or some tasks could be distributed to house-bound women for part-time work, still limiting employment in the center to unmarried and young married women. I would argue that keeping a production unit relatively small not only reduces capital expenditure for buildings and equipment, but also intensifies feelings of solidarity among workers. But there is nothing sacred about smallness per se. Small producers will experience greater difficulty in competing with large industries. A combination of supply-and-demand conditions may well require a larger unit in one location. If so, the opportunity is ideal for maximizing female employment. (Potential labor shortages could be reduced by relaxing the age barriers in order to hire older wives and widows.)

Although criteria for membership in the producers' cooperative should be somewhat flexible, it is important to emphasize the desirability of employing unmarried girls and young married women as a first resort. Government specifications that cooperative membership be limited to men and women eighteen years of age or over should be revised to, say, fourteen years, in order to account for the current and potential employment patterns of younger girls. We have been suggesting that women with three or more children should not be given preference for employment, although workers may decide against a policy of restricting membership in this way. If a woman's allegiance to the work group is to challenge the pronatalist environment of her home, however, it might be appropriate to attach a family-planning condition to her employment in order to stress the contradiction between work and family obligations. Membership among married women could be tied to a promise of spacing early births and to limiting family size to two or three. At the third or fourth pregnancy, then, the woman would have to leave her employment. These qualifications are, of course, based on the premise that the women will have been given instruction regarding contraceptive methods. It might even be feasible to limit employment in some cooperatives entirely to unmarried girls who, upon marriage, would have to leave. Because Hindu girls normally marry outside of their villages, a break with employment would follow naturally. Awareness of this impending cleavage could well induce a girl to try to resist early marriage, especially if she had strong support from her peers and cooperative managers.

Members' Rights and Responsibilities

All employees, with the possible exception of temporary or part-time workers, should become full members of the cooperative with its attendant benefits and obligations. Persons who are not regular workers would be excluded from membership. Many Indian women's cooperatives have a category of member called a "well-wisher" or "sympathizer," usually middle- or upper-class women who wish to be identified with the organization (often as officeholders), who purchase shares, but who do not actively engage in production. They appear mostly on social occasions. This type of membership should be discouraged. The primary obligation of cooperative members is to engage in the daily work of the enterprise, either as producers or as support staff.

All workers would be required to purchase a share in the cooperative as a symbol of their commitment to its ideals and of their economic stake in its success. Naturally, the share size would have to be kept small in order not to exclude any potential members. AMUL Dairy members buy shares of Rs. 5 (55 cents) or Rs. 10 ($1.10) per family; in Rangunia, the IRDP women's agricultural cooperative shares are 10 taka (70 cents).

The value of the share could be contributed through deductions from workers' salaries, with additional shareholdings built up to a specified maximum over several months. All members should also be required to save a fixed percentage of their earnings, say, 10 to 20 percent, in an interest-earning capacity. (Papad makers at Vedchhi save 15 percent.) Shareholdings and savings form a cooperative fund that can be banked in interest-earning accounts or loaned to members. Members may also wish to establish a disability fund, a health insurance plan, or other security schemes.[7] Workers, in turn, receive yearly dividends as part of their membership benefits in proportion to their shareholdings or to their income during the year. Generally, about one-third of cooperative profits are distributed to members in this way, with the balance divided between community projects and business reserves.

Membership meetings should be held frequently, at least once a month, and perhaps once a week in a centrally organized workers' cooperative. (AMUL Dairy cooperative members meet as a group in their village societies once a year only.) Every member has an equal vote regardless of her position in the cooperative or the number of shares she holds. These membership meetings provide a prime opportunity for discussing interpersonal problems that arise at the workplace, proposals for the scheduling of work, ideas for new products, applications from prospective new members, the allocation of cooperative profits to community projects, the division of labor in the workplace, the basis for payment of members (same wages for everyone, differential wages, piecework), and other employment- and community-related issues. They offer a training ground for the development of political skills—members may become managers, and managers may become officeholders in the village panchayats. Weekly meetings also create an ideal audience for talks by community agents on family planning, nutrition, health care, village politics, and other issues. (These meetings are held in addition to the functional literacy classes, which serve as simultaneous consciousness-raising and activating sessions.) Members are also expected to elect a board of directors from among the group. The primary societies of the AMUL Dairy elected nine-, eleven-, or thirteen-member boards depending on their size; cooperatives with less than fifty members might elect five. The workers will also send women away from the village for additional training in production techniques.

The board, along with its elected or hired manager and staff, in turn provides the essential linkages between workers and the local community,

---

[7] According to Sister Bruno of the Corpus Christi Mission, about 250 destitute Muslim women and their children, in Jalchatra in northern Bangladesh, enrolled in a prepaid hospital plan costing 50 paise a week (about 4 cents).

aid agencies, banks, state authorities, suppliers, buyers, secondary societies (federation centers), and other cooperatives. It is primarily responsible for the organization and supervision of day-to-day operations, but it will also make decisions regarding members' requests for loans from cooperative funds, the organization of training programs, and other issues. Great care will have to be taken to ensure that managers are selected not on the basis of their social standing in the community, but on the basis of their motivation, their willingness to travel if necessary, their acceptability to workers and the rest of the community, and their literacy and other relevant skills. Again, class homogeneity among the membership must be emphasized. Extreme inequalities tend to encourage exploitative or corrupt practices among management, such as the misuse of cooperative funds. The UN Research Institute for Social Development (1975, pages 8–9) study of agricultural cooperatives found, for example, that in two cooperatives in Sri Lanka "where land distribution was less unequal and caste influences did not lead to economic controls, the members showed a higher degree of interpersonal trust and the leadership did not engage in corrupt practices such as those found in other Ceylonese and other Asian cooperatives."

Establishing Linkages with Other Cooperatives

The economic importance of developing what Hirschman calls forward and backward linkages in production was touched upon in chapter 4. This chapter is concerned with the organizational importance of establishing vertical and horizontal linkages with other cooperatives and agencies. *Horizontal linkages* are connections with other primary societies performing similar functions; *vertical linkages* are connections with secondary societies acting as federation centers, and with government or other agencies offering services of various kinds.

Most single cooperatives will find it difficult to function alone. In addition, the creation of a single unit requires intensive administrative and training inputs relative to the size of the unit. Per capita investment can be considerably reduced by organizing cooperatives in networks with identical or linked economic functions that are concentrated in one geographic area. The BRAC project in the Sulla area of Bangladesh covers a population of about 120,000 people living in two hundred villages spread over 168 square miles of lowlands (of which 90 percent is flooded during the monsoons).[8] The project area is divided into eleven sectors,

[8]Based on information from the Bangladesh Rural Advancement Committee (1974).

with fifteen to twenty-five villages in each sector. Each sector has an area manager, under the general supervision of an overall field director, to coordinate the activities of four field motivators, each of whom covers about five villages.[9] In addition to the field motivators, who organize community development projects, there are functional literacy teachers, paramedics (one for every five to eight villages), and female family-planning organizers (one in each village). Field motivators and their area manager live in camps close to the villages they serve, but they attend regular meetings at the main camp where the overall field director resides.

Transportation is bound to be a problem in such an extensive area. BRAC's field motivators and paramedics spend a great deal of their time —often five or six hours a day—simply walking from one village to the next. Visits to the main camp for meetings and training sessions are doubly difficult, but essential, if the program is to remain tightly integrated. Transportation between federation headquarters and village societies was also extremely difficult in Rangunia Thana, where administrative boundaries were drawn along rather than across major transportation routes. Representatives from primary societies who were to come into headquarters for training and banking once a week often had to walk long distances across the fields because the roads went in different directions. Clearly, the major communications routes should be taken into account when organizing a network of cooperatives so that each is within relatively easy walking distance from the center. The Jagaroni/Jute Works federation of sika makers found that the long distances between the Dacca headquarters and many of the village societies made supervision of the societies practically impossible and prevented village women from coming regularly to the center for meetings and additional training. (The rapid growth in the number of cooperatives in the federation also posed organizational problems.)

Some of the economic advantages of federation were mentioned in chapter 4. The secondary society can purchase raw materials in bulk, obtain credit, solicit large orders in competition with private industry, distribute orders among the primary societies, introduce strict standardized quality controls, and handle all or part of the pricing and marketing (including export arrangements), among other functions. The Mahila Griha Udyog Lijjat Papad federation centered in Bombay is a case in point. Federation also permits easier arrangements for training and management, reducing the duplication of effort at the local level. The two

---

[9] Field motivators work in agriculture, horticulture, and fisheries, and help organize cooperatives, functional education classes, youth groups, community center construction, health-care, family-planning, and vocational and leadership training programs.

IRDP inspectors of women's cooperatives in Rangunia, for example, attended meetings and helped keep accounts of the five or six groups under their jurisdiction. The Rangunia Thana Central Cooperative Association provided additional services. The more effective among agricultural cooperatives in the UN Research Institute for Social Development (1975, page 17) study were those that "had strong links with outside agencies such as central associations which trained local leaders in adopting new technology, provided credit and other facilities, audited their accounts regularly, and disciplined those responsible for defaults and irregularities."

Small industrial cooperatives are like building blocks. Beginning with a few small local units, the enterprise can be built into a network of integrated mutually supportive production centers around an administrative core. What local decision-making power the primary societies lose by federation (pricing or design, for example) is balanced by the economic and social efficiency of the larger unit—at least up to a limit. Beyond this point one must begin a new federation rather than adding to the original in ways that expand its geographical spread or numbers beyond a manageable sphere.

The Pros and Cons of Government Affiliation

Registration of producers' cooperatives with governments in some states carries a number of advantages such as low interest loans, tax concessions, subsidies of some staff salaries, government purchase of cooperative shares, technical assistance of various kinds, and the right of the cooperative to purchase raw materials from cooperative wholesalers and to sell finished products through government cooperative stores or directly to government buyers (for example, schools or the armed forces).

But government affiliation can also be problematic. For example, centralized administration increases the likelihood that management will be all male, and thus insensitive to the special needs of women producers, and that it will consist of an urban elite insensitive to the needs of rural people. Centralization also produces a top-heavy system of bureaucratic control over local decision making. Standardized policies and operational procedures (membership rules, accounting mechanics, and so forth) fail to account for important variations in organizational structure or membership criteria at the local level. Groups that might function better as loose, informal affiliations are required to adopt an inflexible, formal constitution defining their rights and responsibilities. Registration requirements are also unnecessarily complicated. Procedures need to be

drastically simplified so that illiterate villagers can register their cooperatives without having to pay frequent visits to city offices. Government
field staff should visit villages for these purposes.

In addition, governments sometimes shift their policies toward cooperatives quite abruptly by demanding "impetuous structural changes"
following the findings of cooperative committee or commission investigations (Ahmed, 1973, pages 32–34). Inconsistency can be compounded
by changes of political regime and attempts at political interference and
favoritism in cooperative management.

Governments are sometimes tempted to set unrealistic quantitative
goals for the growth of numbers of cooperatives or numbers of members.
Following heavy floods in 1970–71, the government of Bangladesh, for
example, asked organizers in Rangunia to set up two hundred agricultural cooperatives. The quickly organized units left uneducated members
vulnerable to exploitation by local "touts" who were concerned only with
fattening their pockets and expanding their spheres of influence.[10] As
Ahmed (1973) notes from his experience as registrar of cooperative
societies in the Northwest Frontier Province of Pakistan:

> Cooperatives are first and last people. Care should, therefore, be taken to
> see that the cooperative idea is not imposed from above, but that it is
> genuinely rooted in the hearts and aspirations of the people. True coopera-
> tives can be built up only by the slower process of education helped by
> modern mass media among the masses of the people and not hustled into
> existence by overkeen officials anxious to show results and meet targets
> within a short time. It is no solution for sound cooperative development to
> aim at an official quota of so many societies each year. The problem rests
> in the functioning not the creation of societies. [page 33]

Compulsory or pressured membership negates the basic principle of
voluntary association. In their zeal to organize whole villages into consolidated cooperatives, some government agencies set membership quotas
of a minimum percentage of the population. The Nepalese government,
for example, hopes to include 50 to 75 percent of village household heads
in consolidated rural cooperatives.[11]

Similarly, the promotion of multipurpose, rather than single-purpose,
cooperatives (the latter were disbanded in Nepal) defeats the purpose
of representing particular interest groups. Cooperatives designed to include the majority of villagers in a multipurpose association tend to
become convenient mechanisms for the transmission of government pol-

---

[10] January 1976 interview with David Stockley, agricultural advisor to the Rangunia Thana Central Cooperative Association, Bangladesh.

[11] February 1976 interview with K. P. Manandhar, deputy registrar of cooperatives, Ministry of Land Reform, His Majesty's Government, Kathmandu.

icies rather than alternative structures based on grassroots organization. The new structure inevitably incorporates the social hierarchy of the community and is easily dominated by the powerful and well-to-do.

Government intervention along these lines may also ignore natural bases of social organization within the community. For example, the IRDP wanted to create in Rangunia Thana a single, all-inclusive women's cooperative in each village. Local organizers strongly believe that separate associations for Hindu, Muslim, and Buddhist women were essential.[12]

Under government control, the educational qualifications for managers are frequently set at an unreasonably high level so that most local people, especially women, are excluded from eligibility.[13] In Rangunia the senior woman inspector of cooperatives could not advance any higher in her job because she lacked a secondary-school leaving certificate. Unnecessarily strict government regulations thus block the progress of hard-working local people familiar with community needs and conditions. As a consequence, government employees in cooperative federations (project officers, assistants, accountants, and inspectors) are frequently city-born, city-trained agents with little interest in village life. Carrying no commitment to authentic rural development and demonstrating a disdainful or actively hostile attitude toward villagers, agents prefer to spend their time at headquarters rather than in the field. The low salaries of government agents encourage bribery, cheating, patronage, and subversion of cooperative goals. Illiteracy exposes villagers to manipulation by agents and others in authority. Villagers, in turn, commonly view the educated outsider as a trickster who will use his educational advantage to outwit the innocent.[14] Unfortunately, they are usually right.

Neither organizers nor villagers are induced to promote indigenous leadership or self-reliance. Removing the decision-making power from local members discourages them from active participation in the business affairs of their associations. Members come to identify cooperatives with

[12] January 1976 interview with Joyce Stockley, women's program advisor, Rangunia, Bangladesh.

[13] One rationale for the high qualifications in Bangladesh is to expand employment opportunities for the educated.

[14] In a February 1976 interview conducted in Dacca, Henry Moseley of the Johns Hopkins University pointed out that the theme of cleverness triumphing over simplicity runs through the folk tales in Bengali children's books. Parents frequently fear that their children will become "too smart" if they are sent to school. Banfield (1958, p. 89) discovered a similar theme in southern Italy, quoting a young teacher who was himself of an artisan family, " 'Study and education has helped some people to succeed. It has helped them by giving them an advantage over the ignorant. With their knowledge, they are better able to exploit ignorance. They are able to cheat more dexterously.' "

the interests of the government rather than with their own interests. The resulting apathy or hostility encourages a psychology of dependency and discourages local initiative.

None of these problems is unique to government affiliation, however, for nongovernmental organizations are also vulnerable. Nor are the problems inevitable. Sensitive government policies could maximize state support for rural cooperative industries, while minimizing obstacles such as inflexible bureaucratic administration. Government agents might even be encouraged, in radically revised training procedures, to learn from the people, although such dedication is bound to be difficult to maintain, even among the most committed workers.

TRAINING FOR SELF-MANAGEMENT

Effective training is crucial to developing among village women a new spirit of self-reliance that will derive from, and express itself in, the economic success of their producers' cooperative. Workers should be trained in vocational and managerial skills that will enable them to become self-managing. Indeed, the success of organizers' efforts could well be measured by how completely they are able to withdraw once the new industry shows signs of independence. This is not to suggest that fledgling cooperatives be prematurely abandoned to their own, perhaps inadequate, resources, but only that organizers should make every effort to ensure that cooperatives establish the necessary linkages with other cooperatives, organizations, and government agencies so that village women can turn to indigenous sources for technical assistance, credit, and advice. Some of the most dramatically innovative programs in rural development have collapsed with the death or departure of an extremely dedicated leader because local people were not adequately prepared to carry on the work.

Most training programs for rural women have, unfortunately, not pursued an ideology of self-management or economic self-sufficiency. According to the Committee on the Status of Women in India (1974, page 333), for example, the basic idea of the thousands of village Mahila Mandals (women's groups), organized under the government's Central Social Welfare Board, the Department of Community Development, and by voluntary agencies, "is to create opportunities for rural women *to improve their status as house-wives* and to take part in public affairs" (emphasis added). Toward this end, the Mahila Mandals promote women's programs in nutrition, education, health, mother and child care, home improvement, adult literacy, recreation, cultural activities, and family planning. Programs run by urban, middle-class women's organizations also tend to take on charitable overtones at the expense of a genuine development focus. National organizations, such as India's Grameen Mahila Sangh, the All-Pakistan Women's Association (APWA), the Bangladesh Mahila Samity, and the Nepal Women's Organization (NWO), as well as numerous other women's groups, draw heavily in their leadership from among wives of powerful political and administrative figures (national and local) and in their membership from the educated elite of towns and cities.[15]

Members are not only out of touch with the needs of illiterate rural women, on the whole, but because they are usually matrons in their forties or older, they are also frequently out of touch with the needs of young, educated women of their own class who are seeking personal independence in the avoidance of arranged marriage or the pursuit of a professional career. Defining themselves as enlightened women working for the poor, the groups' programs of uplift generally include literacy classes and training in hygiene, child care, and homemaking. Vocational training emphasizes sewing, embroidery, and other handicrafts that are sold to a relatively small market of upper-class consumers through the organizations' sales outlets.[16] Trainees find themselves dependent on the charity of the elite, who buy their handiwork but do not encourage them to make products with more mass appeal on their own, form into cooperative work groups, or find viable independent sales outlets.

The efforts of the Nepal Women's Organization (n.d., page 1) offer one such example: the group defines its program objectives as (1) the abolition of illiteracy among women; (2) the creation of a "conscious society" by imparting social, economic, and educational consciousness to women; and (3) the inculcation of a spirit of self-reliance among women through improvement in their economic conditions. A model skill-training center in the Bhaktapur District in the rural outskirts of Kathmandu trains about a dozen women at a time in machine sewing in two- to six-month sessions.[17] The trainees (almost all unmarried Newar girls in their late teens or early twenties) come in daily from neighboring villages. While at the center, they work with free fabrics and receive a small salary. But few, if any, can afford to buy a sewing machine of their own once their training is completed, and so they are reduced to handwork which cannot

---

[15] For a discussion of the evolution of women's groups in Pakistan and Bangladesh, see Jahan (1975, pp. 21–28).

[16] APWA, for example, runs approximately 3,000 industrial homes that train women in embroidery, sewing, knitting, mirror work on cloth, woodworking, leatherworking, and weaving. The women work at home following their training period and sell their crafts through APWA shops in the cities (Helbock, 1975a, p. 41).

[17] February 1976 interview with Meera Bhattarai, of the skills development program of NWO, Kathmandu.

possibly compete on the local market. The Bhaktapur center runs a shop in the main temple square that sells some of their crafts, but the women lack the organizational skills necessary to teach others or to form co-operative work groups to buy machines. As a consequence, most of their intensive training goes to waste.

Dissipation of scarce training resources, due to the inappropriate nature of the training itself or to lack of follow-up action, plagues a number of programs. The consequences are particularly disillusioning to women who invested their energies and risked some social disapproval only to find their hopes dashed. In the next section I will propose a procedure for ensuring that village women acquire managerial and vocational skills which they, in turn, will pass on to others within a structured organizational framework. The focus is specifically group-oriented, rather than individual-oriented, in order to create a basis for cooperative production rather than more risky self-employment.

Training Workers at the Village Level

The first requisite is functional education. Most rural female recruits from the economic strata we have been discussing will be illiterate. In Nepal, in 1970, only 2.6 percent of all women (rural and urban) fifteen years of age and over could read and write. In Pakistan (including Bangladesh), in 1971–72, only 8.7 percent of all women, and 3.3 percent of rural women, were literate (Helbock, 1975a, page 22). In India, in 1971, 18.7 percent of females aged five and over were literate, while only 13.2 percent were so in rural areas (Committee on the Status of Women in India, 1974, page 31). Although teenage girls are two or three times more likely to be literate than are older women (9.0 percent of rural girls aged fifteen through nineteen in Pakistan in 1971–72, for example, as compared with 3.3 percent of females of all ages), it would not be surprising to find a village or town in which none of the women who volunteer for employment know how to read, write, or perform simple arithmetic. The Women's Affairs Training and Extension Centre in Jawalakhel, Kathmandu, found that many young women, recruited from remote villages for training as rural workers, could not read simple written instructions, write notes, or measure cloth for fitting patterns. Basic literacy skills had to be taught in conjunction with the substantive training materials.

On-the-job literacy training of the type discussed in chapter 2 is essential. Teachers could be recruited from among local women with some schooling to hold short classes every day, with lessons and discussions clearly related to everyday issues encountered in the workplace, the family, and the community.[18] These lessons offer an ideal forum for introducing materials in health, nutrition, child care, money management, and family planning as well as for stimulating critical discussions of attitudes and practices relating to women's social, economic, and political roles. Political skills of debate, analysis, and decision making can be developed in the literacy classes, as well as in regular membership meetings in which matters pertaining to the cooperative are decided.

Workers, of course, also require training in production techniques. Some are relatively simple and build on skills the women may already possess, such as sun-drying fruit and vegetables, grinding spices, pressing oil, or other types of food processing or handicrafts. The Hindu and Muslim women of Valod already knew how to make papads, for example, although they were instructed carefully in the standards expected of home production; and the tribal women of Golan were taught how to roll papads and worked in a center under supervision. Other skills are far more complex: garment making, including measuring cloth, cutting patterns, assembly, detailed sewing and finishing; assembly and finishing of light manufactured goods; and the more complex techniques required for food processing such as canning or bottling, and so on. For training in relatively simple or standard techniques of production, the cooperative can send two or three trainees to a training center or to another cooperative. Jute handicrafts cooperatives in Bangladesh send women to the Jagaroni training center in Dacca or to one of the primary societies in Dacca (Sri Joni) to learn specific patterns for weaving sikas, skills which the trainees in turn teach their co-workers. For more complex or varied production techniques, on-the-job training of all workers will probably be required. Specialists may have to spend three to six months in the village, training women in proper manufacturing procedures. After each woman is trained in at least one aspect of the work, job rotation should be encouraged in order to expand the range of skills among all workers, to encourage flexibility of work organization, and to reduce the possibility of boredom. Job rotation also offers the workers themselves the opportunity to teach others the skills they have learned and to train new recruits without having to depend on outsiders. Frequent in-service training may be necessary to maintain high levels of quality control or to introduce new techniques or products.

---

[18] Teachers do not need to be highly educated. BRAC found that women with five or six years of schooling could teach others with the aid of their programmed visual aids.

Local Managers and Staff

The managing board of the cooperative is elected by its members and includes production workers. Staff with specialized functions (bookkeepers, designers, technicians) may have to be hired from outside. Where possible, however, both managers and staff should be young, local women drawn from the same socioeconomic sector as the majority of workers. Younger women are more likely than older women to be literate, idealistic, and innovative. Local women are more likely to be familiar with the needs and interests of villagers than are women brought in from the outside who, in any case, will find it difficult to leave the relative comforts of the city to work in a smaller town or village. Managers and staff drawn from the same socioeconomic sector as the majority of the workers are likely to be more accountable in their actions than those drawn from higher-status groups who can more easily manipulate illiterate workers or misappropriate cooperative funds without fear of reprisal. Recall that members of the one all-female milk cooperative affiliated with the AMUL Dairy in Gujarat were so fearful of the possible repercussions of firing two male staff members whom they accused of holding back milk payments that they began selling their milk in a neighboring village rather than facing the issue directly. On-the-job training of managers and staff, although it is a slow and painstaking process, might help to avoid some of these problems.

It is important to stress that board members and staff may not have to be literate at the outset for effective functioning on the job. The women need to *become* literate if they are to participate actively in business decisions and to protect themselves from unscrupulous suppliers, moneylenders, and others. But enthusiasm, commitment, willingness to learn, and the confidence of their co-workers are probably far more important attributes of good managers than are the number of years of formal schooling. Hard-working local women can learn to be "barefoot managers" in some enterprises in much the same way as men and women with little schooling have become barefoot doctors in China.[19] They need a range of tools such as simplified forms of pictorial bookkeeping for keeping accounts of the number of hours worked by each woman or of stockpiled products. Illiterate village midwives in the Mahtlab area of Bangladesh, for example, have learned to keep detailed records of births, deaths, and movements in and out of the village on the basis of daily house-to-house visits.

[19] I am indebted to K. B. Kothari of CARE in New Delhi for the concept of barefoot managers.

One of the major advantages of federation is that many managerial and technical functions can be concentrated at the secondary level in order to reduce the duplication of effort at the primary level. Part or all of the purchasing of raw materials, allocation of orders, quality-control inspection, marketing, and record keeping is carried on in federation headquarters which are, ideally, easily accessible to the primary working centers. If the federation is headquartered in a market town, natural transportation routes ease the movement of people and goods between headquarters and the surrounding network of village production centers. In addition, the town is more likely to contain women with higher educational qualifications for administrative work.

If administrative functions are to be centralized in this way, it becomes necessary to choose secondary-level managers who are sensitive to the needs of rural women workers. In its search for a woman worker who could act as intermediary between Dacca headquarters and the village societies producing jute sikas, the Jagaroni/Jute Works federation stressed the importance of finding someone who was interested in learning *from* the villagers rather than simply carrying strict ideas of formal cooperative procedures or rigid production techniques *to* the villagers as an agent of the central office. Indeed, the importance of maintaining frequent exchanges between rural producers and the federation center, as well as among rural producing units, cannot be stressed too much. Not only should the secondary level be staffed with people eager and willing to travel to the village sites, but village managers and workers should, if possible, meet regularly at the center. In this way, relatively isolated rural producers can learn from one another's experiences, as well as from training agents.

At the same time, social meetings offer social recognition for women who may be considered deviant in their own villages. One is reminded of Medina, the young Muslim cooperative inspector in Rangunia, who was criticized by more conservative members of the community for remaining unmarried and walking about with an uncovered face in the course of her work. If young women are expected to challenge conventional notions of appropriate female behavior, they will need strong social support.

The shortage of trained personnel in low- and middle-level business management runs as a theme through virtually every report on programs designed to promote small-scale rural or urban industry in developing countries. If there are few men trained in efficient business practices, there are even fewer women. In South Asia the problem becomes even more acute because, with some important exceptions, women are rarely found in the marketplace either as buyers or as sellers. The 1971 census of India counted only 500,000 women engaged in trade and commerce out of a total female population of 264 million (Committee on the Status of Women in India, 1974, page 158). Fewer women engage in trade or commerce in northern India, Pakistan, and Bangladesh than in southern India (Boserup, 1970, page 89). In any case, few women will come into the new rural industries with practical experience in business management.

It is not possible here to suggest a recipe for training that will cater to all occasions. As for the workers themselves, the requirements for training of managers and staff depend in large part on the type of industry. The AMUL Dairy sends potential leaders from new villages for one month's training at the dairy and at one of the primary societies. The training process is simplified by the standardized organizational structures and operating procedures, requiring only that an existing village model be duplicated elsewhere, and the new cooperative society receives a great deal of financial, technical, and managerial aid from the cooperative federation. The Rangunia women's cooperatives send managers for training in both agricultural techniques and cooperative principles to the BARD at Comilla. In Pakistan, employees of primary cooperative societies (secretaries, managers, accountants, and clerks), along with employees of Cooperative Departments (assistant registrars, inspectors), are trained at the Cooperative Training College in Lyallpur, in principles of bookkeeping, auditing, business management, and community development. The Pakistan Academy of Rural Development at Peshawar, along with smaller institutes in other provinces, also offers special courses (Ahmed, 1973, page 36). Training courses are also offered by independent development programs such as BRAC, by women's organizations (the NWO runs four regional training centers for rural women), by colleges, voluntary organizations, and other agencies.

India's Small-Scale Industry Development Organization of the Ministry of Industrial Development, Science, and Technology has been cited, along with a pilot Rural Industries Projects Program, as a model for training employees and employers in a wide range of small industries through an extensive network of institutes and extension centers.[20] The centers provide such services as improving product design, assessing industrial opportunities and markets, and advising on project feasibility for financial assistance, and they carry on special programs to "(1) facilitate the manufacture of parts and components by small-scale industry for larger industrial establishments, (2) qualify small firms for government contracts, (3) secure a more equitable allocation of scarce raw materials

---

[20] The following discussion is drawn from Coombs and Ahmed (1974, pp. 49–65 and pp. 137–155). They, in turn, draw on deWilde (1972).

for small businesses, and (4) promote small-scale industrial exports" (Coombs and Ahmed, 1974, page 59).

The Rural Industries Projects Program, designed in part to compensate for the urban bias of the first program, established training courses of one year's duration in centers with facilities for machining and welding, carpentry, tanning, textile dyeing, wool carding, milk chilling, fruit preservation, pottery making, and other skills (Coombs and Ahmed, 1974, page 61). After its initial success, however, the program began to suffer from high costs and inadequate funding, as well as from the trainees' reluctance to spend a year away from home in learning new skills. Indian government agencies offering technical assistance in purchasing raw materials, marketing, finance, and design include the All-India Handicrafts Board, the All-India Handloom Board, the Khadi and Village Industry Commission, the Coir Board, the Silk Board, and state industry and cooperative departments. Cooperative unions at the state level and the National Cooperative Union of India offer classes for managers and members in cooperative organization but not in technical skills (Beniwal, 1976, page 34).

With the exception of women's organizations, few of the sources mentioned above offer training programs specifically for women. In some cases it makes sense to integrate women into current training and assistance programs offered by government departments or ministries of cooperatives, handicrafts, small industries, education, agriculture, or rural development; in other cases special programs catering to the specific needs of rural women will have to be designed. The Jagaroni/Jute Works federation, for example, persuaded the BARD at Comilla to offer accounting classes for their female cooperative managers. Delegates to the All-India Conference on Women and Cooperatives in New Delhi recommended that women's sections be established in the cooperative departments in all states headed by an officer of at least joint registrar level; that special schemes be drawn up to organize women's industrial cooperatives in areas with a concentration of "economically backward" sections of the community; and that the number of women cooperative inspectors and industrial instructors be greatly expanded.[21]

Special Problems of Female Organizers and Members

Given the cultural restrictions on women's freedom of movement so prevalent in Muslim and Hindu societies, it is natural that special problems

[21] See the National Cooperative Union of India (1976a, pp. 11–12). For additional suggestions for central and local governments and private institutions, see Zeidenstein and Zeidenstein (1974, pp. 19–23).

will arise in connection with training women workers and supervising women's industries. The BRAC program for rural development in the Sulla villages of Bangladesh offers a good example. Until recently, BRAC had no full-time female program personnel, even though they were actively promoting rural women's agricultural cooperatives and had set up a number of literacy classes for females and recruited village women to work as female family-planning motivators. One problem was that female staff had to live in all-male camps. To try to overcome some of the housing and social obstacles that impeded the recruitment of full-time female organizers, BRAC decided to set up a separate area camp run entirely by women (Kabir, Abed, and Chen, 1976, appendix A, page 5). The camp opened in the spring of 1976 with a female area manager and three field motivators (two local and one outsider). The staff will carry out ongoing women's activities in functional education, health, family planning, and cooperatives; experiment with potential economic activities for women such as poultry and duck farming, food processing, intensified horticulture, and crafts; and train prospective female leadership from other areas.

BRAC's experiment is still in its infancy. But the story highlights a number of problems facing women who take an active public role in culturally conservative settings. The first is physical mobility. How are women to move about? BRAC's field motivators, for example, are each responsible for visiting five villages regularly, most of them several miles distance from the camp. It is considered unseemly for a woman to walk alone, and riding a bicycle or scooter—even if it were feasible to do so over the rutted mud paths along the dikes at the edge of the rice fields—is out of the question. Formerly, a single female would have to find a male staff member to accompany her; now, with four field motivators living together, the women can walk their rounds in twos or threes. For traveling longer distances, however, or for sending female staff to towns or cities for training, the projects must provide transportation allowances for hiring cycle or scooter rickshaws or send the women in small groups (perhaps even with a chaperon) to protect them from physical or verbal abuse on public conveyances. As time wears on, the extra precautions may well prove unnecessary, but at the beginning, they could spell the difference between confidence and fear.

Housing is another critical issue. With an all-female camp BRAC can now house the women together, but since there is no place for them to stay overnight in the villages their trips must be timed for return before nightfall. Housing was also a problem for the women workers trained at the Women's Affairs Training and Extension Centre in Jawalakhel, Nepal. They were expected to move in pairs from village to village every three months, organizing rural women in literacy, child-care, nutrition, kitchen-gardening, and crafts classes.[22] Wherever women are sent away from their families, housing becomes a dilemma. Whereas a man could lodge with a family overnight or in a hostel without question, a single woman experiences real hardship if she is posted at a location far from her natal village. For example, the chief women workers in the Jawalakhel program, who are sent to rural districts for two- to four-year stints, are usually fearful of leaving the security of their district headquarters for inspection tours of the village programs. Training local women for work in their own areas is one solution to this problem. But even then, it is essential that safe living quarters be provided in villages (preferably at the workplace) for female trainers and inspectors sent to rural areas, and in towns for village women sent for training. Where women's programs are integrated with men's programs they will need separate office space and a place to hold meetings so that the women will not be interrupted by curious male onlookers.

Considering the social and physical difficulties that women workers—and especially the young and unmarried—are likely to face, the need for providing strong social and economic support becomes all the more compelling. We touched on the question of social support earlier in this chapter in the discussions of creating cooperative work groups and establishing linkages with other cooperatives. Sending women to training sessions or on inspection tours in groups of two or three rather than singly also helps to strengthen mutual social support as well as to spread skills, as does the delegation of authority in decision making. But women willing to risk some social ostracism and the physical discomfort connected with travel should also be compensated with adequate financial rewards. This is where women's programs often fall short, even in the context of low pay scales for government workers as a whole. The women workers of Nepal, for example, were posted to rural districts by the government after a year's training at Jawalakhel at a pay scale of Rs. 140 ($11) a month. The chief women workers in a supervisory capacity earned Rs. 210 ($17) a month, and the volunteers—mostly illiterate young women from remote villages, trained for three months at Jawalakhel to help the women workers—were expected to work for nothing. In view of their many problems, it is not surprising that trained and experienced workers were dropping out of the program in considerable numbers.

[22] Information on the Women's Affairs Training and Extension Centre at Jawalakhel was obtained from a report by Padma Shrestha, acting principal in 1976, from an interview with Linley Boulden of UNICEF in Kathmandu, and from my visit to the center in March 1976.

CONCLUSIONS

The central theme of this chapter is the importance of building on indigenous social relationships in order to create a cooperative work group,
a viable organizational structure, and appropriate training in productive
and administrative skills. I have emphasized the need to build from the
ground up so that the new small industries can become self-sustaining.
Developing local leadership and local training processes is the key to in-
stilling a spirit of self-reliance among women workers which should, in
turn, manifest itself in changing roles in the family and in the community.

The willingness of women to work together as a cooperative production unit will depend in part on whether they share common concerns;
shared interests, in turn, depend in part on the socioeconomic homogeneity of the group. The experience of a number of producers' cooperatives (both agricultural and nonagricultural) points to the conclusion
that class homogeneity, and probably also religious and caste homogeneity, is a necessary condition for transcending family loyalties and
factional splits within the work group as well as for avoiding social and
economic control by higher-status members. Rather than trying to draw
workers from diverse socioeconomic backgrounds within the community,
then, the new industries might better recruit from the most "disadvantaged" religious and economic minorities. Existing informal associations
such as savings clubs, labor exchanges, or visiting networks could offer
a natural base on which to build a more formal cooperative structure with
democratic decision making in the workplace. Women's associations
could well form counterinstitutions to the major community associations
dominated by men.

We have argued that organizational structure should evolve from the
needs and interests of the people themselves and from the nature of the
economic activity to be organized. The Rajasthani women who pull heavy
wooden carts through the streets of Ahmedabad clearly face different
problems and have different organizational needs than the Garo tribeswomen of Bengal who plant market gardens communally or the Muslims
in a Punjabi village who embroider dresses and tapestries. Organizational
structure needs to remain flexible in order to account for socioeconomic
conditions unique to each locale. As a consequence, the question of government registration as a formal cooperative should be carefully considered for its potential benefits and drawbacks.

Some general guidelines could nevertheless be offered, each relating to
the desirability of involving workers in decisions about their own lives.
These include the members' obligations to purchase shares or contribute
dues, however small, to the capital fund of their organization and to meet

regularly as a group to decide policy, elect a board of directors, and make other decisions of direct concern. Guidelines include, too, the importance of establishing strong linkages with public and private institutions offering support services, with other primary societies engaged in similar types of production, and with secondary-level societies. Indeed, frequent contact among primary societies and between the societies and their federation headquarters appears to be essential for ensuring democratic operating procedures and mutual social support, as well as for economic reasons. The early success of the BARD Comilla farmers' cooperatives in Bangladesh, for example, has been attributed partly to the coordination of development efforts in villages within a seven-to-eight-mile radius of one another which permitted face-to-face management (Hunter, 1969, page 179). In addition, Comilla stressed four vital principles of organization: frequent meetings of all the cooperatives' members, young and energetic managers chosen for their skills and commitment, regular training of workers and of managers who came to the center once a week, and a concern for members' families and communities, not just the farmers themselves.

Training for self-management upgrades the talents of rural women through basic functional education in literacy, arithmetic, production techniques, marketing, and administrative skills, among others. Young girls already facile in weaving rush mats for the family's own use can extend their skills to more complex products and designs; illiterate women can learn to keep simple accounts and become barefoot managers selected from the ranks of workers; and agents can be sent from government or private institutions to offer on-the-job training, or workers and managers can be sent in small groups to cooperative headquarters or development centers for training. Wherever possible, young local women should be selected for management training, not only to promote local talent but to avoid the problems of importing and keeping female staff from outside the area.

Young women willing to take on new leadership roles in the community are bound to risk social ostracism for themselves and their families. Many will already be considered deviant because their parents sent them to schools where almost all of their classmates were boys, or because at age sixteen or eighteen they are still unmarried in a society that marries off girls as soon after puberty as possible. Some will already have taken on unusual economic roles, perhaps attempting to support themselves in a community offering few economic options for women. It is on these young risk-takers that the major burden of innovation falls, the burden of breaking through prevailing modes of thought that see either individual advancement or cooperative effort as impossible.

No recipe can ensure success. Although the availability of adequate funding, of raw materials, and of assured markets will smooth the way, an enterprise may still not catch hold, or, once established, may subsequently flounder. Organizers with years of field experience find it difficult to predict which of their projects will flourish, for much appears to depend on conditions unique to each place: the mix of personalities, the nature of group interaction, the personal histories of villagers, and the experiences common to their community.

7

POLICY CONCLUSIONS

Although women "hold up half the sky," as the Chinese saying goes, until recently they have remained invisible in most development plans. True, much of the neglect has been benign rather than hostile, but the consequences are similar, no matter what their cause. The participation of rural women in agricultural production, crop processing, petty trading, handicrafts and other nonagricultural production, marketing, other services, and domestic work has been underestimated, undercounted, and undervalued, not only by planning agencies but also by rural men and women themselves. Although women's role in caring for their families has received more recognition and support, many programs aimed specifically at improving the situation of women and children in developing countries have either distorted this role by offering inappropriate training, or overemphasized it at the expense of ignoring women's needs in other activities such as subsistence farming. Where programs have addressed women's productive capacity at all, they have tended to incorporate a welfare bias rather than promoting genuine opportunities for economic independence. As a consequence, rural women in many developing countries find themselves bypassed by the social and economic advantages accruing to men. The former director of the Bangladesh Academy for Rural Development (BARD) in Comilla, Akhter Hameed Khan, has characterized the rural women of Bangladesh as "frogs in a well" who, from the darkness, are able to see only a small circle of light.

Why have women been so ignored by development planners in the past? At least four factors contribute to their neglect:

1. Male dominance in decision making in international and national planning agencies, as well as the underrepresentation or nonrepresentation of women on these bodies
2. The "invisibility" of rural women's productive activities because of their concentration in the informal sectors of the economy, in subsistence agriculture, and in the home
3. The primitive state of technology used by women in domestic work and agriculture which requires solutions in small-scale and inter-

mediate technology rather than the grand schemes so favored by planners

4. The powerlessness of the women themselves, deriving both from their lack of economic leverage and from cultural restrictions that severely limit their ability to press for policy changes on their own behalf (Fageley, 1976, pages 12–13).

In addition, decision makers are beset with myths about women's roles that may blind them to certain policy options (Germain, 1975, pages 165–169; and Kabir, Abed, and Chen, 1976, pages 3–12). Among these are the idea that promoting feminist ideas of autonomy or liberation in other cultures is necessarily a form of Western cultural imperialism; the fear that strengthening women's economic and social position outside the home will undermine the harmony of the family;[1] the myth that employing women will necessarily exacerbate unemployment among men; and the conviction either that development problems must be solved first before attention can be paid to the less compelling issue of reducing inequalities between the sexes, or that most forms of social and economic development benefit everyone so there is no need to design programs for women only.

This latter belief resembles the beloved "trickle-down" theory of economic development and technological change, that is, start innovations at the top, and everyone will eventually share in the benefits. But such faith appears to fly in the face of evidence that benefits tend to stick disproportionately to those who are already advantaged. This natural law is succinctly summarized by Cancian (1977, page 6) in two propositions: (1) "Individuals and classes of people will struggle to improve their lot relative to all other individuals and classes of people"; and (2) "All other things [being] equal, individuals and classes of people who have more resources at the beginning of an isolatable period of struggle will have the advantage in the struggle and in the end improve their position relative to others."

Not surprisingly, the same law seems to apply to the relations between men and women. The theory that economic development and technological change would benefit women equally with men fades in light of considerable contradictory evidence that, at least in some project areas, technological change in agriculture and trade has frequently displaced

---

[1] The United Nations Declaration on the Elimination of Discrimination Against Women reflects this fear in Article 6, which specifies that women should have equal rights with men "without prejudice to the safeguarding of the unity and the harmony of the family, which remains the basic unit of any society. . . ." It is not clear exactly which principle is to be sacrificed to the other if they happen to conflict.

women from their former roles, thus widening the earnings and productivity gap between the sexes (Boserup, 1970; Tinker, 1976; and Van Allen, 1974). These observations suggest a particular strategy; that is, if the phenomenon of disproportionate advantages accruing to the already advantaged is to be circumvented, programs must be aimed *directly* at those who need them most.

Recent proposals for integrating women more fully in development have suggested a broad, multifaceted approach that would involve:[2]

1. Collecting data to establish current levels of female participation and decision making in domestic, agricultural, and nonagricultural activities; to assess the major determinants of female status among different groups; to measure the range of knowledge, skills, and resources currently available to women; and to understand women's "felt needs" and priorities, upon which specific programs could be based[3]
2. Integrating girls and women more fully into current institutions and development programs such as elementary schooling, adult literacy classes, vocational training, agricultural extension work, and credit and marketing cooperatives—both as beneficiaries and as decision makers—in order to reduce discrepancies between males and females in their access to community resources
3. Creating, where necessary, special programs for women to promote economic and social self-reliance by building on knowledge and skills that the women already possess, or by teaching new skills
4. Increasing the productivity and reducing the work load of currently burdensome and time-consuming tasks, such as fuel and water collection, food processing, and subsistence agriculture, through the development and propagation of improved tools and labor-saving devices[4]

[2] Especially noteworthy are the proposals of Germain (1974, 1975, and 1976–77), from which some of these points were taken. For a critical discussion of the concept of "integrating women in development," see Papanek (1977), and other articles in the special issue on women in development in *Signs: Journal of Women in Culture and Society.*

[3] Research projects to collect data on the role of women in rural development have been designed by T. Scarlett Epstein and Ranjit Senaratne of the Institute of Development Studies, Sussex, England; Iftikhar Ahmed of the International Labor Office, Geneva; and Development Alternatives, a consulting firm in Washington, D.C. (United Nations Children's Fund, 1976).

[4] Participants in the 1972 UNICEF-sponsored Lomé Conference on Children, Youth, Women, and Development Plans suggested the following ideas (as quoted in Fagley, 1976, pp. 22–23):

Arranging for a mother or girl to take care of the children of a group of families during the agricultural working day (village day-care group); increasing water points,

5. Encouraging cooperative forms of social organization, such as credit societies, marketing cooperatives, and mothers' clubs, in order to mobilize women as agents of social, economic, and political change at the neighborhood, community, and national levels

6. Offering family-planning information and services in the context of expanding social and economic roles that will reduce women's dependence on men and on children for social and financial support

7. Evaluating the impact on women's status and roles of current and projected programs and policies

8. Promoting massive national campaigns to change traditional attitudes and sex role ideologies that limit women's options in the family, the community, and the society at large. Government leaders, in particular, will have to take an unequivocal stand in favor of abolishing "existing laws, customs, regulations and practices which are discriminatory against women, and to establish adequate legal protection for equal rights of men and women."[5]

The proposal outlined in this volume for establishing a network of small industries for rural women touches on all but the last of these elements. The compelling need for research on rural women (see items 1 and 7) is stressed in the appendix (see page 178), which suggests data requirements for determining project sites; for evaluating the impact of the new employment on rural development, the status of women, and reproductive behavior; and for testing causal relationships in a variety of settings. We should be careful not to let research requirements overwhelm the action component, however. Indeed, it may be necessary to compromise on a number of issues in order to reduce project costs. Preliminary investigators could rely more heavily on informants, for example, rather than undertaking detailed house-to-house surveys or long-term participant observations in the community. Project sites will often be chosen on the basis of prior knowledge or accessibility rather than on criteria which would require extensive investigations of the social structure, economic resources, and cultural attitudes and beliefs of dozens or hundreds of communities. If women's industries are to move beyond the pilot stage,

---

wells and general distribution facilities; reafforestation of land near villages with fast-growing trees for fuel; organizing granaries; introducing light transport facilities such as carts for crops, water, and wood; making available equipment for fishing and fish processing with hand-worked machinery; providing communities with light machinery for grinding millet and grain; introducing improved but cheap cooking and other household utensils and equipment; developing efficient agricultural tools; sharing of duties among men, women and children even if this means breaking down the traditional division of labour.

[5] Quoted from the United Nations Declaration on the Elimination of Discrimination Against Women, Article 2.

techniques for quick and informal evaluation will have to be developed so that programs can be adapted to changing conditions and needs.

The question of integrating females more fully into current institutions and development programs (see item 2) has been raised previously. Is it possible for girls and women to achieve parity with boys and men in the schools, in vocational training programs, in agricultural extension work, and in access to credit and loans, among other areas, or should male-dominated institutions and programs be bypassed in favor of alternative paths for women? The latter option requires a duplication of facilities that may be quite impossible in some situations; for example, the setting up of separate vocational training centers or agricultural extension programs would be prohibitively expensive. On the other hand, attempts to integrate girls and women more fully into current programs may meet with strong cultural resistance from the whole community, often including the women themselves. Clearly, the choice depends on conditions unique to each locale and to each socioeconomic group, as well as on the institution in question.

Because this book has been written specifically with the countries of India, Bangladesh, Pakistan, and Nepal in mind, and because the populations of these countries typically (but not universally) value the ideal of female seclusion, I have recommended that small-scale industries be created that will employ only women, and particularly the more sexually vulnerable group of unmarried girls and young married women. Although the idea of segregating girls and women both physically and occupationally will doubtless appear retrogressive to some critics, I would argue that the "fit" between this policy and prevailing cultural attitudes will permit girls and women to take advantage of the new opportunities outside the home within a setting in which they would otherwise be forbidden to work alongside men. In addition, restricting employment to women could encourage women to develop a sense of solidarity with co-workers that transcends kinship loyalties and to learn vocational and management skills by occupying positions that would otherwise fall to men.

Consistent with the ideals of promoting individual and community self-reliance (see item 3), I have stressed the need to build on women's current knowledge and skills and to utilize locally available material resources in designing small industries. Activities that rural women currently perform in an arduous and relatively unproductive fashion could, in many cases, be upgraded to generate income if the work setting could be reorganized (for example, by locating it in a centralized workplace with more security, better facilities, and some division of labor rather than duplicating efforts on a small scale in separate households), if appropriate skills training is offered in production and marketing, and if operating capital could be made available on a regular basis. I have discussed in some detail the type of products that appear to be especially suited to small-scale, labor-intensive production in rural locations which would not compete directly with large manufacturers. Among these are certain types of food processing (canning, bottling, drying) that do not have large economies of scale and for which there are local markets; garment making; the manufacturing of household and farm implements and of animal feed; crop processing (rice milling, oil pressing), and so on. Particularly promising are industries that can use local resources, such as seasonal fruits, which would otherwise go to waste, that can establish linkages with other centers of production (either producing elements for their use, or using their products), that can substitute locally made items for imports, and that can generate new demands for goods and services.

Women's employment is likely to stimulate a demand for laborsaving devices and procedures that will reduce the domestic work load (see item 4). It makes little sense to offer, under the guise of improving women's position, employment that only adds to their already heavy burden as in the oft-cited case of the poultry schemes in rural Zaire.[6] But where employment opportunities are offered in conjunction with laborsaving improvements, such as centrally located wells, cooking stoves that use fuel more efficiently, small machines for grinding or hulling grain or for pressing oil; and new forms of work organization, such as centralized child care, then two ends will be served. Women will have a strong incentive to adopt the innovations in order to free themselves for more productive activities, and the industries may produce goods (for example, small appliances or prepared foods) that in turn reduce domestic labor throughout the marketing area.

Item 5, encouraging cooperative forms of social organization, has been discussed at length in this volume, as has item 6, the provision of family-planning information and services in the context of expanding women's opportunities outside the home. Again, it should be emphasized that the causal mechanisms linking certain types of female employment with changing reproductive aspirations and behavior are not precisely known, nor is it certain that the immediate effects of increasing women's incomes would be antinatalist. Indeed, women in families currently constrained

---

[6] A report from the Food and Agricultural Organization of the United Nations pointed out that when poultry schemes were introduced in the villages of Zaire without simultaneously providing a source of water, the task of carrying water for the chickens from long distances fell on the shoulders of the women (UNESCO, 1973, p. 22). The report cited this contradiction as one reason why the women were frequently hostile, or at least indifferent, to projects aimed at "improving their own condition."

by extreme poverty from achieving traditional goals of early marriage and high fertility could use their money to fulfill these goals more easily, for example, by raising larger dowries for themselves or for their daughters. The long-term effects on reproductive aspirations and behavior are likely to be less ambiguous, however, as genuine alternatives become more widely available.

During a transitional phase in which girls and women who adopt new forms of behavior are exposed to the risk of social ostracism, perhaps even within their own families, it is extremely important to consider ways in which projects can offer protection and support to their participants. Financial incentives are one inducement: if workers' salaries are sufficiently high to make a significant impact on the level of living of their families, then the mockery of others may soon turn to envy, then to emulation. Additional financial incentives, encouraging young women to delay their marriages or to postpone the birth of the first or subsequent children, could likewise help pave the way to new forms of behavior. The element of social support among co-workers is crucial. In literacy training classes and in more general discussion groups, projects should be designed to encourage women to evaluate critically their own position in the family and the community, and to propose solutions to their own problems. Only in this way can women truly become agents of social change.

In the long run, the risks will lessen. What was once daring and innovative—a young woman walking through the village without a burqa—can become commonplace, sometimes in a remarkably short time. But the process could be greatly facilitated by a strong commitment to change among local, regional, and national leaders (see item 8). Although some governments have paid lip service to the ideal of breaking down the barriers to women's advancement, few have taken specific steps to ensure that discriminatory attitudes and practices are eliminated. Legislative acts, such as raising the minimum age at marriage for females, or specifying women's right to divorce or to inherit property, are important symbolic steps. But the gap between law and practice remains virtually unbridged in many areas. Women remain uninformed of their rights or are incapable of exercising them because of their social and economic dependency.

The overall strategy behind organizing small industries for women is to introduce new agents of change in rural areas, such as those of South Asia, that are currently experiencing high levels of fertility, poverty, and oppression of both women and men. The plan builds initially on indigenous conditions by training barefoot managers, upgrading current economic activities, fitting the division of labor to prevailing norms, and adapting to cultural restrictions on contact between the sexes. But it simultaneously introduces new, more generative ingredients including, among others, money incomes for women, regular contact with other women outside the home, consciousness-raising through functional literacy, access to family-planning knowledge and services, and group decision making. And it introduces these ingredients to the young, to unmarried girls, and to women in the early years of marriage who are most amenable to change.[7] The hope, of course, is that the endeavor will flourish in some quite unanticipated ways, contributing to the transformation of participants, their families, and the community. In Hirschman's words, the new enterprise should create a disequilibrium, a tension that cries out for adjustment, a dislocation that compels further action.[8] In this sense it is quite different from the integrated approach to rural development so favored by planners today.

Among all the possible development strategies, why should we single out small-scale industries for rural women? Other approaches also cry out for attention—the generation and more egalitarian distribution of all forms of employment, as well as of incomes, wealth, and arable land, for example; and the extension to all sectors of the population of elementary schooling, vocational training, adult literacy, health services, improved nutrition, minimal social security, and family planning, among other services.[9] At the same time there are roads to be built and repaired, levees to control the floods, rural electrification, housing, irrigation schemes, and a hundred other compelling needs. The competition for priority is overwhelming. One expert will argue that malnutrition is the single most important factor inhibiting rural development; another, illiteracy; another, the lack of relevant vocational training, or of water, or of fertilizers.

---

[7] Yet it is this generation that is forgotten in most development planning that concentrates on programs for adults and on youth clubs for teenage boys (Childers, 1976, pp. 133–134).

[8] Hirschman (1958, p. 202) offers a perfect illustration of what he conceives as the two functions of government economic policies in development planning: to create pressures for action, and then to react to them. As an example, he writes, "In an unforgettable movie Charlie Chaplin, as glazier, employs Jackie Coogan to throw stones into shopwindows, whereupon he providentially passes by and obtains the job of repairing the damage. The ingenious twist consists here in combining, *under a single command*, the disequilibrating and equilibrating functions."

[9] See, for example, the range of proposals in Ridker (1976, pp. 1–35). One choice would be to concentrate on areas that are both amenable to policy manipulation and that are believed to have a significant impact on reducing fertility. Ridker suggests selecting from the range of possibilities a package that includes more and better primary and secondary education in rural areas (with a content more relevant to rural needs, particularly those of the agricultural sector); higher attendance rates of girls in school; stimulation of the demand for labor, including female labor; the elimination of discrimination against women in the labor force; and the movement of people out of traditional agricultural occupations into more modern sectors of the economy (ideally, without moving people physically to overburdened cities).

The question I am asking is, What form of investment is most likely to reach directly to the poorest sectors of the population, and most likely to stimulate additional changes? Improving the nutritional level of the population, while clearly of central humanitarian concern, cannot by itself generate significant social or economic change and may well result in higher levels of fecundity and fertility. In any case, it is difficult to know how to improve nutrition among the landless poor who cannot afford to purchase most foods, unless one is talking of massive free-distribution schemes that will be plagued with financial shortages and administrative corruption. Even expanding elementary schooling in rural villages could fail to produce significant benefits per se, partly because the poorest rural people will still be unable to send their children to school if they are needed at home or in the fields, partly because girls will continue to be taken out of school early if their education carries no visible subsequent advantages, and partly because children can relapse into illiteracy in the absence of employment that requires the exercise of basic skills—that is, in the absence of a "felt need" to be literate. Indeed, without the expansion of rural nonagricultural employment, more schooling may only intensify the desire among the educated to move into the cities in search of work, compounding problems of urban congestion and unemployment.

One could argue with some certainty, I believe, that most poor people *do* experience a need for money that would enable them to buy or produce the goods and services they need for their basic survival, and beyond that, for some minimal level of social and economic well-being. Infusing new sources of income into rural households—especially into those of the poorest families—thus creates an effective demand for more food, improved housing, better clothing, household utensils, and for health care sufficient to keep the income flowing. In addition, the employment itself, which may tap a range of skills ranging from manual dexterity to quite complicated arithmetic calculations of quantities and prices, creates a need for literacy and perhaps for more advanced forms of vocational training, not only for the worker but also as an investment for the workers' children. In this sense, then, the creation of income-generating, skilled or semiskilled employment has a spin-off effect that other forms of investment are less likely to yield.

Finally, by focusing on employment for young women, we maximize the potential for creating dynamic disequilibrium. So long as girls and women remain bound to unproductive and unpaid labor, or cloistered behind walls in a state of psychological, social, and economic dependency, they will hold back progress, no matter how much is invested in Green Revolutions or other development schemes. They will continue to seek security through early marriage and frequent childbearing and teach their daughters to do the same. Those unfortunate enough to lose the protection of male household heads—as did the war widows of Bangladesh, for example, who banded together from village to village begging a handful of rice—will, by their very example, teach a fearful lesson.

But if networks of industrial cooperatives were organized in villages and throughout the region, offering the possibility either of shifting out of the most exploitative or unproductive labor into paid employment, or of taking a job for the first time, poor women could acquire some of the resources necessary to struggle on their own behalf. They could become an *active force* for change, transcending apathy or resistance. The resources of money, skills, knowledge, and social support that they derive from the workplace could be translated into a more effective bargaining position in the household, the community, and the society at large. The benefits of delaying marriage and spacing and limiting births are likely to become more salient in the context of these new sources of security. Again, I am arguing that employment outside the home in nonexploitative conditions could strengthen the motivation for taking more control over sexual and reproductive behavior, if not in the first generation, then at least in the long run. This particular strategy for change, more than most other policies, is likely to have a significant impact in reducing fertility because it is aimed directly at women in their early childbearing years.

The proposal to restrict the new employment outside the home (where possible) to unmarried girls and married women with no more than two or three children is intended to intensify its demographic impact on delayed marriage and childbearing. For unmarried girls, it may be possible to build simple hostels enabling them to live together at the work site, thus reducing the pressure on their families to find husbands for their daughters at an early age, while enabling the daughters to contribute financially to their families' upkeep. For young mothers, the provision of child-care facilities on the job is crucial. Infant care is particularly important to encourage mothers to breast-feed their young children, both for health reasons and as a natural child-spacing method.

The emphasis on hiring women in their early childbearing years does not exclude older women from participating in upgraded economic production. Cooperatives could be organized around activities generally performed in the home or the fields, such as handicrafts, vegetable gardening, or the raising of poultry or small animals. In some cases these producers' cooperatives could feed directly into the small-scale industries, with older women raising fruit to sell to a local juice-bottling plant, for example.

The major obstacle to the propagation of small-scale industrial cooperatives for women is doubtless their location in scattered, relatively
small rural communities. An urban-based program concentrated in the
largest cities is certainly more feasible from almost every perspective. But
in South Asia the vast majority of the population is not urban: in 1971,
about 74 percent of those in Pakistan lived in settlements of under 5,000
persons; in India, 81 percent; in Bangladesh, 93 percent; and in Nepal,
96 percent (see chapter 2, footnote 6). If programs are to have a national impact, they will have to reach these rural people. Clearly, one
cannot set up a network of cooperatives simultaneously in the half-million
villages of rural India. But one can begin on a small scale, find workable
and adaptable models, and establish networks for administration, purchase of raw materials, credit, marketing, and training that will pave the
way for new enterprises. Some regions will inevitably remain untouched,
but others may thrive in quite unprecedented ways under the stimulus of
these new forms of production.

APPENDIX: RESEARCH ISSUES IN FEMALE EMPLOYMENT

In the preceding chapters I have covered a wide range of questions relating to rural development, the status of women, and reproductive behavior. Many assertions implying cause and effect remain highly speculative and require detailed investigation to test their validity. This volume is intended not only to offer models for creating industrial cooperatives as an income-generating activity for rural women, but also to stimulate research. We need preliminary investigations before deciding on appropriate sites for small-scale rural industries; evaluative research to measure the impact of the new employment on rural development, the status of women, and reproductive behavior; and comparative research to test causal relationships under a variety of cultural and structural conditions.

What style of research is most appropriate? I would argue that large, one-time surveys of individuals' attitudes and behavior, such as the numerous KAP surveys on family-planning motivation, are less useful in most situations than are more intensive, long-term field studies combining in-depth interviews of a rather small sample of persons over a period of time, with direct observation of families within a particular community.[1] Although large surveys can serve a purpose in collecting baseline information on the social, economic, and demographic characteristics of populations, they are far less helpful in picking up subtle nuances of attitudes, in revealing contradictions between professed attitudes and practices, in exploring patterns of interpersonal relations, or in illuminating change on the individual or family level. Too, the sudden appearance of a strange interviewer in the village can cause considerable commotion so that private questioning becomes virtually impossible. Rural women asked about their knowledge, attitudes, and practices of family planning, for

---

[1] KAP (knowledge, attitude, and practice) surveys have been used for twenty-five years to collect information on family planning and to derive policy. About four hundred KAP surveys were conducted in sixty-seven countries from 1950 to 1970 (Ratcliffe, 1976, p. 322). For some basic critiques of KAP methods and interpretation see Ratcliffe (1976), Cleland (1973), and Hauser (1967). On the limitations of survey research techniques in studying Indian women, see Singh (1975, pp. 197–198). Recommendations for research on the role of women in rural economies are also outlined in Mickelwait, Riegelman, and Sweet (1976, pp. 99–103).

example, will be influenced not only by the higher status of the educated interviewer but by the throngs of children, neighbors, and family members who have crowded into the room or yard to share in the excitement.[2] In contrast, a researcher who can spend several months in the village will find more opportunity to talk to women and men alone in their daily rounds of activities as well as to record events and sentiments common to the community as a whole.

Failure to consider the nature of the village community in its entirety and of its composite neighborhood and household units accounts for some of the inadequacies of survey research in dealing with certain questions. Problems of interpreting data on the relationship between female employment and fertility, for example, derive in part from the gap in information between characteristics of individuals and aggregate data for states or nations. Critics of the use of traditional sociological survey methods in developing countries claim that the entire village is a relevant unit of analysis (and of policy formation) insofar as residents, at least partially, identify their own interests with those of other members and share a common administrative structure (or other form of social control) and recognized territorial boundaries.[3] Households also constitute logical units of analysis insofar as members share common economic and social needs and interests and are integrated into a decision-making structure that not only shapes personal desires but mediates between desires and behavioral outcome. Beyond the single household there may be a compound of households related by common descent, such as the *bari* of Bangladesh, forming another natural unit of analysis; beyond this, the neighborhood or quarter of the village in which residents are likely to share a particular economic status, occupation, religion, caste, and language. Some villages are highly nucleated, while others consist of dispersed dwellings that defy the outsider to distinguish the point at which one village ends and another

---

[2] Ellickson (1976, p. 7), interviewing young rural women in Bangladesh about their food habits and preferences, describes the setting this way: "But the moment I singled out one woman for questioning she would be overcome by embarrassment and unable or unwilling to speak. The other women would continue to talk and volunteer answers for their tongue-tied cohort. At the same time the children would start to shout what they considered very funny answers. By my questioning I succeeded in silencing only the unfortunate individual on whom I had focused my attention. She would giggle, cover her face and protest ignorance." Ellickson also reports that older women believed that *they,* rather than the younger women, should be interviewed, yet they often felt threatened by the interviewer's questions for fear of losing face. The women were concerned that there were "right" and "wrong" answers to questions, including those about their personal preferences or opinions.

[3] The policy implications of using the village as a unit of analysis are spelled out in McNicholl (1975, p. 8).

begins. But the underlying structure is clear to its residents: among the households scattered across the rice fields of Comilla Municipality in Bangladesh, for example:

> The villagers, including the women, are aware of the village boundaries. In most cases the village is surrounded by other villages. In some cases a road, the river or a swamp forms the village boundary. The villages are divided into two to five "paras" [neighborhoods]. Paddy fields, roads, the railway track or fallow lands separate the "paras." Several "baris" in a cluster form a "para." The "baris" are not numbered and are known by the name or the title of the male head of the family, such as the "Haji Bari" or the "Mazumdar Bari." A few families live in a "bari." [Abdullah, 1974, page 6]

Appropriate units of analysis will be specified in the discussion of research questions that follows.

Research sensitive to the complexities of local conditions will also require direction or full collaboration by social scientists native to the country in question. Although biases are by no means eliminated by this move—consider, for example, Mamdani's (1972, pages 30–48) critique of the class biases of the family-planning research conducted in the Khanna Study in India—they will be reduced somewhat. At the very least, researchers will become aware of a wider variety of possible methodological approaches and interpretations. Ratcliffe's (1976) innovative experiment in subjecting identical data sets from Bangladesh fertility surveys to interpretation by experts of varying familiarity with the local culture reveals important differences in both the number and nature of "explanations" for particular fertility relationships offered by Western professional analysts never having visited the Indian subcontinent, Western professionals having spent at least two years in Bangladesh working in KAP surveys, Bengali professional analysts working in KAP surveys (many of whom were at least partly Western-educated), and Bengali nonprofessionals experienced in interviewing respondents and coding data. Ratcliffe (1976, page 330) suggests that the differences in the interpretation of data between those familiar and those unfamiliar with the local culture may also extend to the basic conceptual level, and that foreigners may therefore be "unable to formulate or select questions that can elicit data relevant to a foreign culture." Neither side necessarily holds the ultimate truth, however, for local nonprofessional or professional people may also be blind to certain cultural aspects that are taken for granted. The foreigner may be able to provide the valuable insights of an outsider. Papanek (1975, page 197) declares that good research *requires* full collaboration with local colleagues, not only for their cultural insights but for their familiarity with indigenous data sources and methods of investigation. She warns strongly against attempting to bypass local scientists or turning local collaborators into "native assistants," an untenable role for good working relationships.

In the following sections I will suggest guidelines for research in three areas: investigations preliminary to deciding on a site for organizing small-scale industries; evaluations of the impact of ongoing programs; and comparative analysis in the causal relationships implied in the discussions of female employment, the status of women, and reproductive behavior. These topics, however, by no means exhaust the possibilities for research and policy formulation relating to women's role in population and development.[4]

SELECTING A SITE FOR RURAL INDUSTRIES

Throughout this book I have contended that one goal of employing women in small rural industries is to reduce income inequalities between urban and rural areas, among economic classes within rural areas, and between men and women. Areas containing a high proportion of groups at the bottom of the economic scale, such as landless peasants, small subsistence or tenant farmers, and certain religious or ethnic minorities, are good potential sites so long as they are reasonably accessible. The Vedchhi Intensive Area Scheme in Gujarat, for example, designed its broad developmental program for the "backward" classes of the area— that is, scheduled-caste Hindus, members of scheduled tribes, Muslims, and women of all groups—in a specific attempt to reduce inequalities by improving the social and economic conditions of the poorest sectors of the population.[5] To the extent that these marginal groups also (but not always) marry earlier and bear more children, the program could reduce demographic inequalities as well.

A number of additional site conditions must be met. Some have been discussed in the foregoing chapters: in chapter 4, products suited to small-

---

[4] For additional research and policy proposals, see Chaney (1973); UN Food and Agriculture Organization (1975); Germain (1975); Papanek (1975); Tinker and Bramsen (1976, pp. 129–233); and UN Department of Economic and Social Affairs (1973), among others.

[5] The population of Valod Taluka (Surat District) of 52,000 in 1971 was 72 percent scheduled tribe (Adivasi), 1 percent scheduled caste (also Adivasi), and 26 percent non-Adivasi (mostly Hindu with a small Muslim minority). Half of Valod's working population were farm laborers compared with 32 percent in Surat District and 22 percent in Gujarat as a whole. Over one-quarter of Valod females were defined as employed compared with 19 percent in the Surat District and 10 percent in Gujarat (Vedchhi Intensive Area Scheme, n.d., pp. 26–27).

scale manufacturing; in chapter 5, incentives and disincentives to female employment outside the home; and in chapter 6, appropriate forms of organization and training. They will be reviewed only briefly here. If preliminary inquiries as to the feasibility and desirability of establishing a cooperative project are conducted in a group of interconnected villages within a single geographic area, the most promising site can be selected for the initial experiment and additional cooperatives added in neighboring centers as markets are established and interest spreads.

Community Accessibility

In most cases the economic success of the industry will depend on year-round accessibility by road, rail, or water for the import of raw materials (if not of local origin) and the export of finished products (if not for local markets) as well as for regular supervision and training. Probably the best that more isolated regions can hope for is to increase their self-sufficiency through higher productivity and diversification. Staley and Morse (1965, pages 310–316) propose locating small industries in "intermediate growth points" (towns, not villages) in order to promote contact with urban markets and to take advantage of "modernizing influences" in towns. I have suggested that small industries could be located in larger villages and smaller towns so long as linkages can be established among them. Ideally, a federation of cooperatives producing the same or complementary products would be organized around an easily accessible administrative center in the market town at the core of the radial network. To begin, then, does such a network exist? What is the quality of the main road linking the village with the market town and with other villages? Is it flooded or otherwise impassable for part of the year? What distances separate the villages and how are these translated into actual travel time? What kinds of transport are available (cycle rickshaws, scooter rickshaws, bullock carts, cars, buses, trains, boats), and how frequent is the service? How far is the market town from a major urban center? Does the village contain a post office, a telegraph, a telephone?

Population Characteristics

Information could be collected from the census, from district records, or from a house-to-house survey on the total population size of the village, the number of households, the religious and caste composition of its residents, patterns of land ownership (number of landless farmers, tenant farmers, and landowners according to size of holding), and occupations (including artisans and service workers). Which of these groups is most likely to include young women who will be able or willing to seek employment? Do groups contain enough households to offer a sufficiently large potential labor pool? Vital statistics records or household surveys can yield further information on the timing of marriages, timing and number of births, levels of infant and child mortality, and patterns of migration into or out of the village.

Community Power Structure

Identify the leadership of the village, including the religious elite (priests, other persons of high ritual status), the economic elite (wealthy landowners, moneylenders, merchants), and the political elite (panchayat members, village elders, political activists). How do the elites exercise their power? What kinds of decisions does each control? And what are the major factions in the village? Along what religious, economic, political, or family lines are these factions drawn, and what are the history and current state of their conflict? Clearly, little can be accomplished if village leaders oppose the project. There is always the danger that a project favored by one faction or elite group will be resisted on principle by another. Extreme care will have to be taken in the initial stages to win the support of key figures and to avoid alienating others through their jealousy of new alliances or their fear of losing economic or political control. Ultimately, of course, the goal of creating producers' cooperatives is to provide an economic and political base for challenging elite control. But the battles cannot all be fought at the beginning.

Major Service Institutions

Preliminary research should identify and evaluate major village service institutions or development programs—such as schools, health centers, family-planning clinics, social welfare programs, agricultural extension centers, and agricultural cooperatives—as well as financial institutions—such as agricultural development banks, private banks, moneylenders, and credit cooperatives. Who controls these institutions, and who are their primary beneficiaries? What segments of the population are generally excluded from their services? What is the history of the success or failure of these projects? Do any offer a promising base around which women's cooperatives could be organized in order to win the trust of intended participants, or should the new industries try to avoid the possible taint of existing programs? What can be learned from the experience of these institutions about problems most likely to plague the new enterprise, such as possible takeovers by powerful local families, and how they might be avoided? This review of services offered by existing community programs will also reveal the unmet needs of the groups most likely to seek employment.

Material Resources for Production

What raw materials are available locally, either seasonally or year-round, that could form the basis for small industry? These include not only agricultural products such as cotton, jute, fruit and vegetables, fish, dairy animals and poultry, or goats (for fine leather), but also natural products such as bamboo, cane, and good-quality clay, wood, and other resources. What is the potential for expanding or diversifying local production to produce a steady supply of materials at reasonable and secure prices? What are the major threats to steady local production (floods, drought, cyclones, fluctuations in market prices, unsteady supply of seeds or fertilizers, and so forth)? Even if local production cannot satisfy the demand for raw materials for small industries, the surrounding region or even more distant centers can be considered, depending on such factors as the cost of importing the materials, their bulk, the security of the supply, and their ease of transport.

Energy and other resources needed for processing raw materials are also critical. Some forms of production will make heavy demands on fuel (electricity, gas, wood, and so forth) or on water supplies (for canning fruit and vegetables, and so forth). Production will depend on a steady supply of these resources without drastic price fluctuations or shortages. Are they available?

Potential Markets

Deciding on an appropriate product for small-scale manufacturing is a crucial step in ensuring the economic success of the enterprise. In chapter 4 we outlined several strategies for deciding on a product, including the possibilities of manufacturing goods locally that are currently imported, of filling an unmet local or urban need for a product, or of producing goods now on the market either better or more cheaply. An inventory is needed of the products sold in the local village and in neighboring town markets (both seasonal and year-round) and of patterns of consumption of local people with spendable incomes. Can the community support an industry by itself, or must markets be sought in more distant places, including export? What type and volume of goods can export markets bear? Careful preliminary investigation is required to establish the existence of a relatively steady outlet with stable prices. Cooperatives could provide neighboring industries with partially processed raw materials, perform one stage in the production process (polishing, finishing, packaging), or manufacture component parts, all for a single assured buyer.

Financing

Some kinds of manufacturing require little additional equipment; others require expensive equipment, heavy transport, and plentiful secured space. Are premises for a central workshop already available or will they have to be constructed? How much will purchase, renovation, or construction cost? What are the special equipment needs, and what will they cost? What transport will have to be purchased, and what will it cost?

Even if the initial infusion of money for capital expenditures, preliminary training, and operating costs (including salaries) comes from outside funding agencies, indigenous sources of capital will have to be found to ensure the ultimate independence of the cooperative. Will suppliers of raw materials offer credit? Are local cooperatives, government, or private banks willing to extend loans for operating costs and seasonal outlays? How much support will be needed before the cooperatives can become economically self-sustaining?

Women's Current Role in Production

It will be necessary to identify the economic activities in which women currently engage, both inside and outside the home. Knowledgeable informants or household surveys could provide simplified time-budget data on the nature of women's everyday tasks, such as cooking, collecting water, gathering fuel, and tending animals, and the time typically devoted to them.[6] How do these differ according to the socioeconomic status of the

---

[6] Accurate time-budget data are extremely difficult to collect because of problems of recall, time recording or estimation, distinguishing separate activities, daily and seasonal fluctuations, and so on. Nor, under some conditions, should they be taken too seriously, for activities can expand to fit the time available. Wolf (1972, p. 222) describes the old women of rural Taiwan who managed to stretch the wash-

household and the woman's position within it? How do they vary seasonally? Can daily and seasonal tasks be shortened or redistributed so that a sufficient number of young women will be able to take on full-time employment outside the home? If current obligations appear to impede the possibility of employment, can working hours or seasonal operations in the new industries be adjusted to fit these constraints? And what additional steps could be taken to reduce the time and energy currently spent on domestic tasks? Installing a tubewell, finding a new fuel source, or cultivating high-yield animal fodder on wasteland near the village could cut down on women's long trips to distant gathering sources. Time–budget studies would help considerably in revealing these needs.

It is important to note the current range of women's activities outside the home. One may find large numbers of girls or young women who either regularly or seasonally work as agricultural laborers, service workers, market women, or in some other capacity. Which of these economic activities actually provides a cash income, and how much does it provide? Is the money considered the personal property of the woman or does it become part of the joint household income? In what other ways are women currently contributing to the support of their families through either money incomes or indirect sources, such as shares of the crop they harvest? To the extent that females already engage in work outside the home, one would expect community resistance to their employment to be considerably reduced.

Discovering the range of women's economic activities also helps in deciding on a product. Current activities such as weaving, pottery making, or poultry raising could possibly form the core of the new industry. Tasks normally allocated to women in the sexual division of labor may be particularly suitable for upgrading into small industries as a means of circumventing conflict over jobs with men.

Range of Available Skills

The household interviews should include an inventory of skills which women already possess. Anwar and Bilquees (1976) found a wide range of productive skills among the Muslim women that they interviewed in a

---

ing of a few items of clothing over a whole morning in order to visit with others at the river. And the Gurungs of one village north of Pokhara in Nepal varied widely from day to day the time they took to collect wood from the mountains and perform other tasks, depending on what else they had to do (MacFarlane, 1976, pp. 126–152).

Punjabi village. Virtually all of the women knew how to spin, weave straw baskets, and make pickles; over half could embroider, crochet, and weave elaborate tape belts; over one-quarter could sew and knit; and one-tenth made clay pottery. Young women typically engaged in a wide range of crafts, while older women did little except spinning. This preliminary skill assessment is useful in evaluating the extent of vocational training necessary for new workers and in designing training programs around existing knowledge. Household surveys should also collect data on reading and writing skills, simple arithmetic skills, such as those required in buying and selling in the market, and accounting skills, among others.

Women's Position in the Family

Recruitment of female workers will depend on the current position of women in the family, as indicated by such factors as the scope and degree of their decision-making power or influence, and by whether a bride must leave her natal home in order to take up residence with her husband's family in another village.[7] A research proposal to UNICEF in Nepal on village women's role in child health and nutrition is equally relevant for mobilizing village women for employment. Research would include studies of:

> ... The marriage system, the position of women with respect to their natal family before and after marriage, the position in husband's family, rights of married women, and customary inheritance. Authority and affection relationships within the family would be studied both in their ideal structures and in actual process. Since societies often invest most of the overt power and formal authority in men, the project will need to focus on the indirect strategies (often capitalizing on inherent conflicts and weak points in the idealized family structure) which women use to achieve their aims. Special attention will be directed to detecting and understanding the working of such "underground" power systems as they influence family decisions about childrearing, family planning, ... use of family food and financial resources. [Bennett, 1974]

Understanding these "underground" power systems is also crucial to discovering the extent to which young women may find ways to volunteer for income-earning employment and ultimately to negotiate for later

---

[7] Hindu girls in northern India must marry outside their village, for example, whereas in the south they frequently remain in their own village, sometimes marrying cousins (Das, 1975, pp. 81–82). Muslim girls generally marry within the village.

marriages or deferred births, even in the face of apparent disapproval by persons in authority in the household.

Women's Associations in the Community

In chapter 6 I mentioned building on existing patterns of association among women in creating a cooperative work group. Yet these linkages are likely to be particularly elusive to the outside observer and the methods of uncovering them unclear. The Nepalese UNICEF proposal quoted above addresses the question this way:

> Through observation of meeting places and communication patterns, individual friendships and formal and informal groups, an attempt would be made to understand the organization and workings of the women's community at a given site. Factors which determine group cohesion, as well as factors which tend to cause tension within and between groups, would be explored. A related question would be the role of the women's community vis-à-vis the men's community. That is, do women's factions reinforce, mediate or simply ignore the various factions that may exist among the men? How does the process of conflict resolution among women differ from that among men? Who if anyone are the female community leaders? Do they tend to be found among the members of certain age-groups, ritual status or economic standing? How have they gained and used their power? There are many questions in the area of community relations and organization, and the strategic importance of understanding this area for successful program implementation can hardly be over-stated. This is particularly so because one of the project's central aims is to utilize as much as possible what the social structure of a given group already has to offer. [Bennett, 1974]

Discovering patterns of association and cleavage in the community of women is particularly important for finding groups who would be eager and willing to work together, for identifying potential managers who have already earned their neighbors' confidence and trust, and for stimulating interest among women who are too shy or afraid to come forward during the initial stages. Of course, care must be taken to ensure that the most privileged women of the community do not dominate the planning in ways that exclude or treat as charity cases the very women who stand in most need of economic and political mobilization.

The scope of the research defined here as "preliminary to deciding on a site for rural industries" is clearly much too broad to accomplish in a brief period; indeed, many of the proposals would require sensitive investigations by persons living in the community over a period of at least several months. What, then, are the priorities? Two preconditions are probably essential to deciding on whether to continue the research: (1) a group of women should be interested in organizing a cooperative, and (2) their efforts should have the support of community leaders.

The first requirement is to consult with community leaders about the possibilities of undertaking such a project, eliciting their suggestions and criticisms; the second is to hold a series of community meetings in which project organizers, under the aegis of respected leaders or service institutions, consult with groups of families most likely to participate in the project. In some villages separate meetings will have to be organized for men and women, with males addressing the men's meetings and females the women's. It may be difficult to persuade people from scheduled-caste, tribal, or other religious and economic minority groups to attend, but it is exactly these groups who should be encouraged to articulate their needs.

If women express no interest in the project, even after learning about some of its possible forms and benefits, then there is no point in proceeding further. If the women express interest but qualify it with such objections as "Our husbands would never allow us to do this," or "We would like to earn some money but we have no spare time as it is," then debate could be encouraged on how some of these obstacles might be overcome. The women themselves should be totally involved in discussions about laborsaving devices, possible activities in which they could engage, where they might obtain raw materials, what kind of skills they already have, and so on. One of the main problems in the beginning may be to build their confidence to a point at which they understand that they do have useful skills and knowledge that could be put to good use, and goals that they are unable to achieve on their own can be accomplished through cooperative effort.

If community interest is assured, only then does it make sense to embark on a detailed analysis of production possibilities, financing, recruitment of workers, and so on. Some of the research ideas outlined above, such as those on the decision-making role of women within the family, will form a baseline against which changes can be measured after the project gets underway. But once the preliminary research is accomplished, what if women's enthusiasm is met only with dismal predictions about the success of a small industry? In these cases, alternative ideas should be proposed and debated so that the women can decide on some smaller project, perhaps a cooperative market garden for raising fruit or vegetables, a handicraft association, a savings club, a literacy class, or some other venture. Adhering to a strict model of the ideal industrial producers' cooperative, only to reject the idea completely if all the preconditions are not met, does everyone a disservice. Organizers should be flexible in recognizing alternative forms of organization that would fit more closely with the current interests, needs, and resources of the community.

EVALUATING THE IMPACT OF THE NEW INDUSTRY

I have argued throughout this volume that introducing small-scale industrial cooperatives for rural women is a prime means of promoting rural development, improving the status of women, and creating conditions favorable to delayed marriage and birth control. Research designs to evaluate the impact of the new cooperatives are necessarily plagued with problems. We could collect extensive baseline data on prevailing conditions prior to the introduction of the cooperative and supplement these with periodic or continuous evaluations of how conditions change once the cooperative gets underway. Yet this "before–after" comparison is insufficient for attributing causality. Conditions might change without the cooperative too. The technique of undertaking similar research in a control village is not only time-consuming and expensive, but it would be virtually impossible to find a setting in which all other things are equal except for the new project. Changes deriving from the women's project would be difficult to sort out from those deriving from other programs operating in the same community. In the Vedchhi Intensive Area Scheme, for example, households in which women earn regular incomes from the papad cooperative are also likely to contain members of credit societies, agricultural producers' cooperatives, or other schemes. The confounding effects of all these forces would be extremely difficult to untangle.

An alternative to selecting an experimental village and a control village is to compare, *within* the experimental village, members of women's producers' cooperatives with nonmembers, and members' families with nonmembers' families, trying to match for basic socioeconomic characteristics such as religion, caste, occupation of the household head, and family composition. This strategy at least eliminates the problem of trying to match whole villages, but it simultaneously introduces the problem of selectivity among workers. At first, women who are interested in joining a cooperative, and their families who tolerate or support their endeavors, are likely to differ significantly in their attitudes and practices relating to women's roles from those who remain in the home.[8]

Both these strategies carry some risk. Focusing all of one's energies on the evaluation of a single project exposes one's research to the risk that

---

[8] Additional discussion of possible research designs for evaluating rural cooperatives can be found in Dixon (1976b, pp. 316–321).

some unforeseen event will ruin the enterprise—that the cooperative will fold because a severe drought dries up the source of agricultural produce on which it depends for raw materials, or because a scandal throws the project into disrepute. Ideally, then, research would include a number of cooperatives so that the conditions under which they are likely to succeed or fail, and their impact on rural life, can be more clearly defined.

The guidelines that follow must be considered in the most adaptable way. They encompass a number of questions that could be asked regarding a project's impact on rural development, the status of women, and reproductive behavior. Specific research designs would have to be tailored to the unique conditions of each setting.

Effects on Rural Development

The definition of rural development proposed in chapter 1 includes (1) general improvements in levels of living; (2) decreasing inequality of income distribution; and (3) the capacity to sustain continuous improvement over time. These concepts need to be operationalized so that information can be gathered at several different levels of analysis: the individual worker, her family–household–compound, the neighborhood from which the majority of workers come, and the community as a whole.

Data on individual workers (and on a matched group of nonworkers, if possible) would be collected before the cooperative begins and at periodic intervals thereafter. Some of this information would be part of the cooperative's records; some, public knowledge; some, obtained from structured interviews; some, from informal observations on the job, in the community, and in the home.

Levels of living at the individual level include the woman's earned income in cash or other goods or services; the number of hours worked for this income and the nature of the work; the extent and nature of unpaid labor within and outside the home; her formal or informal schooling; indicators of general levels of health and nutrition; consumption of food, housing, clothing, and other consumer goods and services; access to labor-saving amenities such as water, electricity, transport; and extent of personal ownership (and control over) wealth such as land, jewelry, and cash savings. The central questions are whether the material conditions of women's lives improve in a significant way as a result of their new employment and whether cooperative members are better off than similar nonmembers, taking into account initial differences between the two groups. Such improvement can by no means be assumed, for one of the major criticisms of many women's employment schemes is that they add to already heavy burdens of labor. In addition, the money that women earn may be lost in gambling, spent on an elaborate wedding feast for a marriageable daughter, or diverted to some other "unproductive" expenditure.[9] Research at this stage could suggest needed changes in the structure or functioning of the cooperative such as enforced savings schemes, the adoption of new laborsaving devices, or more flexible working hours.

The "capacity to sustain continuous improvement" could include, at the individual level, indicators of the likelihood of maintaining or improving a woman's personal level of living over time and her attitudes about the possibility of improvement in the social and material conditions of the individual or the group.[10] Does a young woman's experience in learning new skills and earning an independent income alter her consciousness about what is possible in the future for herself, her children, and the community as a whole? Does the work experience provide a sense of personal efficacy in bringing about social, economic, political, or cultural change?

Similar data could be collected on households or the extended family compound as a unit (depending on the extent to which resources and decisions are shared by the group), the neighborhood (if workers are drawn from a relatively well-defined area of the community rather than from widely dispersed households), and the community as a whole. Family–household information (including matched households of nonmembers) would encompass the combined before–after incomes of all household members and the dependency burden on these incomes; the nature of the division of both paid and unpaid labor within and outside the home by age, sex, and relationship to the household head; level of schooling of all household members; indicators of their health and nutrition; household consumption of food, housing, clothing, consumer goods and services; and family ownership of land, money, and other capital. An example of one possible unforeseen consequence of women's new earning capacity is that male family members may decide to work less so long as previous levels of household income can be maintained.[11] Evaluation research questions should be particularly sensitive to these possibilities.

The distribution of income and of other benefits within the family becomes relevant at this point. Does the new employment narrow or close

[9] Many of these so-called unproductive expenditures carry important social rewards, however. The amount of money a family spends on a wedding feast will be actively debated by community members for years to come. For one example of how increased incomes can be dissipated, see Nair (1961, pp. 55–57).

[10] I refer here to the idea of the "group-focused" and "individual-focused" images of change raised by Hirschman (1958, pp. 11–20).

[11] A man's decision to work less so long as basic survival needs are met can be quite rational in view of the time and energy it takes to earn only a few rupees at hard labor.

the income gap between male and female family members? Is the division of labor within the household redistributed as a consequence? Who in the household benefits most from the new income, and who the least? Does female employment stimulate a reallocation of investment priorities within the family so that, for example, girls begin to receive the same schooling, food, and health care as do boys?

Indicators of the "capacity to sustain continuous improvement" within the family refer to the extent to which the employment of young female household members has altered the family's perceptions of the possibilities of long-term improvement in their lives. It may be that family elders view the employment primarily as an interim phenomenon that just happens to fill the time (though in a profitable way) until a suitable mate can be found for a marriageable young girl, or until a husband earns enough to keep his wife at home. On the other hand, the new employment could significantly affect the family's aspirations for themselves and their children.

Neighborhood measures of levels of living become salient when workers are drawn from a particular spatial area in the community. Social and material conditions refer here, not only to individual improvements in housing or in other forms of consumption in the neighborhood, but also to visible improvements in the condition of the neighborhood as a whole. Unlike individual entrepreneurs, cooperatives should be investing a portion of their profits in community projects, such as health centers, schools, tubewells, or improved roads, rather than absorbing the profits individually. Former inequalities in the distribution of incomes and services within the neighborhood should be reduced, and the neighborhood group should begin to feel a sense of confidence in their ability to organize for group advancement. Do these consequences actually follow, or do they not?

The same argument holds for the community at large. Does the evaluation indicate significant improvements in the levels of living of the entire village, both individual and collective, that can be attributed, at least in part, to the new industries? Women of the Valod papad cooperative, for example, brought $50,000 of earnings into their town of six thousand people in 1974–75. Almost two-thirds of the households of Valod are said to benefit from these incomes, most of them low-status Muslims and Hindus. A central question of evaluation research would be how these incomes are spent or invested and what some of the indirect consequences are. Have other industries sprung up either as suppliers or users of the cooperative's products? Has the employment of women generated an effective demand for new goods and services such as appliances, laundries, prepared foods? How have these incomes affected the distribution of earnings, wealth, and access to community services such as health care and schooling? Has the industry stimulated an attitudinal and organizational breakthrough in the community which offers new possibilities for innovation and change? The outcome will depend on collecting good baseline measures of these phenomena and on careful observation of community events.

Effects on the Status of Women

The status of women, as defined in chapter 1, refers to women's access to material resources (money, food, land, and so forth) and social resources (knowledge, power, prestige) in the family and the community, measured both in absolute terms and relative to men. Part of this definition has been subsumed in the discussion above of levels of living, which included incomes in cash, kind, or services; consumption of food, housing, and other amenities; and ownership of wealth (all material resources), as well as schooling (access to knowledge). In this section I am concerned with a purely social aspect of women's status, that is, access to power and prestige. *Power* includes the ability to control others' behavior, even in the face of initial opposition, through the exercise of force, legitimate authority, or influence and persuasion, and the ability to control one's own behavior, even in the face of initial opposition, by acting autonomously. *Prestige* refers to the esteem, value, or respect in which one is held by others. These elusive concepts are extremely difficult to measure. Their operationalization will probably vary from place to place, depending on the structural and cultural conditions of the group under investigation.

Because the concepts of power and prestige take on meaning only in the context of group interaction (power and prestige in the family, the neighborhood, the community as discussed below), their measurement on the individual level appears problematic. But the individual aspects are important. I refer here to women's perceptions of their own power and their self-esteem, that is, to the subjective aspects of their objective situation.[12] One would need to construct sensitive measures of women's general feelings of control over the major decisions or events shaping their lives, including control over others and control over self.[13] This latter dimension

---

[12] Mukherjee (1974, 1975a) has attempted to develop indicators of the status of women relevant to Indian society. For an anthropological approach to measuring women's status in tribal and agrarian societies, see Sanday (1973). Indicators of female status more appropriate to industrial societies are developed by Dixon (1976a) and Safilios-Rothschild (1971a), among others.

[13] Rural men and women alike—and especially young people—are likely to indicate low levels of control over the major events of their lives. Their perceptions are probably a good reflection of reality.

would tap women's sense of self-reliance or autonomy in areas of behavior including those of which others may disapprove. To what extent, and under what conditions, does a woman feel justified in going against the wishes of others, for example, in practicing birth control without her husband's knowledge or in leaving the house to visit relatives without soliciting his consent?[14] Self-esteem could be tapped by questions relating to women's estimates of the prestige with which they are viewed by others and to their feelings of value or self-worth. Do they feel they have important skills or contributions to make to their families and to society? Do they have confidence in their own abilities? Some of the evidence collected may be quite impressionistic. For example, the supervisor of a group of Muslim women (most of whom had never worked outside the home before) enrolled in a YWCA handicraft training course in Dacca reported that, at first, the women were extremely shy, poorly dressed, and lacking in self-confidence, "scattering like mice" whenever a supervisor came near. After a few weeks of training, working together, and earning money, they began to take a real interest in their appearance and to assert themselves by making demands on the job.[15] Through informal observations and interviews it should be possible to construct measures for individual women, permitting comparisons of both cooperative members and matched nonmembers over time.

There are probably as many different approaches to measuring family power structure as there are studies attempting to do so. Safilios-Rothschild (1970) summarizes a number of conceptual and methodological problems of family power studies by noting that they often present a one-sided view by interviewing wives only; fail to differentiate concepts of power, influence, and authority; equate the family power structure with decision making; and give equal weight to decisions of varying levels of import and frequency, among other shortcomings.[16] In addition, Western studies tend to focus exclusively on the husband–wife dyad. Mistaken even in the Western context, failure to include other family members who are likely to become involved in certain decisions becomes a critical deficiency in studies of the distribution of power within extended families, whether or not members all live together in a single household.

The central question of interest here is the extent to which women's income-earning employment increases their power within the family. First,

---

[14] A surprisingly high percentage of Egyptian women in one large study said yes when asked, "Do you agree that a woman should go ahead and use a contraceptive, even if her husband disagrees?" About 30 percent of the total rural and urban sample agreed, ranging from 11 percent in rural Kena Governate to 37 percent in rural Sharkia and 38 percent in the urban areas. Literate wives were more likely than illiterate wives to agree with the statement (Khalifa, 1973, p. 219).

[15] February 1977 interview with Mrs. Das, supervisor of the YWCA in Dacca.

[16] See also Cromwell and Wieting (1975).

what are the most salient everyday and periodic decisions, and how important are they? In South Asian studies these would certainly include, among other elements, decisions about the division of labor by age and sex within the household and outside it; the distribution of communal resources (how money is spent, for example); the allocation of resources such as food, clothing, health care, and schooling among family members (especially between daughters and sons); decisions relating to the timing of marriage of sons and daughters and the selection of a spouse; decisions relating to the frequency of sexual intercourse between husband and wife and the timing and number of births; patterns of deference and demeanor within the home; the nature and frequency of religious observances; whether to buy or sell land; when to plant and harvest crops; borrowing money; and so on. Some are everyday decisions that can be observed directly or discovered through interviews, such as who controls the money spent for household needs; some arise periodically and can be directly observed, such as the search for a suitable marriage partner; some are latent, "settled" decisions such as the deferential behavior of a young daughter-in-law in standing in the presence of her husband's father and older brothers and covering her head in their presence—decisions that become activated only when norms are violated and conflict occurs. Concentrating only on conscious decision making thus ignores other facets of the family power structure such as patterns of segregation within the household and restrictions on the spatial mobility of some members outside the home.[17]

Second, it is not sufficient to ask simply, Who makes the decisions—the husband, the wife, or both together, not only because other people may be involved, but also because these questions generally elicit a culturally accepted definition of who *should* make the decisions rather than any indication of the dynamics of the process. We want to know how power is *exercised*—is it through force, legitimate authority, or influence and persuasion? *Force* means the actuality or threat of physical restraint or abuse. *Authority* endows a person with a socially or culturally approved right to exercise power, its legitimacy deriving from the person's privileged position in the family (for example, the eldest member), from special expertise (the most educated person), or from some other source. Influence refers to overt or covert pressure such as direct verbal persuasion, indirect verbal pressure (persuading a more favored family member

---

[17] Goldberg (1974, pp. 5–6) isolates three dimensions of family "modernism" as they affect fertility in his analysis of interviews with women in Ankara and Mexico City. *Power* refers to the wife's perception of who makes, and should make, decisions in the family; *segregation,* to her perceptions of the differentiation of sex roles within the family; and *containment,* to her perception of her husband's restrictions on her activities, particularly those outside the home.

to act as advocate), or indirect nonverbal pressure (setting the stage through offers of food, sexual favors, and so on).[18] Particular attention should be paid to the ways in which women achieve their aims by so-called subversive acts that do not directly challenge cultural norms, or by ignoring norms and acting autonomously even in the face of expressed or implied disapproval.

Women's prestige within the family can be measured by other family members' definitions of her value or worth, by the frequency with which her opinions are sought, and by the respect with which she is treated. Does her income-earning ability increase her prestige? Perhaps not, especially if the cost is delayed marriage or fewer births. Do other family members envy her? Mock her? Women's prestige has traditionally grown from a low point immediately after marriage, through the birth of children (especially sons), to a high point when married sons bring daughters-in-law and grandchildren into the home (although it may decline after widowhood). Whether the acquisition of new social and economic skills and earning money can provide an alternative source of prestige remains an open question. I noted in chapter 5 that in some situations the prestige of the whole family will suffer if a woman goes out to work.

Finally, measures of women's power and prestige in the neighborhood (if relevant) and in the community would include observations of their actual participation in decisions reflecting the community at large and their own group interests, and by the general esteem in which women as a whole, and particular women leaders, are held. One indicator of the political success of a women's cooperative is the extent to which it serves as a training ground for community involvement. This may be the sphere most resistant to change, however. The cooperatives described in chapter 3 had only the most limited impact on women's political activities. Although in some cases small groups were beginning to express an interest in public affairs, few had actually invaded the male domain of community meetings and panchayat government.

Effects on Reproductive Behavior

Data would be collected on women's attitudes and practices relating to the timing of marriage, the timing of the first birth, the spacing of births,

---

[18] Wolf (1972, chap. 4) gives a fascinating account of how rural Taiwanese women can influence family decisions through either the implied threat or the actuality of gossip. A woman who feels unfairly treated carries her tale to her neighbors, among whom the incident is actively debated. A husband or mother-in-law accused of harsh treatment may incur scorn or severe criticism. According to Carstairs (1975, p. 233), fears of female witchcraft can also keep men in line.

and the total number of births—again, comparing cooperative members with a matched group of nonmembers where feasible. These would include the actual age at marriage of girls currently within the group, the age at marriage of all female family members, the expected age at marriage of unmarried daughters, and the ideal age at marriage for girls in general and for those within the household in particular. Although not directly relating to reproductive behavior, it would be interesting to include information on other attitudes and practices relating to marriage, such as the ideal age gap between bride and groom, expectations regarding the social standing of the groom, the size of dowry or dower, and other patterns of marital exchange. The key issue here is whether the employment of unmarried girls can, in fact, defer their marriages for several years, and, even if it does, whether cultural values have actually changed or have merely been compromised by the delay. Specific incentive schemes for delayed marriage such as payments to the family for keeping a daughter unmarried, at least until age twenty (or later, if possible), would require special research designs to evaluate their impact in comparison with other employment schemes in which incentives are not offered. Of course, participants could be asked whether the fact of the girl's earning money, or an incentive payment, had influenced the decision as to the timing of her marriage, but responses are likely to be difficult to interpret. Comparisons of the timing of the marriage of cooperative members with that of nonmembers should provide one of the more measurable effects, although even here the problem of selectivity interferes.

The timing of the first birth depends heavily on the timing of marriage (or more accurately, of its consummation, which varies far less across groups than the timing of the marriage ritual itself).[19] It is unrealistic, given the extreme cultural pressures to produce children early in marriage, to expect that couples will adopt birth control before the first pregnancy. But the spacing of subsequent births is another matter. Family planning, offered in the context of delaying an additional birth until the first child has finished breast-feeding (or, more specifically, has attained a specific body weight) and until the mother is in good health, is likely to meet with

[19] The child brides of India usually wait several years before consummating the marriage in a *guana* ceremony; the earlier the marriage, the longer is the waiting period. One study of 100 middle-class and 50 lower-class women in Delhi reported the average age at marriage and at *guana* of the former group as the same—about nineteen years—with the first child born on the average when the mother was twenty-three. Women in the latter group were married on the average at about 13½ years, consummated their marriages at about 15½, and bore their first child at 18 (Dubey, Bardhan, and Garg, 1975, pp. 41–42). Among 150 married women construction workers in Delhi (all scheduled caste), 91 percent had married before age sixteen, 74 percent had consummated their marriage before sixteen, and 18 percent had borne their first child before sixteen (Ranade and Sinha, n.d., p. 10).

far more receptivity than efforts aimed at delaying the first birth or limiting total births. In any case, the ongoing research would include precise measures of contraceptive knowledge, contraceptive practice, and the timing of births. Of particular interest is the extent to which women begin to think of contraception as something that is their "right" or responsibility, regardless of possible resistance from their husbands. What methods do they choose? Financial incentives for spacing births could also be evaluated in this context.

Data should also be collected on current variations in completed family size, expected total births, and ideal total births, including sex composition. To what extent can employment outside the home alter women's reproductive intentions for themselves and their marriageable children? Can cooperative members be persuaded to stop at two, if they have a son and a daughter, or stop at three whatever the sex ratio?[20] I have suggested that one incentive for birth limitation would be to deny women with more than two or three children employment in the cooperative. An alternative would be to concentrate on positive financial incentives backed by group pressures. Incentives could be offered for sterilization, for abortion, or for maintaining other forms of birth control successfully over a specified number of years. Once again, the question is not only whether the behavior can change but whether cultural attitudes or values will change too. Although the demographic results are the same, birth deferral or limitation for the sake of immediate financial need has different social and psychological consequences than the same behavior resulting from genuinely broadened aspirations or goals.

Dramatic transformations will not occur overnight. It may take several years for individuals, families, and communities to respond visibly to the new industries. Material conditions are likely to be the first affected: a young woman buys a new sari; families begin to eat two regular meals a day instead of one; they pay off debts, repair their house, and save money for a bullock and cart. Slowly the appearance of the compound, the neighborhood, and the village begins to change as the new incomes filter through the community to the shoemaker's, the fruit seller's, and the weaver's. Social changes follow, although slowly perhaps. Young women initially fearful of leaving their homes now walk openly through the streets to their work; they gain confidence in their dealings with the outside world from their new literacy skills and from having a little spending money of their own. Ultimately, they begin to assert their needs and interests more forcefully in the home. Purposive deferral of marriage and childbearing

[20] The reader will recognize these options as the model proposed by several state governments of India for their sterilization schemes.

may not appear for several years. But if the impact of the new employment does not show clearly on the first generation of participants—a transitional group that may be embarking on entirely new roles—it will appear in their younger sisters and their daughters who are exposed to a wider range of possibilities for women. They will see that women can support themselves and make a major contribution to their families' support. They will see that an unmarried girl of twenty is not an economic burden to her family, but rather that she may be able to buy things for herself and her family that were formerly only dreamed of. They will see that women can organize politically around issues of concern to them. A sensitive research design encompassing a variety of approaches should be able to tap some of these subtle changes.

CAUSAL ANALYSIS OF THE RELATIONSHIP BETWEEN FEMALE EMPLOYMENT, AGE AT MARRIAGE, AND FERTILITY

Rather than performing long-term evaluations of a few projects, one could classify economic activities in which women are already engaged in a variety of situations along such dimensions as whether the work is paid or unpaid, "essential" or "inessential" to the group's or family's survival, inside or outside the home, regular or sporadic, and so on, and then measure the effect of these activities on rural development, the status of women, and reproductive behavior. Or, research could focus on the more specific issues of the mechanisms by which different types of economic activity influence the timing of marriage and the timing and number of births. What types of economic activity serve as a resource for females that can be translated into power in other spheres? Is participation in subsistence agriculture enough, or must the work produce income over which women have some control? Is even this enough? Sanday's (1973, page 1695) analysis of twelve tribal societies, for example, finds that women's contribution to essential agricultural production is a necessary but not sufficient condition for the development of higher status for females in economic and political spheres. The question of how higher status for females influences reproductive behavior forms the core of this section because of its sociological interest and its relevance to policy decisions. We need to discover the circumstances under which female employment *can* lead to reproductive change, and to identify the sequence of events (primarily within the individual and the family) through which this change occurs. One set of hypotheses is set forth in figure A-1; more valid models will emerge from the research process.

Under what conditions does employment generate income, skills, and social contacts? Female economic activities could be classified as ranking low, medium, or high on each of these dimensions in order to test their independent effects comparatively.

Most economic activities in which rural women of South Asia commonly engage are unpaid (domestic work in their own homes, subsistence agriculture), paid only sporadically in cash or in kind (occasional wage labor in agriculture, periodically selling small amounts of ghee or other produce for cash), or paid indirectly (home crafts, such as weaving, in which "the husband is the employer"). They are largely unskilled in the sense that they do not require literacy or independent decision-making skills. In many cases, the social contacts engendered through female employment are limited to the extended family. Even wage labor in agriculture often consists of family members working together.

Some occupations for rural women offer a high degree of income, skills, and social contacts (the small minority of professional workers in rural communities); others may not, depending on individual circumstances (market women, for example). The underlying hypothesis is that the higher an activity "scores" on each of these dimensions, the greater

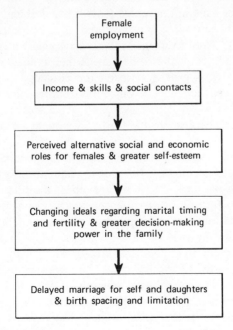

Fig. A-1. One causal sequence through which female employment could influence reproductive behavior.

are the resources a woman brings into her family and the higher the probability that her reproductive behavior will ultimately be affected. This hypothesis has shaped the theme and structure of the producers' cooperatives proposed in this report.

Under what conditions do relatively high levels of income, skills, and social contacts create in women a perception of socioeconomic alternatives to traditional female roles? Is female employment a necessary or sufficient condition?

One would assume that earning an independent income would cause women to perceive that they do not have to depend on a father, brother, husband, son, or other male relative for economic support. This perception would depend on the amount of the woman's income relative to average male wages and to those of the men in her immediate family, and on the dependability of her future employment. A key question is whether a wife or unmarried daughter earning money even considers the possibility that her economic dependence on men is reduced or eliminated. The same question can be asked of certain types of skills which, whether currently producing income or not, could be performed for an income. If a woman is a skilled basket weaver, for example, and there is a potential market for her goods, does she perceive this as an alternative role that might become activated at some time in the future (say, if her husband should divorce her), or one that could serve as an economic alternative to early marriage for her daughter? And do women whose economic activities commonly bring them into contact with people outside their immediate family, especially in solidary work groups, perceive this contact as a resource which reduces their social dependence on family relationships or approval in any way?

Taking the argument somewhat further, we might ask whether the employment is viewed as currently incompatible with traditional family roles. *Incompatibility* refers here both to normative conflicts (the belief that women should devote their full time to their families) and to conflicts in the allocation of time and energy. Much of the literature on female employment and fertility has focused on this key concept in explaining why some occupations seem to require women to choose between remaining on the job and having additional children, while others do not. But how do women themselves perceive these options? They may view some occupations as perfectly consistent with, or even as being an expected component of, traditional roles (handicraft production in the home, for example, or transplanting and weeding rice) and others more clearly as alternatives (wage labor that takes women away from home on a regular basis over a long period of time).

We also ask under what conditions relatively high levels of income, skills, and social contacts can increase women's self-esteem. Are they either necessary or sufficient? One would predict that the higher her activities rank on each of these three dimensions, the higher are her feelings of self-worth. But her valuation naturally depends on others' opinions. In societies in which women's power and privilege derive almost entirely from childbearing, women who marry early and bear many children (especially sons) may well value themselves more highly (and be more highly valued by others) than those who marry later and bear fewer children, even if the latter earn income or practice skills of some importance. Mukherjee (1974, page 13), in a sample of married women from Haryana, Tamil Nadu, and Meghalaya, found no significant correlations between the employment of rural women outside the home and their self-perceived status within the home, although most employed women were cultivators or laborers. The question is whether the cultural value ascribed to women's productive, relative to their reproductive, roles can be challenged by women at the individual level and, ultimately, at the societal level as well. Of course, if the relative values are first challenged on the societal level, then individual conformity follows more easily. Reports on China suggest that strong peer-group pressures are exerted on young women in the new, semiindustrial rural jobs to remain at work rather than drop out, even temporarily, to bear children. The ideology into which the women are socialized, stressing community interests before family interests, rewards those who do so with high social status (Salaff, 1972, page 254).

Are women's perceptions of alternative social and economic roles, together with a heightened sense of self-esteem, either necessary or sufficient to change their marital and fertility ideals or to increase their decision-making power in the family? It is quite possible that in some situations women who are fully aware of their ability to support themselves will nevertheless adhere tenaciously to traditional expectations regarding the ideal timing of marriage and the timing and number of children, viewing their economic activities merely as an instrument for realizing these expectations more effectively. Saving money for a dowry to ensure an appropriately early marriage is one example. Even in industrialized countries, studies frequently find that women in the paid labor force hold similar views of the ideal number of children (and desire as many for themselves) as do nonemployed women.[21] It may be that an additional ingredient—work commitment—is necessary in order to activate a change in ideals.[22] Work commitment could result from some personal predisposition antecedent to a particular job, from a strong ideological campaign as in the

---

[21] See Ware (1965) and other examples cited in her work.

[22] This ingredient would partially explain why women in professional positions most frequently express deliberate intentions to postpone or forego marriage or childbearing in order to remain at work. For a review of the problems of measuring work commitment, see Safilios-Rothschild (1971 and 1972).

Chinese example, or from structural aspects of the job itself. One would predict that the higher the income, the greater the skills, and the more varied or intense the social contacts an occupation offers, the more strongly a woman would be committed to her work; and, in turn, the more she would value the work for herself and for others as a genuine alternative to early (or any) marriage and high fertility.[23] This is certainly a testable proposition.

A heightened sense of self-esteem may also be used to achieve traditional goals, while adhering to traditional norms could enhance rather than detract from a woman's estimation of her own value. Presumably, then, the perceived alternatives and self-esteem outlined in figure A-1 are not sufficient to alter women's ideas about marital timing and fertility, although research may well find them to be necessary.

What of the effect of perceived alternatives and heightened self-esteem on decision making? A wide variety of evidence suggests that women who are employed outside the home play a greater role in family decision making than do those who are not employed, although the findings are not entirely conclusive. In some contexts, cultural expectations regarding who should make the decisions apparently override the effect of any additional material or social resources that employed women might use to their advantage.[24]

Are changing ideals regarding marital timing and fertility in the context of women's greater decision-making power in the family either necessary or sufficient to produce actual delays in female marriage and the spacing and limitation of births? In many cases, the marriages of young girls have been increasingly delayed, *not* because of changing ideals but because adherence to traditional ideals proved to be impossible. That is, early marriage is seen as no less desirable, but as less feasible because of a scarcity of money or of potential marriage partners. Escalating requirements for

[23] The idea that female employment might be seen as an alternative to *any* marriage has not been developed in this study because of the virtual universality of marriage for women in the South Asian countries under discussion. But it remains a logical possibility. Topley (1975) includes a fascinating description of two forms of marriage resistance (taking a vow never to marry, or, once married, not to live with the husband) that occurred in nineteenth-century China among women silk workers living in the Canton delta. These women lived together in hostels, worked together in the silk factories, and formed a quasi-religious (and in some cases sexual) "sisterhood." They enjoyed a considerable degree of social and spatial freedom which, according to Topley, raised their status "considerably above that of the conventionally married woman."

[24] Mukherjee (1974, p. 13) found no significant correlations between rural women's employment status and their role in household decision making in three states in India. For ways in which cultural values may intervene between resources and decision making, see Cromwell, Corrales, and Torsiello (1973); Oppong (1970); Rodman (1972); Safilios-Rothschild (1970); and Salaff (1976b).

dowries are commonly believed to be a source of marital delays throughout South Asia, a condition which frequently occurs in combination with a shortage of available mates engendered by increasing educational expectations for young men (Gore, 1968, page 53). Apparently, changing ideals are not necessary conditions for delayed marriage, although they may be sufficient so long as they are shared by other decision makers.

The idea of shared ideals raises the question of whether women's increased decision-making power within the family is, itself, either a necessary or sufficient condition for delayed marriage for herself or her daughters. Her power becomes salient only when she disagrees with others. If she shares with them a traditional view of early marriage or shares a willingness to postpone, then greater power on her part will serve only to reinforce this behavior. If she holds a more conservative view, then her increased power could shift marital timing toward an earlier date. Only when she values later marriage, in contrast with more conservative views of other decision makers, does her power have the potential of altering behavior in the desired direction. The effectiveness of her persuasion may depend considerably on the kind and amount of resources she has at her disposal. It is at this point that the income contributed to the family by an unmarried daughter could become a critically persuasive device.[25]

Finally, we might ask how changing ideals and greater female decision-making power alter the timing and number of births. Some theorists argue that a general level of awareness of fertility as a potentially controllable phenomenon (that is, not simply "God's will" or "up to fate to decide"), in combination with birth-control knowledge and services, are preconditions for fertility decline; others argue that all couples know how to limit fertility, if only through abstinence or withdrawal, and that unavailability of knowledge or services simply begs the question of motivation (Davis, 1967). In any case, the extent to which a woman's changing ideals about the timing and number of births can be translated into behavioral change will depend on her role in decision making. A number of studies conclude that couples in which the wives participate more actively in household decisions in general, and in discussion about family planning in particular, are likely to want fewer children and to practice birth control more effectively.[26] A woman's access to resources, such as social support from peers

[25] See, for example, Salaff (1976a and 1976b). The latter paper includes a detailed account of the percentage of the family budget contributed by a small sample of working daughters in Hong Kong together with the spheres of family decision making in which the daughters participated.

[26] See Goldberg (1974); Mitchell (1972); Mukherjee (1975b); UN Economic Commission for Asia and the Far East (1973); among others.

or financial independence, could also be translated into a decision to act autonomously in spacing or limiting births so long as she has private access to methods such as injections, the IUD, abortion, or sterilization.

The wife's motivation to defer or limit births is not sufficient for reproductive change if her husband is able to overrule her, nor is it even necessary, for the same reason. A husband may himself act unilaterally in practicing birth control. A study of Muslim couples in a low-income government housing colony in Dacca found that a high level of communication or agreement was *not* necessary for the adoption of family planning, nor were husband-dominant couples necessarily less likely to practice it. Carlaw and coauthors (1971, page 583) report, "The data suggest that a domineering husband can also be a progressive husband, and his wife might agree heartily with his decisions even though she has not participated in making them."

The resource theory of reproductive change that underlies the hypotheses in figure A-1 quite clearly has its limits. From this brief review it is apparent that female employment, even for money outside the home, probably leads through the full sequence of events culminating in delayed marriage and fewer births in a minority of cases only. In particular, strong cultural pressures toward early marriage and high fertility can negate the potential influence of resources on reproduction. These observations suggest that a full ideological onslaught may be necessary to activate the causal sequence.

One study (Ranade and Sinha, n.d., pages 1–16) of 150 unskilled female laborers on nine major construction sites in Delhi shows more vividly than any abstract argument the limitations of a pure economic resource theory. Virtually all of the sample of married women twenty years of age or older were illiterate, scheduled-caste Hindus from rural Rajasthan whose husbands worked as construction laborers on the same sites. They crushed bricks, carried loads of earth, mortar, or bricks, or worked hand pumps. Two-thirds were under thirty years of age. Most earned the same wage as their husbands, about 50 cents a day (below the legal minimum), or $11 to $14 a month for a six- or seven-day week. These women provide an ideal test of the impact of equal wages on family power and reproductive behavior.

First, their employment had no effect on the timing of their own nuptials because they generally began work after marriage. More than 90 percent had been married before they reached their fifteenth birthday, and over 40 percent had been married before the age of ten. None knew her husband before marriage; elders had arranged the marriages and given dowries in all cases. Nor did their employment challenge traditional attitudes about marriage: 86 percent believed that girls should be married before they start menstruating and more than half believed in marriage before the age of ten.

Of the 150 respondents, 137 had children; of these, 80 percent had their first child before the age of twenty. With a mean age of about thirty years, the women had given birth to an average of five children each, although 40 percent of those born had died. In spite of the fact that most women worked right up until their eighth or ninth month of pregnancy (one-quarter worked until the day of delivery), only five women said they knew about methods of family planning, and only two said they were practicing birth control.

Although most of the women earned as much income as their husbands, Ranade and Sinha (n.d.) reported that their position within the family was apparently powerless:

> Only about 8 percent of women said that they had a say in making decisions in respect of matters like daily expenditure, education and marriage of children and selection of jobs. The rest of the respondents said that the decisions were taken by their husbands or by the parents-in-law in case they lived with the respondents. When asked about their opinion in regard to status of wife vis-à-vis her husband an overwhelming majority (92 percent) felt that the status of husband should be higher. Many of them said that a woman without husband would have no status at all. It was the husband who carried the name of the family and he was like God to his wife. All the respondents stated that they had to show due deference to the male members of the family and most of them (82 percent) could take their meals only after the male members of the family had eaten. [page 16]

Why did the wage employment of these female construction workers have so little influence on their status with their husbands and their husbands' families, and on their own reproductive behavior? It would seem that the tremendous strength of cultural pressures toward early marriage, high fertility, and a patriarchal role relationship could not be challenged by the limited resources these women commanded. Indeed, the women's commitment to their work was, not surprisingly, very low. Most were working solely from poverty, with the active encouragement of their husbands and in-laws. Eighty-five percent said they would leave their jobs if their husbands could earn enough money. The work provided wages, true, but barely enough to feed their families—if that. (Most were also in debt because of daily expenses and unforeseen events such as illness; only four were able to accumulate small savings of their own.) The jobs were unskilled and exhausting. Rather than status-enhancing, they were status-depressing. Most women were too worn out to work past the age of thirty-five or forty.

The type of employment described above, a far cry from the model set forth in chapter 2, clearly illustrates that the causal sequence from employment to status to reproduction does not always follow. But some forms of employment *can* improve women's status and serve as a genuine alternative to early marriage and frequent childbearing. Comparative research on this question could help enormously in the design of development plans that would augment the positive effects of integrating women in development while minimizing its exploitative potential.

CONCLUSIONS

A number of research strategies have been outlined in this chapter for discovering promising sites for rural industrial cooperatives, evaluating ongoing programs, and understanding the causal sequence of events leading from female employment to delayed marriage and birth control. Perhaps the most direct conclusion that could be drawn is that the questions significantly outnumber the answers. Indeed, the success of this review of gaps in our knowledge might well be measured by the degree to which it has undermined the efforts of the preceding chapters in spelling out a model for social change. Instead of statements of fact and assurances of success, we are left with an unsteady feeling of lost ground and a host of unanswered—and in some cases unanswerable—doubts.

The natural inclination is to decide, as academics are wont to do, that "further research is necessary." It is. But I would argue that the research must be undertaken in conjunction with a variety of action programs designed to promote rural development, to raise the status of women, and to postpone and limit marriages and births. Only through the interplay of theory and practice can we discover the cultural and structural conditions under which social experiments such as this will succeed in bringing about desired change. In the Muslim and Hindu regions of South Asia the need for experimentation becomes all the more pressing in view of the paucity of ongoing programs even approaching the model of the producers' cooperatives proposed here. We simply do not know what type of programs might be effective. Elsewhere in Asia, and in some regions of Africa and Latin America, one can more easily find examples of rural women working in cooperative groups or as individual entrepreneurs for money incomes in agriculture, manufacturing, and service trades. But with the exception of China, nowhere are rural women mobilized into agriculture and industry on a massive scale.

The idea of social experimentation elicits an image of persons unwittingly deployed as pawns in a game of whose rules they are innocent.

In part, the negative connotation derives from a conviction that experimentation upsets the natural course of events through artificial manipulation. This is so. But the natural course of events in many countries holds little hope for improvement in the human condition. And the contrast between "natural" and "artificial" poses a false dichotomy that ignores the strong social, economic, political, and cultural forces currently shaping human behavior, including reproduction, through a complex system of differential rewards and punishments.[27] The term *experiment* means only that planning will be accompanied by ongoing evaluations of the effectiveness with which program goals are achieved. A negative connotation derives also from the fear that persons will be exposed to risks, the outcome of which is uncertain. This, too, is true: farmers are persuaded to accept new seeds or fertilizers with the expectation, but not the certainty, that crop yields will improve; young women are encouraged to defer marriage and childbearing with the expectation, but not the certainty, that they will be able to find a suitable husband and to conceive a child at a later time. To counter the possibility of loss, programs should contain safeguards to ensure that participants are at least no worse off than they might otherwise have been: crop insurance against the risk that the new seeds will not germinate; social and economic insurance through female employment against the risk of never marrying or of remaining childless. Planners should be prepared with a solution for the worst that could happen if the program fails. They will need a firm system of economic and social supports for those who are asked to take a chance.

[27] For a further discussion of this point, see Blake (1973).

REFERENCES

Abdullah, Tahrunnessa Ahmed. 1974. "Village Women As I Saw Them." Un-published paper (Dacca, The Ford Foundation).

Ahmad, Imitiaz, ed. 1973. *Caste and Social Stratification Among the Muslims* (New Delhi, Manohar).

Ahmad, Perveen. 1976. "The Role of Women in Cooperative Development in Bangladesh," in International Cooperative Alliance, *Regional Conference on the Role of Women in Cooperative Development, Kuala Lumpur, Malaysia, 21–28 July 1975* (New Delhi, International Cooperative Alliance) pp. 23–27.

Ahmed, Akbar S. 1976. *Millennium and Charisma Among Pathans* (London, Routledge and Kegan Paul).

———. 1973. *A Strategy for Cooperation: A Study of the North-West Frontier Provinces* (Peshawar, Pakistan, Sarhad Cooperative Union and the Board of Economic Inquiry, University of Peshawar).

Ahmed, Wajihuddin. 1975. "The Husband is the Employer," *Ceres* vol. 8, no. 2 (March–April) pp. 28–31.

Ali, Masarrat S. 1976. "The Role of Women in Cooperative Development in Pakistan," in International Cooperative Alliance, *Regional Conference on the Role of Women in Cooperative Development, Kuala Lumpur, Malaysia, 21–28 July 1975* (New Delhi, International Cooperative Alliance) pp. 95–102.

American Council on Education, Overseas Liaison Committee. 1977. "Small-Scale Industries," *Rural Development Network Bulletin* no. 7 (September).

Anwar, Seemin, and Faiz Bilquees. 1976. "The Attitudes, Environment and Activities of Rural Women: A Case Study of Jhok Sayal." Research Report no. 98 (Islamabad, Pakistan Institute of Development Economics).

Baldwin, C. Stephen. 1977. "Policies and Realities of Delayed Marriage: The Cases of Tunisia, Sri Lanka, Malaysia, and Bangladesh," *Population Reference Bureau Report* vol. 3, no. 4 (September).

Banfield, Edward C. 1958. *The Moral Basis of a Backward Society* (Glencoe, Ill.: The Free Press).

Bangladesh Rural Advancement Committee. 1974. "Sulla Project Phase II Interim Report" (Dacca, April).

Bean, Lee L. 1968. "Utilisation of Human Resources: The Case of Women in Pakistan," *International Labour Review* vol. 97, no. 4 (April) pp. 391–410.

Beniwal, Kamla. 1976. "Background Paper on Women and the Cooperative Movement in India," in International Cooperative Alliance, *Regional Conference on the Role of Women in Cooperative Development, Kuala Lum-*

pur, Malaysia, 21–28 July 1975 (Delhi, International Cooperative Alliance) pp. 33–38.

Bennett, Lynn. 1974. "Mobilization of Women for Improved Child Health Care and Nutrition at the Village Level: A Proposal to UNICEF/Nepal" (Kathmandu, UNICEF).

————. 1973. "Two Water Case Studies," Department of Local Development/UNICEF Paper no. 5 (Kathmandu).

Béteille, André. 1975. "The Position of Women in Indian Society," in Devaki Jain, ed., *Indian Women* (New Delhi, Government of India, Publications Division, Ministry of Information and Broadcasting) pp. 61–68.

————. 1974. *Studies in Agrarian Social Structure* (Delhi, Oxford University Press).

Bhatt, Ela. 1976. "Organizing the Self-employed Women Workers into Labour and Cooperatives: An Experiment." Paper presented at All-India Conference on Women and Cooperatives, sponsored by the National Cooperative Union of India, New Delhi, 22–23 March.

Bhatty, Zarina. 1975. "Muslim Women in Uttar Pradesh: Social Mobility and Directions of Change," in Alfred de Souza, ed., *Women in Contemporary India* (Delhi: Manohar) pp. 25–36.

Bindary, Aziz, Collin B. Baxter, and T. H. Hollingsworth. 1973. "Urban-Rural Differences in the Relationship Between Women's Employment and Fertility: A Preliminary Study," *Journal of Biosocial Science* vol. 5, no. 2 (April) pp. 159–167.

Birdsall, Nancy. 1974. "An Introduction to the Social Science Literature on 'Women's Place' and Fertility in the Developing World," in *Annotated Bibliography* vol. 2, no. 1 (Washington, D.C., Interdisciplinary Communications Program, Smithsonian Institution).

————. 1976. "Women and Population Studies," *Signs: Journal of Women in Culture and Society* vol. 1, no. 3, pt. 1 (Spring) pp. 699–712.

Blake, Judith. 1973. "Coercive Pronatalism and American Population Policy," in Charles F. Westoff and Robert Parke, Jr., eds., *Aspects of Population Growth Policy* vol. VI of Commission on Population Growth and the American Future Research Reports (Washington, GPO).

Boserup, Ester. 1970. *Woman's Role in Economic Development* (New York, St. Martin's Press).

Boulding, Elise. 1977. *Women in the Twentieth Century World* (New York, Halsted).

————, Shirley A. Nuss, Dorothy Lee Carson, and Michael A. Greenstein. 1976. *Handbook of International Data on Women* (New York, Halsted).

Bruce, Robert. 1975. "Some New Indian Developments in Small Scale Spinning and Weaving," *Appropriate Technology* vol. 2, no. 3 (November) pp. 9–10.

Buvinić, Mayra. 1976. *Women and World Development: An Annotated Bibliography* (Washington, Overseas Development Council).

Cancian, Frank. 1977. "Can Anthropology Help Agricultural Development?" *Culture and Agriculture* no. 2 (March) pp. 1–8.

Carlaw, Raymond W., Richard Reynolds, Lawrence W. Green, and N. I. Khan. 1971. "Underlying Sources of Agreement and Communication Between Husbands and Wives in Dacca, East Pakistan," *Journal of Marriage and the Family* vol. 33, no. 3 (August) pp. 571–583.

Carr, Marilyn. 1976. *Economically Appropriate Technologies for Developing Countries: An Annotated Bibliography* (London, Intermediate Technology Publications).

Carstairs, G. Morris. 1975. "Village Women of Rajasthan," in Devaki Jain, ed., *Indian Women* (New Delhi, Government of India, Publications Division, Ministry of Information and Broadcasting) pp. 231–235.

Chaney, Elsa. 1973. "Women and Population: Some Key Policy, Research, and Action Issues," in Richard L. Clinton, ed., *Population and Politics: New Directions in Political Science Research* (Lexington, Mass., D. C. Heath) pp. 233–246.

Chatterjee, Atreyi. 1975. "Landless Agricultural Women Workers," *Indian Farmer* vol. 25, no. 8, pp. 31–33.

Chattopadhyay, Kamladevi. 1976. "Women's Participation in Industrial Co-operatives in India," in International Cooperative Alliance, *Regional Conference on the Role of Women in Cooperative Development, Kuala Lumpur, Malaysia, 21–28 July 1975* (New Delhi, International Cooperative Alliance) pp. 39–57.

Chaudhury, Rafiqul Huda. 1974. "Labour Force Status and Fertility," *The Bangladesh Development Studies* vol. 2, no. 4 (October) pp. 819–838.

Chesnais, Jean-Claude, and Jacques Vallin. 1975. "Les Populations au Sud de l'Himalaya," *Population* vol. 30, no. 6 (November–December) pp. 1059–1110.

Childers, Erskine. 1976. "The Development Approach to Liberation: Suggestions for Planning," in Irene Tinker and Michèle Bo Bramsen, eds., *Women and World Development* (Washington, Overseas Development Council) pp. 129–137.

Christian Science Monitor. 1977. 18 March, p. 6.

———. 1978. 14 February, p. 18.

Cleland, J. 1973. "A Critique of KAP Studies and Some Suggestions for Their Improvement," *Studies in Family Planning* vol. 4, no. 2 (February) pp. 42–47.

Coale, Ansley J., and Edgar M. Hoover. 1958. *Population Growth and Economic Development in Low Income Countries* (Princeton, N.J., Princeton University Press).

Committee on the Status of Women in India. 1974. *Towards Equality: Report of the Committee on the Status of Women in India* (New Delhi, Government of India, Department of Social Welfare).

Coombs, Philip H., with Manzoor Ahmed. 1974. *Attacking Rural Poverty: How Non-formal Education Can Help* (Baltimore, Johns Hopkins University Press).

Cromwell, Ronald E., Ramon Corrales, and Peter M. Torsiello. 1973. "Normative Patterns of Marital Decision-making Power and Influence in Mexico and the United States: A Partial Test of Resource and Ideology Theory," *Journal of Comparative Family Studies* vol. 4, no. 2 (Autumn) pp. 177–196.

————, and Stephen G. Wieting. 1975. "Multidimensionality of Conjugal Decision-making Indices: Comparative Analyses of Five Samples, *Journal of Comparative Family Studies* vol. 6, no. 2 (Autumn) pp. 139–151.

Dandekar, Kumudini. 1959. *Demographic Survey of Six Rural Communities* (Poona, Gokhale Institute of Politics and Economics).

Das, Veena. 1975. "Marriage Among the Hindus," in Devaki Jain, ed., *Indian Women* (New Delhi, Government of India, Publications Division, Ministry of Information and Broadcasting) pp. 71–86.

Davis, Kingsley. 1975. "Demographic Reality and Policy in Nepal's Future." Paper presented at Nepal/Berkeley Family Planning/Maternal and Child Health Conference on Family Planning, Population and Development in Nepal, Berkeley, California.

————. 1967. "Population Policy: Will Current Programs Succeed?" *Science*, vol. 158, no. 3802 (November 10) pp. 730–739.

D'Cruz, Margaret. 1976. "Review of Women's Cooperative Activities in South East Asia," in International Cooperative Alliance, *Regional Conference on the Role of Women in Cooperative Development, Kuala Lumpur, Malaysia, 21–28 July 1975* (New Delhi, International Cooperative Alliance) pp. 12–22.

deWilde, John C. 1972. *Nonformal Education and the Development of Small Enterprise in India*, ICED Case Study no. 4 (Essex, Conn., International Council for Educational Development).

Dhamija, Jasleen. 1975. "Handicrafts: A Source of Employment for Women in Developing Rural Economies," *International Labour Review* vol. 112, no. 6 (December) pp. 459–465.

Dixon, Ruth B. 1976a. "Measuring Equality Between the Sexes," *Journal of Social Issues* vol. 32, no. 3 (Summer) pp. 19–32.

————. 1976. "The Roles of Rural Women: Female Seclusion, Economic Production, and Reproductive Choice," in Ronald G. Ridker, ed., *Population and Development: The Search for Selective Interventions* (Baltimore: Johns Hopkins University Press for Resources for the Future) pp. 290–321.

————. 1970. "The Social and Demographic Determinants of Marital Postponement and Celibacy: A Comparative Study" (Ph.D. dissertation, University of California, Berkeley).

D'Souza, Victor S. 1975. "Family Status and Female Work Participation," in Alfred De Souza, ed., *Women in Contemporary India* (Delhi, Manohar) pp. 129–141.

Dubey, D. C., A. Bardhan, and S. Garg. 1975. "Fertility Behaviour of Working and Non-Working Women." Monograph Series no. 24 (New Delhi, National Institute of Family Planning).

Duza, M. Badrud, and C. Stephen Baldwin. 1977. *Nuptiality and Population*

Policy: An Investigation in Tunisia, Sri Lanka, and Malaysia (New York, Population Council).

Ellickson, Jean. 1975. "Rural Women," in Women for Women Research and Study Group, *Women for Women: Bangladesh 1975* (Dacca, University Press) pp. 81–89.

———. 1976. "Women of Rural Bangladesh: Variation in Problems of Self-Perception." Paper presented at Conference on Women and Development, Wellesley College, Wellesley, Mass.

Epstein, T. Scarlett. 1973. *South India: Yesterday, Today and Tomorrow. Mysore Villages Revisited* (London, Macmillan).

Fagley, Richard M. 1976. "Easing the Burden of Rural Women: A 16-hour Workday," *Les Carnets de l'Enfance/Assignment Children* no. 36 (October–December 1976) pp. 9–28.

Finkle, Jason L., and Barbara B. Crane. 1975. "The Politics of Bucharest: Population, Development, and the New International Economic Order," *Population and Development Review* vol. 1, no. 1 (September) pp. 87–114.

Fisher, Douglas. 1968. "A Survey of the Literature on Small-Sized Industrial Undertakings in India," in International Committee for Social Sciences Documentation, *The Role of Small Industry in the Process of Economic Growth* (The Hague, Mouton) pp. 117–215.

Fong, Monica S. 1976. "Female Labor Force Participation and Fertility: Some Methodological and Theoretical Considerations," *Social Biology* vol. 23, no. 1 (Spring) pp. 45–54.

Freire, Paulo. 1972a. *Cultural Action for Freedom* (London, Penguin).

———. 1972b. *Pedagogy of the Oppressed* (London, Penguin).

Germain, Adrienne. 1976–77. "Poor Rural Women: A Policy Perspective," *Journal of International Affairs* vol. 30, no. 2 (Fall/Winter) pp. 161–172.

———. 1974. "Some Aspects of the Roles of Women in Population and Development." Paper presented at International Forum on the Role of Women in Population and Development, 25 February–1 March 1974. ESA/SDHA/AC.5/3 (8 February 1974) and ESA/SDHA/AC.5/3/Add.1 (13 February 1974). New York: United Nations.

———. 1975. "Status and Roles of Women as Factors in Fertility Behavior: A Policy Analysis," *Studies in Family Planning* vol. 6, no. 7 (July) pp. 192–200.

Giele, Janet Zollinger, and Audrey Chapman Smock. 1977. *Women: Roles and Status in Eight Countries* (New York, Wiley).

Goldberg, David. 1974. "Modernism: The Extensiveness of Women's Roles and Attitudes." Occasional paper no. 14, World Fertility Survey.

Goldstein, Sidney. 1972. "The Influence of Labour Force Participation and Education on Fertility in Thailand," *Population Studies* vol. 26, no. 3 (November) pp. 419–436.

Gore, M. S. 1968. *Urbanization and Family Change* (Bombay, Popular Prakashan).

Hass, Paula H. 1972. "Maternal Role Incompatibility and Fertility in Urban Latin America," *Journal of Social Issues* vol. 28, no. 2, pp. 111–127.

Hauser, Philip M. 1967. "Family Planning and Population Programs," *Demography* vol. 4, no. 1, pp. 397–414.

Helbock, Lucy. 1975a. "The Changing Status of Women in Islamic Pakistan" (Islamabad, Pakistan, U.S. Agency for International Development).

————. 1975b. "Women in Pakistan: An Annotated Bibliography of Materials Dealing with Women's Social and Economic Conditions (Islamabad, Pakistan, U.S. Agency for International Development).

Hertzberg, Ruth, Beatrice Vaughan, and Janet Greene. 1975. *Putting Food By.* 2nd ed. (New York, Bantam).

Hirschman, Albert O. 1958. *The Strategy of Economic Development* (New Haven, Yale University Press).

Hossain, Hameeda. 1975. "Third World Craftsmen and Development: The Bangladesh Experience" (Dacca, Bangladesh Cooperative Handicrafts Federation).

Hunter, Guy. 1969. *Modernizing Peasant Societies: A Comparative Study in Asia and Africa* (New York, Oxford University Press).

Husain, A. F. A. 1958. *Employment of Middle Class Muslim Women in Dacca.* (Dacca, Dacca University Socio-Economic Research Board).

International Confederation of Free Trade Unions. n.d. "The Aurangabad Experiment: A Program for Rural Workers' Family Welfare" (New Delhi).

International Cooperative Alliance. 1976. *Regional Conference on the Role of Women in Cooperative Development, Kuala Lumpur, Malaysia, July 21–28, 1975* (New Delhi: International Cooperative Alliance).

————. 1974. *Report on the Proceedings of the ICA Regional Women Co-operators Seminar, Kampala, 14–18 January 1974* (Moshi, Tanzania, ICA, Regional Office for East and Central Africa).

International Labour Office. 1974. *Cooperative Education and Population: A New Field of Action in Africa* (Geneva, ILO).

International Labour Organisation. 1973. "Status of Rural Women, Especially Agricultural Workers." Paper presented at the Economic and Social Council, Commission on the Status of Women, 25th Session. E/CN.6/583/Add.1. 17 December.

Jaffe, A. J., and K. Azumi. 1960. "The Birth Rate and Cottage Industries in Underdeveloped Countries," *Economic Development and Cultural Change* vol. 9, no. 1, pt. 1 (October) pp. 52–63.

Jahan, Rounaq. 1975. "Women in Bangladesh," in Women for Women Research and Study Group, *Women for Women: Bangladesh 1975* (Dacca, University Press) pp. 1–30.

Jain, Devaki. 1976. "Creation of Employment Opportunities for Women Through Cooperatives." Paper presented at the All-India Conference on Women and Cooperatives, New Delhi, 22–23 March, sponsored by the National Cooperative Union of India.

————. n.d. "From Dissociation to Rehabilitation: Report on an Experiment to Promote Self-Employment in an Urban Area," in Indian Council of Social Science Research, *Women in a Developing Economy,* vol. 1 (New Delhi, Allied Publishers).

Kabir, Khushi, Ayesha Abed, and Marty Chen. 1976. "Rural Women in Bangladesh: Exploding Some Myths" (Dacca, Ford Foundation).

Kaira District Co-operative Milk Producers' Union. 1971. "The Amul Story: A Saga of Co-operative Effort, Silver Jubilee, 1946–1971" (Anand Press, Gujarat, India).

————. 1975. "Amul" (Anand Press, Gujarat, India).

Karim, Mehtab S. 1974. "Fertility Differentials by Family Type," *The Pakistan Development Review* vol. 13, no. 2 (Summer) pp. 129–144.

Kerri, James Nwannukwu. 1974. "Anthropological Studies of Voluntary Associations and Voluntary Action: A Review," *Journal of Voluntary Action Research* vol. 3, no. 1 (Winter).

Khalifa, A. 1973. *The Status of Women and Family Planning in Egypt* (National Center for Social and Criminological Research).

Khan, M. Ali, and Ismail Sirageldin. 1975. "Education, Income and Fertility in Pakistan," cited in Steven W. Sinding, *Considerations in Long-Term Planning for Fertility Decline in Pakistan* (Islamabad, U.S. Agency for International Development).

King, Timothy, ed. 1974. *Population Policies and Economic Development: A World Bank Staff Report* (Baltimore, Johns Hopkins University Press).

Kocher, James E. 1973. *Rural Development, Income Distribution, and Fertility Decline* (New York: Population Council).

Kolenda, Pauline M. 1967. "Regional Differences in Indian Family Structure," in Robert I. Crane, ed., *Regions and Regionalism in South Asian Studies: An Exploratory Study*. Duke University Program in Comparative Studies on Southern Asia, Monograph no. 5 (Durham, N.C., Duke University Press) pp. 147–226.

Leser, C. E. V. 1958. "Trends in Women's Work Participation," *Population Studies* vol. 12, no. 4 (November) pp. 100–110.

Lindenbaum, Shirley. 1974. "The Social and Economic Status of Women in Bangladesh" (Dacca, Ford Foundation).

————. 1968. "Woman and the Left Hand: Social Status and Symbolism in East Pakistan," *Mankind* vol. 6, no. 11 (June) pp. 537–544.

Lohani, Narayani. 1976. "Women and Cooperation in Nepal," in International Cooperative Alliance, *Regional Conference on the Role of Women in Cooperative Development, Kuala Lumpur, Malaysia, 21–28 July 1975* (New Delhi, ICA) pp. 91–94.

MacFarlane, Alan. 1976. *Resources and Population: A Study of the Gurungs of Nepal*. Cambridge Studies in Social Anthropology 12 (Cambridge, England, Cambridge University Press).

McNicholl, Geoffrey. 1975. "Community-Level Population Policy: An Exploration," *Population and Development Review* vol. 1, no. 1 (September) pp. 1–21.

Major, Alan. 1975. "Third World Craftswomen and Development: Report of a Seminar Held June 20, 1975, at the International Women's Year Tribune, Mexico City" (New York City, Planning Assistance, Inc.).

Mamdani, Mahmood. 1972. *The Myth of Population Control: Family, Caste, and Class in an Indian Village* (New York, Monthly Review Press).

Mascarenhas, Aloma. 1975. "A Report on Rural Women of Bangladesh" (Dacca, U.S. Agency for International Development).

Mauldin, W. Parker, Nazli Choucri, Frank W. Notestein, and Michael Teitelbaum. 1974. "A Report on Bucharest," *Studies in Family Planning* vol. 5, no. 12 (December) pp. 357–395.

Mazumdar, Vina. 1975. "Women in Agriculture," *Indian Farming* vol. 25, no. 8 (November) pp. 5–9, 64–65.

Meng, Molly Foo Yut. 1976. "Women's Role in Promoting Thrift and Their Participation in Thrift and Credit Societies," in International Cooperative Alliance, *Regional Conference on the Role of Women in Cooperative Development, Kuala Lumpur, Malaysia, 21–28 July 1975* (New Delhi, ICA) pp. 82–90.

Mickelwait, Donald R., Mary Ann Riegelman, and Charles F. Sweet. 1976. *Women in Rural Development: A Survey of the Roles of Women in Ghana, Lesotho, Kenya, Nigeria, Bolivia, Paraguay, and Peru* (Boulder, Colo., Westview Press).

Mitchell, Robert E. 1972. "Husband–Wife Relations and Family-Planning Practices in Urban Hong Kong," *Journal of Marriage and the Family* vol. 34, no. 1 (February) pp. 139–146.

Mukherjee, Bishwa Nath. 1975a. "A Multidimensional Conceptualisation of Status of Women," *Social Change* vol. 5, nos. 1–2 (March–June) pp. 27–44.

———. 1975b. "Status of Women as Related to Family Planning," *Journal of Population Research* vol. 2, pp. 5–33.

———. 1974. "The Status of Married Women in Haryana, Tamil Nadu and Meghalaya," *Social Change* vol. 4, no. 1 (March) pp. 4–17.

Naik, J. P. n.d. *Elementary Education in India: A Promise to Keep* (Delhi, Allied Publishers).

Nair, Kusum. 1961. *Blossoms in the Dust: The Human Element in Indian Development* (Bombay, Allied Publishers Private).

National Board of Bangladesh Women's Rehabilitation Programme. 1974. "Women's Work" (Dacca, Bangladesh Co-operative Book Society Ltd).

National Cooperative Union of India. n.d. *National Seminar on Cooperatives and Population Problems: Conclusions and Recommendations.* New Delhi, 16–19 December 1974 (New Delhi, National Cooperative Printing Press).

———. 1976a. "All-India Conference on Women and Cooperatives, New Delhi, 22–23 March 1976. Proceedings and Recommendations" (New Delhi, National Cooperative Union of India).

———. 1976b. "Review of Progress of Women's Participation in Cooperative Movement." Background paper prepared for All-India Conference on Women and Cooperatives, New Delhi, 22–23 March.

Nelson, Cynthia. 1974. "Public and Private Politics: Women in the Middle Eastern World," *American Ethnologist* vol. 1, no. 3, pp. 551–563.

Nepal, Ministry of Land Reform, Department of Co-operatives. 1975. *Co-operatives at a Glance. On the Grand Occasion of the Auspicious Coronation of His Majesty King Birendra Bir Bikram Shah Dev* (Kathmandu, Ministry of Land Reform, Department of Co-operatives).

Nepal Women's Organization. n.d. "Outline of the Programme of the Nepal Women's Organization" (Kathmandu).

Nortman, Dorothy, assisted by Ellen Hofstatter. 1975. "Population and Family Planning Programs: A Factbook," *Reports on Population/Family Planning* no. 2, 7th ed. (October).

Opondo, Diana. n.d. "Handicraft Industries as a Development Strategy" (Moshi, Tanzania, International Cooperative Alliance, Regional Office for East and Central Africa).

Oppong, Christine. 1970. "Conjugal Power and Resources: An Urban African Example," *Journal of Marriage and the Family* vol. 32, no. 4 (November) pp. 676–680.

Oza, Ghanshyambhai. 1975. "Women in Rural Industries," *Social Welfare* vol. 22, no. 8 (November) pp. 27–28.

Papanek, Hanna. 1977. "Development Planning for Women," *Signs: Journal of Women in Culture and Society* vol. 3, no. 1 (Autumn) pp. 14–21.

———. 1971. "Purdah in Pakistan: Seclusion and Modern Occupations for Women," *Journal of Marriage and the Family* vol. 33, no. 3 (August) pp. 517–530.

———. 1973. "Purdah: Separate Worlds and Symbolic Shelter," *Comparative Studies in Society and History* vol. 15, no. 3 (June) pp. 289–325.

———. 1975. "Women in South and Southeast Asia: Issues and Research," *Signs: Journal of Women in Culture and Society* vol. 1, no. 1 (Autumn) pp. 193–214.

Park, Hyung Jong, D. Lawrence Kincaid, Kyung Kyoon Chung, Dal Sun Han, and Sea Baick Lee. 1976. "The Korean Mother's Club Program," *Studies in Family Planning* vol. 7, no. 10 (October) pp. 275–283.

Pastner, Carroll McClure. 1974. "Accommodations to Purdah: The Female Perspective," *Journal of Marriage and the Family* vol. 36, no. 2 (May) pp. 408–414.

———. 1971. "Sexual Dichotomization in Society and Culture: The Women of Panjgur, Baluchistan" (Ph.D. dissertation, Brandeis University).

Piepmeier, K. B., and T. S. Adkins. 1973. "The Status of Women and Fertility," *Journal of Biosocial Science* vol. 5, no. 4 (October) pp. 507–520.

Pohlman, Edward. 1971. *Incentives and Compensations in Birth Planning.* Monograph no. 11 (Chapel Hill, N.C., Carolina Population Center).

Ranade, S. N., and G. P. Sinha. n.d. "Women Construction Workers: Reports of Two Surveys," in Indian Council of Social Science Research, *Women in a Developing Economy,* vol. 2 (New Delhi, Allied Publishers).

Raper, Arthur. 1970. *Rural Development in Action: The Comprehensive Experiment at Comilla, East Pakistan* (Ithaca, N.Y., Cornell University Press).

Ratcliffe, John W. 1976. "Analyst Biases in KAP Surveys: A Cross-Cultural

Comparison," *Studies in Family Planning* vol. 7, no. 11 (November) pp. 322–330.

Repetto, Robert. 1974. "The Relation of the Size Distribution of Income to Fertility, and the Implications for Development Policy," in Timothy King, ed., *Population Policies and Economic Development: A World Bank Staff Report* (Baltimore, Johns Hopkins University Press).

Rich, William. 1973. *Smaller Families Through Social and Economic Progress* (Washington, D.C., Overseas Development Council).

Ridker, Ronald G., ed. 1976. *Population and Development: The Search for Selective Interventions* (Baltimore, Johns Hopkins University Press for Resources for the Future).

———, and Robert J. Muscat. 1973. "Incentives for Family Welfare and Fertility Reduction: An Illustration for Malaysia," *Studies in Family Planning* vol. 4, no. 1 (January) pp. 1–24.

Rodman, Hyman. 1972. "Marital Power and the Theory of Resources in Cultural Context," *Journal of Comparative Family Studies* vol. 3, no. 1 (Spring) pp. 50–69.

Saeed, Kishwar. 1976. *Rural Women's Participation in Farm Operations* (Lyallpur, West Pakistan University).

Safilios-Rothschild, Constantina. 1971a. "A Cross-Cultural Examination of Women's Marital, Educational, and Occupational Options," *Acta Sociologica* vol. 14, nos. 1–2 (Spring).

———. 1972. "The Relationship Between Work Commitment and Fertility," *International Journal of Sociology of the Family* vol. 2, no. 1 (March).

———. 1970. "The Study of Family Power Structure: A Review 1960–1969," *Journal of Marriage and the Family* vol. 32, no. 4 (November) pp. 539–552.

———. 1971b. "Toward the Conceptualization and Measurement of Work Commitment," *Human Relations* vol. 24, no. 6 (December) pp. 489–493.

Salaff, Janet W. 1972. "Institutionalized Motivation for Fertility Limitation in China," *Population Studies* vol. 26, no. 2 (July) pp. 233–262.

———. 1976a. "The Status of Unmarried Hong Kong Women and the Social Factors Contributing to Their Delayed Marriage," *Population Studies* vol. 30, no. 3 (November) pp. 391–412.

———. 1976b. "Working Daughters in the Hong Kong Chinese Family: Female Filial Piety or a Transformation in the Family Power Structure?" *Journal of Social History* vol. 9, no. 4, pp. 439–465.

Sanday, Peggy R. 1973. "Toward a Theory of the Status of Women," *American Anthropologist* vol. 75, no. 5 (October) pp. 1682–1700.

Sattar, Ellen. 1975. "Village Women's Work," in Women for Women Research and Study Group, *Women for Women: Bangladesh 1975* (Dacca, University Press) pp. 33–65.

Shah, Nasra M. 1975a. "Female Labour Force Participation and Fertility Desire in Pakistan: An Empirical Investigation," *Pakistan Development Review* vol. 14, no. 2 (Summer) pp. 185–206.

————. 1975b. "Work Participation of Currently Married Women in Pakistan: Influence of Socio-Economic and Demographic Factors," *Pakistan Development Review* vol. 14, no. 4 (Winter) pp. 469–492.

Simon, Julian. 1968. "The Role of Bonuses and Persuasive Propaganda in the Reduction of Birth Rates," *Economic Development and Cultural Change* vol. 16, no. 3 (April) pp. 404–411.

Singh, Andréa Menefee. 1976. *Neighborhood and Social Networks in Urban India* (New Delhi, Marwah).

————. 1975. "The Study of Women in India: Some Problems in Methodology," in Alfred de Souza, ed., *Women in Contemporary India* (Delhi, Manohar) pp. 189–218.

————. 1977. "Women and the Family: Coping with Poverty in the Bastis of Delhi," *Social Action* vol. 27 (July–September) pp. 241–265.

Srinivas, M. N. 1970. *Caste in Modern India* (Bombay, Asia Publishing House).

Staley, Eugene, and Richard Morse. 1965. *Modern Small Industry for Developing Countries* (New York, McGraw-Hill).

Stycos, J. Mayone. 1965. "Female Employment and Fertility in Lima, Peru," *Milbank Memorial Fund Quarterly* vol. 43, no. 1 (January) pp. 42–54.

————, and Robert N. Weller. 1967. "Female Working Roles and Fertility," *Demography* vol. 4, no. 1, pp. 210–217.

Teitelbaum, Michael. 1974. "Population and Development: Is a Consensus Possible?" *Foreign Affairs* vol. 52, no. 4 (July) pp. 742–760.

Tendler, Judith. 1975. *Inside Foreign Aid* (Baltimore, Johns Hopkins University Press).

Terry, Geraldine B. 1974. "A Theoretical Examination of the Relationship Between Fertility and Female Employment." Paper presented at the annual meetings of the Population Association of America, April.

————. 1975. "Rival Explanations in the Work-Fertility Relationship," *Population Studies* vol. 29, no. 2 (July) pp. 191–205.

Tinker, Irene. 1976. "The Adverse Impact of Development on Women," in Irene Tinker and Michèle Bo Bramsen, eds., *Women and World Development* (Washington, Overseas Development Council) pp. 22–34.

————, and Michèle Bo Bramsen. 1976. *Women and World Development* (Washington, Overseas Development Council).

Topley, Marjorie. 1975. "Marriage Resistance in Rural Kwangtung," in Marjery Wolf and Roxane Witke, eds., *Women in Chinese Society* (Stanford, Calif., Stanford University Press) pp. 67–88.

Torasker, Asha. n.d. "A Brief Review of the Progress of Women-Participation in Co-operative Movement with Special Reference to Indira Mahila Co-operative Bank, Bombay" (Bombay, Indira Co-operative Bank).

United Nations. 1975. "The Integration of Women in the Development Process as Equal Partners with Men; Item 10 of the Provisional Agenda." United Nations World Conference of the International Women's Year, Mexico City, 19 June–2 July, E/CONF.66/4.

United Nations Children's Fund. 1976. "Four Current Research Projects Concerned With Reducing Women's Workload," *Les Carnets de L'Enfance/ Assignment Children* no. 36 (October) pp. 93–100.

———. League of Arab States, and Arab States Adult Functional Literacy Centre. n.d. *Role of Arab Women in National Development, Report of a Conference, 24–30 September 1972, Cairo, A.R.E.* (Beirut, Middle East Copy Centre).

United Nations, Department of Economic and Social Affairs. 1973. *Report of the Interregional Meeting of Experts on the Integration of Women in Development.* Sales No. E.73.IV.12 (New York, United Nations).

———. 1975. *Status of Women and Family Planning.* Sales No. E.75.IV.5 (New York, United Nations).

United Nations, Economic and Social Council (UNESCO). 1973. "Status of Rural Women, Especially Agricultural Workers." Report prepared by the Food and Agricultural Organization for the Commission on the Status of Women, 25th Session. E/CN.6/583/Add.2 (27 December). (New York, United Nations).

United Nations, Economic Commission for Africa. 1975. "The Role of Women in African Development." Report prepared for the United Nations World Conference of the International Women's Year, E/CONF.66/BP/8 (10 April).

United Nations, Economic Commission for Asia and the Far East. 1973. "The Status of Women and Family Planning." Background paper prepared for the United Nations Regional Seminar on the Status of Women and Family Planning, Jogjakarta, Indonesia, 20–30 June.

United Nations, Food and Agriculture Organization. 1975. "The Role of Women in Rural Development." Report prepared for the United Nations World Conference of the International Women's Year. E/CONF.66/BP/ 11 (24 March).

United Nations, Research Institute for Social Development. 1975. *Rural Cooperatives as Agents of Change: A Research Report and a Debate.* Report no. 74.3 (Geneva, United Nations Research Institute for Social Development).

Van Allen, Judith. 1974. "Women in Africa: Modernization Means More Dependency," *The Center Magazine* vol. 7, no. 3 (May–June) pp. 60–67.

Varadappan, Sarojini. 1976. "International Women's Year: Its Impact." Press release 178/76-F, Press Information Bureau, Government of India.

Veblen, Thorstein. 1934. *The Theory of the Leisure Class: An Economic Study of Institutions* (New York, Modern Library).

Vedchhi Intensive Area Scheme. n.d. *Building from Below: Third Five-Year Plan, 1975–79, Valod Taluka* (Valod, Gujarat, India).

von Furer-Haimendorf, Christoph. 1960. "Caste in the Multi-Ethnic Society of Nepal," *Contributions to Indian Sociology* vol. 4, pp. 12–32.

———. 1967. *Morals and Merit* (London, Weidenfeld and Nicolson).

Von-Harder, Gudrun Martius. 1975. "Women's Role in Rice Processing," in Women for Women Research and Study Group, *Women for Women: Bangladesh 1975* (Dacca, University Press) pp. 66–80.

Ware, Helen. 1965. "Fertility and Work-Force Participation: The Experience of Melbourne Wives," *Population Studies* vol. 30, no. 3 (November) pp. 413–427.

Weller, Robert H. 1968. "The Employment of Wives, Role Incompatibility and Fertility: A Study Among Lower and Middle Class Residents of San Juan, Puerto Rico," *Milbank Memorial Fund Quarterly* vol. 46, no. 4 (October) pp. 507–526.

Wilensky, Harold L. 1968. "Women's Work: Economic Growth, Ideology, Structure," *Industrial Relations, A Journal of Economy and Society* vol. 7, no. 3 (May) pp. 235–248. (Berkeley, Calif., Institute of Industrial Relations, University of California).

Wiser, William H., and Charlotte Viall Wiser. 1971. *Behind Mud Walls 1930–1960, With a Sequel: The Village in 1970* (Berkeley, University of California Press).

Wolf, Marjery. 1972. *Women and the Family in Rural Taiwan* (Stanford, Calif., Stanford University Press).

Youssef, Nadia H. 1974a. "Muslim Women and Agricultural Production: Are They Undercounted or Actually Dispensable?" Revised paper presented at Seminar on Prospects for Growth in Rural Societies with or Without Active Participation of Women, Agricultural Development Council, Princeton, New Jersey, December.

―――. 1974b. *Women and Work in Developing Societies,* Population Monograph Series no. 15 (Berkeley, University of California, Institute of International Relations).

Zachariah, K. C., and R. Cuca. n.d. *Population Projections for Bank Member Countries 1970–2000* (Washington, D.C., Population and Human Resources Division, International Bank for Reconstruction and Development).

Zeidenstein, Sondra. 1975. "IRDP Pilot Project on Population Planning and Rural Women's Cooperatives: Report and Commentary on the First Year." (Dacca, Integrated Rural Development Program).

―――, and Laura Zeidenstein. 1974. "Observations on the Status of Women in Bangladesh," *World Education Issues* no. 2 (July).

INDEX

Agriculture, 3, 16
technical advances, 83–84
women's role, 17–20, 50, 82–84, 126–127
Agricultural cooperatives, 10, 13, 29, 42, 43, 44–45, 141–142, 151, 165
female participation, 50, 53–55
milk cooperatives, 42, 43, 50–56, 71, 72
social impact, 49, 56
women's cooperatives, 45–50, 53, 71, 84, 95, 158, 162
All-India Handicrafts Board, 89, 96, 161
All-India Handloom Board, 96, 161
All-Pakistan Women's Association (APWA), 99, 155
Amoral familism, 114, 140
Anand Milk Union Ltd. (AMUL), India, 10, 42, 50–56, 72, 128, 141, 146, 148, 158, 160
Artisan systems, 24, 57–63, 90, 146. *See also* Handicrafts.
Aurangabad Experiment, India, 141

Bangladesh Academy for Rural Development (BARD), 45, 49, 55, 72, 111, 160, 161, 165
Bangladesh Handicrafts Cooperative Federation (KARIKA), 45–46, 58, 59, 62, 79
Bangladesh Mahila Samity, 155
Bangladesh Rural Advancement Committee (BRAC), 16, 37, 82, 113, 142, 146, 149–150, 160, 162
Banks, 94
women's, 93, 96–98

Banking cooperatives, 96–98
Bargaining power, 15, 68, 72, 97, 131–132, 136, 176
Birth control
financial incentives, 39–40, 69, 199
resistance to, 1, 113, 114
spacing of children, 198–199, 205–206
See also Family planning.

Capacity to sustain continuous improvement, 6, 192, 193
Capital
overfunding, 102
raising, 46, 93–104, 185
Carpet weaving, 42, 43, 69–71
Caste system, 109, 117–118, 121
overcoming, 54, 141
scheduled caste, 22, 56
Central workplace, 25–27, 62, 65, 112, 146
education programs, 69
Change
agents of, 32, 33, 140, 173–174, 176
encouraging, 170, 173
images of, 139–140
resistance to, 123, 140. *See also* Cultural obstacles.
Childcare, 38, 130, 132, 135
Community
accessibility, 76, 182
composition, 179–180
factionalism, 141
income, 71
levels of living, 193–194
power structure, 183
women's role in, 72–73, 188–189
Construction work, 22–23, 206–207
Cooking, 129–130

Library of Congress Cataloging in Publication Data

Dixon, Ruth B.
  Rural women at work.

  Bibliography: p.
  1. Women—Employment—South Asia. 2. Producer
cooperatives—South Asia. 3. Rural development—South
Asia. 4. Population policy—South Asia. I. Title.
HD6182.57.D58   331.4'0954   78-5825
ISBN 0-8018-2124-X